Bobby Baker

'Performance artist and painter Bobby Baker has daringly confronted the fragilities and pleasure of human existence with challenging honesty. In a powerful feminist tradition of speaking herself – speaking her own truth – she has ranged from hilarity to the deepest pathos. Her vision, sometimes excruciating, has produced a singular and profoundly important body of art work about the struggle and the joys of living.'

GRISELDA POLLOCK, University of Leeds

'Finally, a book on Bobby Baker! Here is an important artist – important to visual art, to performance art, to culinary art, to frank and brave art. Here is a book essential for anyone invested in questions of mental health, feminism, hilarity, pain, everyday life on the planet, and the crushing honesty of the banal detail. Here, too, is a beautiful book, full of images and insights, smartness and hope.'

REBECCA SCHNEIDER, Brown University

Bobby Baker is one of the most widely acclaimed and popular performance artists working today. This fully illustrated book brings together for the first time an account of Baker's career as an artist with critical commentary by reviewers and academic practitioners. It includes:
• Bobby Baker's own 'Chronicle' of her work as artist and performer
• Transcripts of Baker's performances and other original materials reproduced here for the first time
• Illuminating critical writing about Baker's shows, carefully edited and contextualised
• Significant new essays by Michèle Barrett and Griselda Pollock and a new interview with Bobby Baker by Adrian Heathfield.

Under the guiding editorial hand of distinguished cultural theorist Michèle Barrett, this volume is a hugely absorbing and accessible account of Baker's work, and an essential text for students interested in performance, gender, and visual culture.

Photography by Andrew Whittuck

Bobby Baker

Redeeming Features of Daily Life

Edited by
Michèle Barrett | Bobby Baker

Routledge
Taylor & Francis Group

LONDON AND NEW YORK

First published 2007
by Routledge
2 Park Square, Milton Park, Abingdon, Oxon OX14 4RN

Simultaneously published in the USA and Canada
by Routledge
270 Madison Ave, New York, NY 10016

Routledge is an imprint of the Taylor & Francis Group, an informa business

Book design by Jennie Smith Design

Printed and bound in Great Britain by Bell & Bain Ltd, Glasgow

British Library Cataloguing in Publication Data
A catalogue record for this book is available from the British Library

Library of Congress Cataloging in Publication Data
A catalog record for this book has been requested

ISBN13: 978-0-415-44410-1 (hbk)
ISBN13: 978-0-415-44411-8 (pbk)

ISBN10: 0-415-44410-1 (hbk)
ISBN10: 0-415-44411-X (pbk)

Inside covers: *How To Live* (2004).
BITE, Barbican Theatre, London
'Dancing Peas'.
Page vii: *Kitchen Show* (1991).
Preparatory drawing.

For Andrew, Dora and Charlie Whittuck

Contents

Preface   viii
Acknowledgements   x

PART 1: THE ARTIST   1
The Armature of Reason   3
Michèle Barrett

A Historical Artist
The Tale of the Early Years   23
Chronicle of Selected Artworks   28
Bobby Baker

PART 2: THE WORK   81
Risk in Intimacy   83
Adrian Heathfield

Comment   93
Aisling Foster

The Rebel at the Heart   95
of the Joker
Marina Warner

Integrity: The Essential   109
Ingredient
Geraldine Harris
with Elaine Aston

Upstaged by the Foodie Gaze   117
Helen Iball

Feminist Performance as Archive   129
Elaine Aston

Saying the Unsayable   135
Adrian Heathfield

Comment   145
Roy Foster

PART 3: THE SHOWS   146
Drawing on a Mother's Experience
Transcript   149
David Tushingham   155

My Cooking Competes
Lynn MacRitchie   159

Daily Life 1: Kitchen Show
'Action No. 3' Transcript   161
13 Actions: text   164
Lesley Ferris   172
Griselda Pollock   178
Helen Iball   185

Daily Life 2: How to Shop
Geraldine Harris   191

Daily Life 3: Take a Peek!
Lisa Jardine, Nigel Slater   197
Elaine Aston   200

Daily Life 4: Grown-Up School
Lauris Morgan-Griffiths   207

Daily Life 5: Box Story
Transcript   211
Michèle Barrett   224
Deirdre Heddon   230

Comment
Franko B, Maria LaRibot,   239
Tim Etchells

Spitting Mad
Sarah Gorman   241

How to Live
Jon Snow, John Daniel   244, 246

Diary Drawings
Griselda Pollock   251

Bibliography & sources   268
Permissions   271
Index   273

Preface

Michèle Barrett is Professor of Modern Literary and Cultural Theory in the School of English and Drama at Queen Mary, University of London. She is an editor of Virginia Woolf's *A Room of One's Own* and *Three Guineas* (Penguin) and *Women and Writing* (Harcourt), and the author of many books in the areas of feminism and cultural theory. She is currently working on the First World War, exploring the literary representation of its psychological damage. Her next book, *Casualty Figures: Five Survivors of the First World War* is forthcoming from Verso.

Opposite: *Baseball Boot Cake* (1972). Drawing from sketchbook.

I FIRST MET Bobby and Andrew in early 1989, a playground encounter with other parents at a north London primary school. Bobby integrated her work as an artist with her role as a parent and we were all quickly caught up with benefit performances in the school hall or going off to see *Drawing on a Mother's Experience* in the local church. Over the years, I got to learn more about her artwork and how she put it together. As time went by, we talked about some of the theoretical ideas inflected in her shows and I came to understand more about her complex relationship to the academic world in which these theories are usually batted around.

Bobby Baker's work transcends the boundaries often erected and defended around specific art forms, as they are around specific academic disciplines. *Redeeming Features of Daily Life* is about the work of an artist whose work breaks down any easy distinction between the performing and the visual arts. Funding for this book from Arts Council England has made it possible to present a photographic archive of her performances and it has also allowed us to include many of her sketches and watercolour drawings, doing justice to her visual art. This book is the result of collaboration between an artist and an academic. The collaboration has provided a cultural context in which the artist has felt free to articulate, in her own words, her intentions and reflections at various times, at an angle to the artwork itself. Critical commentary on Bobby Baker's work has emerged from several different academic disciplines and sources. A selection of this analytic and interpretative work is presented here in relation to, but necessarily independent of, the work of the artist. Some of these writings concern Bobby Baker's work in general, and others are presented here as commentaries on specific works. So the aim of the book is to present Bobby Baker's artwork, to add her own reflections on that work, and to put forward a selection of the views of others about that work. The book is consequently hybrid in form – part art book, part academic book, part memoir, part criticism, part case-book: at one and the same time all, and none, of these categories.

MICHÈLE BARRETT

21.10.73
Baseball Boots. Baseball Boot Cake. Birthday Cake
Birthday Boot Cake.
? ? CAKE ?

Start o. Ready Steady. Bang

Acknowledgements

BOBBY BAKER: *Redeeming Features of Daily Life* is a book that combines a record of, and reflections on, thirty five years of an artist's work. Andrew Whittuck's work, as may readily be seen from this book, has registered the visual imagery of Bobby Baker's performance in the art of the photographer, and has provided an archive of her visual art that is of the highest professional photographic standard. This longstanding collaboration between artist and photographer, from 1974 to the present, underwrites the exceptional visual quality of the book.

Much of the work that is recorded here was created, particularly in recent years, in collaboration with others. So the most important debts to record are to those who have been part of, or helped with, the creation of the artworks which the book documents, illustrates and explores.

Artsadmin has been producing Bobby Baker's work since 1990. Especial thanks are due to them for their crucial role in the development of her work since that time, as well as the significant part they have played in this book. Judith Knight, Director, created in Artsadmin an organisation which developed a radically new way of working – as producers, administrators, managers and collaborators – for artists who choose not to fit into traditional artistic categories. Work like this is often on the outside, but the artist also needs to belong to a set of creative institutions, to be part of a creative world. At Artsadmin there is vision, and dedicated long-term commitment. As well as Judith Knight, Bobby would like to thank Stephanie Allen, Bill Gee, Jo Hammett, Gill Lloyd, Kate Mayne, Bia Oliveira, Bibi Serafim and Jessica Williamson.

Many of the key performances, particularly of the *Daily Life* series, were made with Polona Baloh Brown – a huge thank you to her. The extent of her involvement in the making of these shows is reflected in this book. She has provided an exceptional 'outside eye' and has collaborated on many projects since 1990. In addition, as the drawing on p. 52 indicates, she is a good friend.

Steve Wald, Bobby's production manager, has the highest level of technical expertise in his job. Furthermore, his contribution frequently strays into what he regards as 'the art department'. Many thanks to him for his continuing collaboration, which has run from 1993 to the present. Sîan Stevenson, who met Bobby in 1994, was first involved in her shows with *Take a Peek!* in 1995, in which she performed. Since then she has played a variety of roles, including choreography, performance, touring direction and the cracking of many jokes. Deborah May's considerable creative input into the website – *Houseworkhouse* – has also been complemented by her documentation of performances, and development of brilliant audio-visual and 'special' effects in recent shows. Thanks also to Charlie Whittuck for his work on the sculptures for *A Model Family*.

Composer Jocelyn Pook agreed in 2000 to provide what turned out to be stunning choral music for *Box Story*, and has continued to collaborate since, alongside Harvey Brough as Director of Music. Their striking performance singing voices are complemented by the *Box Story* choir (Jeremy Avis, Jacqueline Dankworth, Sianed Jones, Melanie Pappenheim, Tony Purves, Kim Scrivener, Brooke Shelley, Belinda Sykes) and, for *How to Live*, the English Chamber Choir.

Mark Storor has brought energy and a vivid imagination to the project of involving people from a variety of new communities to the making of Bobby's artwork, starting with the workshops of *Grown-Up School*. The most technically ambitious of Bobby's shows, *How to Live*, benefited from the exceptional creative talents of Frank Bock (performer and sidekick), Miranda Melville (production designer), Chahine Yavroyan (lighting designer) and Simon York (set builder extraordinaire, from Miraculous Engineering).

Many other people have contributed to her work. Bobby would particularly like to thank Lucy Cash, Richard Hallam, Carole Lamond, and Lewis Nicholson, as well as Clare Allan, Ian Brown, Shirley Cameron, Helen Chadwick, Fraser Dyer, Daria Gibson, Nick Foley-Oates, Fraser Brown McKenna Architects, Albert Herbert, Marilyn Imrie for Catherine Bailey Ltd, Andrew Johnson, Stephanie Lamb, Ted Little, M J W Productions, Roland Miller, Jacqueline Palmer of Grand Union Design, Antonia Payne, Stephen Rolfe, Jo Scanlon, Swanky Modes, Dave and Pat Tomlinson, Chris Winter and Jess York.

The skill, ingenuity and dedication of technicians and crews who have worked on many productions, and touring, has made the shows happen – and provided great company all over the world.

Many people have contributed voluntarily, including students and interns. Their work added enormously to the shows and is much appreciated.

On the performance side, we could start with all the men who have long-sufferingly been painted in *Cook Dems*, who deserve a special vote of thanks (particularly George Hinchcliffe of The Ukelele Orchestra of Great Britain whose stomach Bobby burnt, panicking during a stony reception in a feminist conference). Duncan Glasse is the star of the *Cook Dems* performance in the DVD set. Finally, thanks to Patricia Varley (*How to Shop*) and Tamzin Griffin of *Take a Peek!*

Arts Council England has supported Bobby Baker's work for many years and its contribution to the production of this book has been particularly appreciated, as has the support of many individual officers over the years. The Arts and Humanities Research Council has funded Bobby Baker's Creative Fellowship at Queen Mary, for which thanks are due. Several of the shows represented in the book have been commissioned or facilitated by arts organisations, and particular individuals within them. Bobby Baker would like to thank Lois Keidan of Live Art Development Agency, the London International Festival of Theatre, Rose Fenton, Lucy Neal, BITE Barbican, Louise Jeffreys, Daniel Hinchcliffe, Sîan Ede, The Wellcome Trust and the London Centre for Arts and Cultural Enterprise. Specific thanks go to the past and present trusty trustees of Daily Life Ltd – John Besford, Fraser Dyer, Valerie James, Jonathan Lichtenstein, Jacquie Richardson, Katy Sender and Lynne Silver (Chair).

Making a book that would do justice to this work was a challenging order. We would like particularly to thank Adrian Heathfield, who encouraged both the project and the collaboration between the two of us. We are extremely grateful to all the contributors to the book. Some of them wrote new work for it, others agreed for their work to be reprinted in this new context, and others again agreed to have their work edited in order to facilitate a particular focus that we were seeking. Everyone has been very positive about the book and we thank them all. Information about publication permissions and rights can be found at the end of the book, and details of how to locate and find out about all the contributors are given throughout. We also want to thank Hugo Glendinning for the photograph of *Pull Yourself Together*.

At Routledge we would like to thank our Commissioning Editor, Talia Rodgers, for putting such faith into this hybrid project, and Production Editor, Susan Dixon, who oversaw an unusually complex book. Jennie Smith brought a superb level of design imagination and skill to the book, and takes the credit for its impressive final appearance. Work on the picture archiving was done by Tova Holmes and Louise Owens, and scanning by Ray Crundwell. The editorial side of the book has been no less complex than the work concerned with images: we would like to thank Nadia Atia for editorial help at an early stage, and Ruthie Petrie for help at the proof stage. Duncan Barrett has done considerable editorial work, has made the two new transcripts published here, of *Box Story* and 'The Housewife's Philosopher', and has also cleared the permissions – we thank him for his energy and precision. Katy Deepwell made the transcription of *Drawing on a Mother's Experience*, which was originally published in *n.paradoxa*. Several people helped with reading drafts of various parts of Part 1 of the book, and we are grateful to them for their comments: Stephanie Allen, Bill Briscombe, Bridget Escolme, Jo Hammett, Judith Knight, Bia Oliveira, Jen Harvie, Miriam Hodson, Maria Thorsnes and Dora Whittuck.

This book, mooted for many years, has finally materialised while both of us have been working in the School of English and Drama at Queen Mary, University of London. Our joint thanks to Julia Boffey, Jen Harvie, Paul Heritage, Amy Neale, Philip Ogden and Morag Shiach. More personally, Bobby Baker would like to thank Keith Broadbent and the staff of Oscar Hills, staff at the Pinestreet Day Centre, Drayton Park Women's Project and Highbury Grove CNC along with all at the Goodinge. Her thanks to her family are reflected in the dedication. Deepest thanks also to David Baker and 'Person J': Joyce Astell (formerly Taylor, Baker).

BOBBY BAKER AND MICHÈLE BARRETT
London, August 2007

Friday 14th June

Give me 14 hours non stop effort &
I will achieve an immense amount

20 min

Part One
The Artist

IN THE FIRST part of the book I give a general introduction to Bobby Baker's work, which is followed by a detailed chronological account of it by the artist herself. I look at Bobby Baker's training as a painter and the influence of conceptual art on her work; discuss her career as a performance artist; and consider her recent artistic explorations of 'unreason' and mental health issues. Bobby Baker then presents a historical account of her early life, in so far as this affects an understanding of her work, which is followed by a 'chronicle' recording her development as an artist. She is remarkably candid about the works that failed, believing that it is from failure that any artist learns, and moves forward. The chronicle covers the major artworks of Bobby Baker's career to date, and is illustrated (since his arrival on the scene in 1974) by Andrew Whittuck's photographs.

MICHÈLE BARRETT

Opposite:
Timed Drawing (1984).

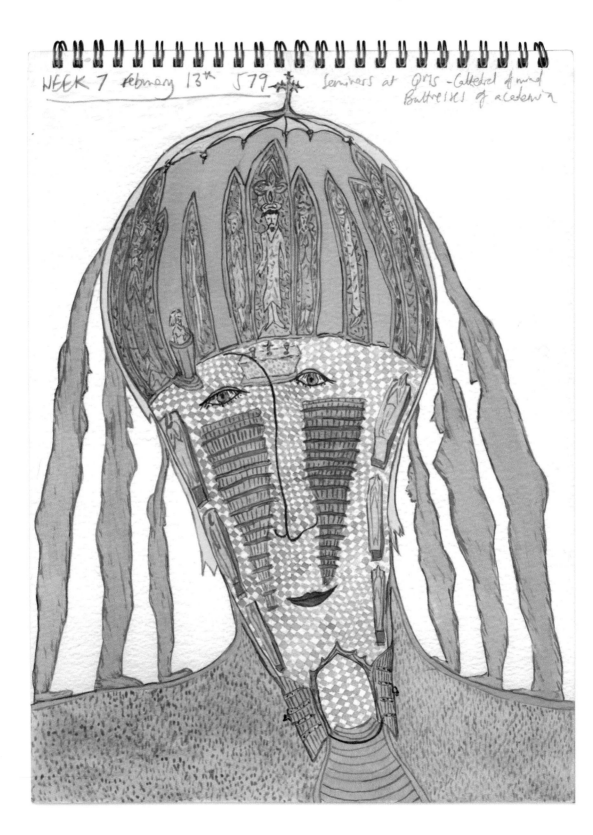

The Armature of Reason MICHÈLE BARRETT

EARLY IN 2007, as we were putting this book together, I glanced at the arts page of the newspaper. Top of the Critics' Picks column (*Guardian*, 20 January 2007) was 'the incomparable Bobby Baker', appearing at the Oxford Playhouse that night. The word 'incomparable' tells us something about the unique complexity of Baker's work. She is best known for her performance work, running from *Drawing on a Mother's Experience* in 1988, through the *Daily Life* quintet of shows in the period 1991–2001, and on to *How to Live*, which opened in 2004. These shows have toured around the world. Baker's work as a performance artist has raised issues about femininity, families and food in sufficiently complex and interesting ways to have inspired many academics and commentators to try to tease them out. These debates are reflected in this book, which includes contributions from scholars with expertise about these issues. Few of these commentators on Baker's performance work, with the exception of Marina Warner, have paid much attention to the specifically visual aspects of this artist's work. Perhaps what is most interesting in Baker's work, an ingredient of the adjective 'incomparable', is that her work cuts across any strong distinction between the visual and the performing arts. One aim of *Redeeming Features of Daily Life*, is to illustrate (not least, literally) the complementary forms of artistry running through her work.

1 '...PROPER FOR HER OWN USE'

In recent years, Baker has been quite forthcoming, in interviews, about her training as a painter, and her rejection of the assumptions of the art world of her student days at St Martins School of Art (now known as Central St Martins College of Art and Design) in London in the late 1960s. In those days St Martins was dominated by Anthony Caro and the 'British School' of sculpture – they created huge works in heavy materials such as iron, often in the form of large industrial flats and girders. Caro was an influential figure at St Martins in Baker's time there. Baker felt that it was 'inconceivable' that complex and difficult ideas could be expressed in these massive art forms, and also felt that they were typically masculine in their size and pretension. She retreated from them, and tells us that she spent her time endlessly re-reading the works of Jane Austen and Virginia Woolf. She retreated also from what, as Roy Foster points out, she regarded as the 'golf club of art', the institutions of the art world in which successful men would rise to the top. Some of her cohort at St Martins did that – Graham Crowley, Richard Deacon, Bill Woodrow. Bobby Baker felt, all the time at St Martins, an anxiety that someone would tap her on the shoulder and say, 'you can't be an artist, you are a woman'.

Antony Caro, *Sculpture 2* (1962).

Baker says that she read *A Room of One's Own* approximately once a month when she was at art school. What did Woolf have to say about Austen in that essay?

> The sentence that was current at the beginning of the nineteenth century was something like this perhaps: 'The grandeur of their works was an argument with them, not to stop short, but to proceed ...' That is a man's sentence; behind it one can see Johnson, Gibbon, and the rest. It was a sentence that was unsuited to a woman's use. ... Jane Austen looked at it and laughed at it and devised a perfectly natural, shapely sentence proper for her own use and never departed from it.
>
> (Woolf, 1929: 69–70)

Here is a context for Baker's *Baseball Boot Cake* of 1972, which she describes in detail in her own 'Chronicle' (see pp. 28–29). She made the cake, carved the boot, decorated it with icing, and looked at it. The revelation that she then describes, the 'new thought' that shone, was that this cake was no more a cake, it was a sculpture. It was a work of art, just as Anthony Caro's huge sculptures were. 'I had discovered my own language, material, form – something that began to echo my fleeting thinking.' Using food as an artistic medium became the hallmark of Baker's work. She had made a significant discovery, and she dates her distinctive work as the artist 'Bobby Baker' from that 1972 baseball boot made of cake.

That revelation has several components. An object not usually considered as art can become so when defined as such by either an artist or an art gallery: art is simply what we call art; as when galleries in the West exhibit the cooking pots and religious artefacts of other cultures as art; or when Duchamp put his urinal on display as a 'fountain', dramatising a whole tradition of discovering art in found objects. Then there is the particular fact of the object being a cake. Baker had taken a domestic object, and one that expressed women's skill, as well as their ambivalent relationships to their own eating and bodies, and to the task of feeding their families. The cake is carved and it is iced, an activity in which Baker developed a professional level of skill. The revelatory moment was far more complex than the way Baker's work with food is often portrayed – she did not simply say 'food is my language', she said she had found a 'language', a 'material', a 'form'. Baker's aestheticisation of her baseball boot cake was not simply poking fun at the Anthony Caros of the world (though it certainly was that: 'I just laughed with delight at the sheer irreverence'). Nor

Baseball Boot (1972). Anerley, London. Bought Madeira cake, icing sugar, food colouring, grandmother's cake plate.

was it simply an attempt to elevate women's domestic trivia to the status of art (though it certainly was that too: 'this decision to name such a pathetic, poorly crafted object A Work of Art of Great Significance'). More complex is how to think about the way in which our perception of an object changes when it is placed in an artistic context. Baker herself has said recently that her images of her own mental suffering, some of them very painful to look at, are made more bearable for the viewer through the distance of their being photographed, framed and exhibited as art, and this provides a clue to the contextual meaning we seek.

Baker went on to become an aficionado of using food as an artistic material, and many of her best-known performance pieces involved the creation, on stage, of an artwork made from various foods. At the beginning, however, she did not herself fully recognise the significance of the choice she had made – Baker works through intuition and an absolute certainty as an artist as to how something has to be and look, often only later understanding why she has done what she did. The early iced cake was soon followed by meringues, used in many of her works. Can she say, or we see, why a particular form is chosen? In the recent interview with Adrian Heathfield, Baker says she is surprised that she is not more often asked why she has chosen a particular image or action.

In October 1973 Baker went to London's Goldsmiths College to take the Art Teacher's Certificate, a professional qualification enabling Fine Art graduates to practise as art teachers in schools. Her Goldsmiths notebook carries, on the inside front cover, a summary of ideas taken from Ben Shahn's work on the definition of form (Shahn, 1957: 70):

> Form is based on a supposition, a theme. Form is a marshalling of materials, of inert matter. Form is a setting of boundaries, of limits ... an outer shape of idea. Form is the relating of inner shapes to the outer limits, the initial establishment of harmonies. Form is the abolishing of excessive content, of content that falls outside the true limits of the theme. It is the abolishing of excessive materials. Form is thus a discipline, an ordering, according to the needs of content.

On 22 November 1973, Baker attended the first of several seminars led by Barbara Reise: an 'incredible experience'. They changed the way she thought about perception, experience, the art object and herself. For the second meeting of the group, Baker made, as agreed with Reise, for discussion in the seminar group, nine 'ladies' in meringue, decorated with piped icing. 'There were eight people there and when they had all eaten one there would be one left to look at.' Baker says that she 'knew indistinctly what Barbara wanted to use the cakes for' but in the event it was an 'amazing experience'. As she recorded it in her notebook:

> Martin [a fellow student] said afterwards that he had never really been able to understand why my cakes should have any sort of reason for existing within an art context but the way it was explained tonight – or should I say, the way it happened

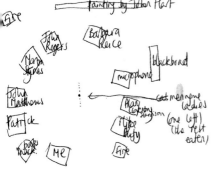

Above: diagram of seminar with Barbara Reise, Goldsmiths College, London (1973). Right: drawings and notes from sketch book (1973).

and the kinds of things that emerged from this – put the whole thing in a totally different light for him – and in a way it happened for me too – it reaffirmed what I had been thinking and feeling about them and it was particularly encouraging that everyone else should understand and perceive things in much the same light (this really became apparent during the discussion).

This seminar, in which Barbara Reise evidently facilitated a collective recognition of the meringues as works of art, was sufficiently important for Baker to draw the event in her notebook. Baker and Reise are the only women in the room. Baker still produces meringue ladies, particularly in large numbers for celebratory events.

Barbara Reise was an American art historian who came to work in Britain. She was an inspirational figure in the movements of minimal and conceptual art in the 1960s and 1970s, until she took her own life in 1978. She played a key affirming role for Baker at this crucial moment, but the meaning of the artistic move was as yet unresolved in Baker's own mind. In early December of that year, Baker wrote in her journal a draft statement, going through the arguments about how her work was exciting and had enormous potential, and why the Royal College of Art should accept her for further study. She acknowledged to herself the gap between her intuitive aesthetic conviction and her understanding of the work: 'But at no point yet have I really got down to what the cakes represent to me or to anybody. If you can't explain it then surely the logical thing to do is to explain *why* you can't explain it – the difficulty of summing up an experience – a conviction – in convincing terms.' Baker's subsequent work, particularly her performance art, has demonstrated to diverse audiences the imaginative and metaphorical possibilities in using food as an artistic medium, but in this early moment a lot of courage was required. The next entry in the journal is rather sad: 'sitting in waiting room at New Cross Gate waiting for the last train home – all sorts of insults (subtle) but I take them', to which she has added in small writing, 'fight rubbish'.

Baker's conceptual move, in 1972, of defining the baseball boot cake as a sculpture, and Reise's endorsement, the following year, of the meringue ladies as works of visual art, were formative moments in her work. Sol LeWitt, one of the artists at the centre of the conceptual movement from the 1960s onwards, stated baldly in his 'sentences on conceptual art' that 'no form is intrinsically superior to another', and that 'successful art changes our understanding of the conventions by altering our perceptions', also insisting that 'conceptual artists are mystics rather than rationalists' (LeWitt, 1969). As we can see from her own 'Chronicle' of the period from 1972 to 1980, there followed a series of artistic interventions, installations, and performances, including the key work, in 1976, *An Edible Family in a Mobile Home*.

But Baker's own question, of 'what the cakes represent', remains an important one. Her criticisms of St Martins as a junior branch of the art golf club were articulated in several drafts of her application letter to the Royal College of Art (she was rejected without interview). She argued that St Martins 'encouraged me to believe that the only valuable work was that of a painter and that a painter was necessarily divorced from normal life and considerations' and that these assumptions were never questioned, or even brought into the open. Baker's dissent from them was evident in both the artwork that she made for her degree show (assigned Upper Second Class honours), some of it included in her 'Chronicle' here, and the main piece of her written work: a dissertation on 'The Relationships between Art and Food and Society using the works of Virginia Woolf, Claes Oldenburg and Gilbert and George'. How prescient of the work she was later to make was this particular combination of figures!

The performativity of Gilbert and George, who met at St Martins in 1967, was inspirational to Baker in those early days. She described their work in her essay as 'conceptual art', in which 'they literally incorporate themselves into some of their works of art', and commented on their peculiarly English precision of dress and manner. Of greatest interest to her was the event 'The Meal', staged in 1969 and defined as 'an important art occasion', in which they drew attention to the formalised rituals around dinner parties.

Claes Oldenburg, *Floor Burger*, (1962).

In 1960, Claes Oldenburg decided to make artworks from everyday objects, including food. Baker was particularly concerned with the issue of artistic context, arguing that Oldenburg was not interested in food as such, but 'uses food purely as an image of the society ... which he can remove from its normal setting in order to transform it into an art-form'. The point is to make objects 'stand at a certain remove from reality'. By using objects, such as food, with which the viewer is familiar, and changing their size, Oldenburg wrenches viewers away from a specialised response to 'art' and reduces the estrangement of the gallery experience.

Baker's student account of Gilbert and George, and Oldenburg, throws light on the conceptual art background of her later performance work. What she described as her own 'fleeting thinking' is echoed in her comments on Oldenburg's remark that 'it is important to me that a work of art be constantly elusive': he wanted it to mean different things to different people. In one of her own sketchbooks of the time, across the top of a drawing in crayons, Baker has written 'there is no final, positive image which can be firmly stated – it must always be suggested – as in life'. The same point comes through in her discussion of Virginia Woolf's rendering of Mrs Ramsay in *To the Lighthouse*: the reader is never given Woolf's knowledge of the character, is never taken into

Woolf's confidence, but is given Mrs Ramsay as she is reflected in, and as she affects, the other characters in the novel.

Beyond the elusiveness of artistic truth lies another important point, and one that is significant for the question of 'what the cakes represent'. In Oldenburg's work 'quite common things ... can now seem to contain the poetry and mystery of reality'. This could be seen, continues Baker, 'as an attempt to find the spiritual in the material, the transcendent in the commonplace'.

Her third artist finds her way into the dissertation via the famous *boeuf en daube* of *To the Lighthouse*, where Mrs Ramsay has the curious sense that the dish ('with its shiny walls and its confusion of savoury brown and yellow meats and its bay leaves and its wine') will celebrate the engagement of Paul and Minta but also calls up, for her, 'the seeds of death' (Woolf, 1927: 115-16). The point that Baker makes here is true of Woolf's work in general: that 'exterior events lose their hegemony and serve to release and interpret inner events'. Woolf, in this reading, submits to what Baker calls 'the random contingency of real phenomena', celebrating the 'little daily miracles' observed by the painter Lily Briscoe.

The art student Lindsey Baker (as she then was) is picking up on Woolf's anti-rationalism, her mysticism, her phenomenological philosophy of 'the moment'. The elevation of the transitory and the mundane to the status of spiritual truth is a form of mysticism based on *this world* rather than an external deity. It is found in Woolf, but is a feature more common in the work of visual artists. It is not necessarily incompatible with conventional religious beliefs and practices, as in fact is the case with Bobby Baker herself. Stanley Spencer, another this-worldly mystic of Woolf's time, painted in his First World War memorial chapel at Sandham many images of men engaged in mundane activities, such as making beds, or doing the laundry. But their significance was transcendental for him: 'Had I not known and been completely assured that this painting was to form part of a scheme in which Christ would be receiving the resurrected soldiers I would not have been able to compose that picture of the man scrubbing the floor' (Rothenstein, 1962: 3).

Stanley Spencer, *Scrubbing the Floor* (1927).

Bobby Baker's first period as an artist, and her later return as a performer, was based on a rejection of the assumptions of the art establishment, and the conventions of painting and sculpture. Her time at art school may have been a contested and difficult period, but some of the insights shown in her own artwork, and in her writing from this period, provide a context for reading her later work. I turn next to the work for which she is best known, her performance art from 1988 to the present. But the person who rejected painting as a public art form never gave it up. Through the whole of this period, privately, Baker was drawing and painting. All of her performance art shows were extensively visualised, in her sketchbooks, during the process of imagining and devising them. Her private life, with family and friends, was also drawn and painted, often in restful or happy moods. Most importantly of all, as we shall see last, her suffering with what she describes as 'severe and enduring mental health problems', and the emotional experiences and political battles that she has had within British mental healthcare systems and practice, have been visually documented in an astonishing collection of watercoloured 'diary drawings'.

2 THE PERFORMING BOBBY BAKERS

Bobby Baker's performance work, starting with *Drawing on a Mother's Experience*, which she has performed live more than 200 times since it first appeared in 1988, has generated a considerable amount of academic analysis and interpretation. In the 'Chronicle' that Baker has compiled, there is an illustrated description of, and a note of any intentions for and reflections about, each piece of work. In Part Two of this book, we print two interviews with her conducted by the leading performance studies academic, Adrian Heathfield. The first, 'Risk in Intimacy', was published in 1999; they met again, to discuss performance issues for this book, in late 2006. The tenor of Baker's work has deepened and darkened in the intervening eight years: the new interview is entitled 'Saying the Unsayable'. Marina Warner's essay, 'The Rebel at the Heart of the Joker', commissioned in 1995 by the Arts Council in relation to *Take a Peek!*, discusses Baker's work up to that point in a manner that many readers have found illuminating. Warner's insightful essay has been much reprinted, but we include it here as the *'Ur-text'* of Bobby Baker Studies, cited and discussed by many subsequent scholars. Geraldine Harris and Elaine Aston offer a very helpful conspectus of Baker's work, from a performance studies point of view, in their discussions of feminism and autobiography, Baker's stage persona, form and action, her care of the audience, authorship and collaboration, and integrity and authenticity. Part Three of the book provides a selection of published work by specialists in performance studies, edited to facilitate discussion of the individual works. We have also included, for general interest, brief comments on these works by other artists, (Tim Etchells, Franko B, Maria LaRibot) and from appreciative members of live audiences over a period of time (Roy Foster, Aisling Foster, Jon Snow, Lisa Jardine, Nigel Slater). The context of the material selected is made clear, and a full bibliography appears at the end of the book.

Coming to this performance discussion from outside its disciplinary base, I am struck by a number of the general issues in play in these debates. In many of them, Bobby Baker's work seems to fit very unevenly, and to destabilise assumptions – perhaps

Above: *Timed Drawing* (1984).
'Tuesday 26 Feb.
Thrill me for 9 minutes, ideas'.

a reason why it has generated so much interest. In some ways, Baker's work has been the epitome of the performance ideal. The site-specific productions of the *Daily Life* quintet might be good examples – those live performances in her own kitchen, in her children's school, in the local church, were unrepeatable. When Baker says in her 'Chronicle' that she got a better reception from the punters in the National Exhibition Centre than she did when performing in reverential art galleries, this is the heart of a live performer speaking. She says she wanted to stand up in the street and perform rather than be defined by an art context. Similarly, *Pull Yourself Together*, with the unpredictability of how the public in central London would respond to Baker loud-hailing them from a truck, is 'live' art, is classically performative art. This ethic of performance has stayed with her over time – as she says to Adrian Heathfield in the latest interview, there is a 'window' of a few years during which she feels able to repeat live shows, after which she has changed too much for that to be possible.

The most eloquent summary of the pure performance position comes from Peggy Phelan: 'Performance's only life is in the present. Performance cannot be saved, recorded, documented, or otherwise participate in the circulation of representations *of* representations: once it does so, it becomes something other than performance. To the degree that performance attempts to enter the economy of reproduction it betrays and lessens the promise of its own ontology' (Phelan, 1993: 146). That word 'ontology' is very important in performance studies. Its usual source is the distinction in philosophy between epistemology and ontology, the former being the study of the basis of knowledge, and the latter being the study of the basis of being, or existence. So when we speak of ontology we speak of something to do with existence as such, as opposed to knowledge of it. The 'ontological' attribute of performance is its existence now, and the fact that no copy will be made. 'Performance is the attempt to value that which is non-reproductive, nonmetaphorical' (Phelan, 1993: 152).

But Baker herself has increasingly been moving away from live performance. In many significant respects, her work does not, never did, fall under a strict 'performance' rubric, certainly as defined by Phelan. In the first place, since she met Andrew Whittuck in 1974, her every move has been captured by a professional photographer. Often they worked on these photographs as a project that was independent of the actual shows – the cover image on this book is a staged photograph rather than one taken during a performance. This book is wholly indebted to Andrew Whittuck's photographs. The performances, too, have been accompanied by striking photographs, such as the cards that were distributed at *How to Shop*.

Bobby Baker has taken a deliberate path away from the pure performance ideal. Increasingly, she has developed versions of her shows in order to make them work in other contexts. At first, there were touring versions, removed from the original site but still live performances. Next, the film of *Kitchen Show*, a radio version of *Box Story*, a dedicated DVD version of *How to Live* and a website, currently being upgraded to house many digital variants of her work. Baker is increasingly complementing live performance and making work that will translate into other media. The *Daily Life* series was largely a collaboration between her and the co-director, or 'outside eye', Polona Baloh Brown. Her more recent productions have involved bigger and bigger teams of collaborators – composer, film-maker, structural engineer and so on. This change triggers the debate around live performance and the recorded, archived event, currently a source of much discussion.

A related issue is touring. Baker's 'Chronicle' indicates the extent of the world touring she has done and Helen Iball raises interesting issues about this in relation to the 'globetrotting' *Kitchen Show*. Baker herself is very conscious that her touring has tended to be anglophone, or in international festivals, and is unwilling to tour shows in which food is destroyed to countries that don't have enough. Also, Baker is now concerned about the carbon impact of international touring – sending containers with sets around the world is becoming environmentally irresponsible, she says. Another factor is physical and mental stress, as we see from the drawings showing the inner cost of these performances – Baker is currently developing a new version of *How to Live*, to be fronted by a young black woman who mocks Bobby's middle-aged, middle-class, and very white, stage persona.

Geraldine Harris and Elaine Aston have set out a generic account of Baker's work – their discussions of particular shows, and those of others printed here, have explored the purchase of many cultural theories, as tools to open up the meanings of Baker's work. Her emphasis on the significance of the everyday, for instance, lends itself to a reading through the work of Michel de Certeau and *The Practice of Everyday Life* (de Certeau, 1974). Similarly, Judith Butler's work on performativity (Butler, 1990) is an obvious source of interest in a performer who ritually reiterates her sex at the beginning of each performance. Baker followers may be interested to see, from her 'Chronicle', that the hostile reviewer, whose scorn led her to stop working for a year, had assumed that Bobby Baker was a man and not attended enough of the event to find out differently. That fact adds something to one's perception of the unrelenting introductory repetition of her sex in Baker's shows. A number of writers discuss Baker's plural and complex stage personas, often using ideas about the fragmented self, or constructed selves, drawn from psychoanalytic theory and from Michel Foucault's work on 'technologies' of the self (Foucault, 1988). Heddon extends these with an exploration of Baker's work in terms of Foucault's account of confession (Foucault, 1976).

Issues of autobiography, of the self, and of authenticity, have been fully explored, as have questions about feminism and femininity. Baker's presentation of self as a housewife and mother, from which position she invariably mocks the whole set-up, is a focal point.

One idea recurs in studies of Baker's performances: abjection. Perhaps we can start with her response to Adrian Heathfield's comment that disorder, and 'a certain kind of abjection', has been 'a strong refrain' in her work. She replies that she sees the abject as something 'pathetic and defiled', a commonsense definition of the word, and also as 'exposed, raw innards', which also suggests that the popular Kristevan notion of abjection has made an impression on her. Baker then goes on to say that she explores abjection, strays very close to it, but 'always with a level of control and knowingness that for me is not abject'. Marina Warner refers to this same artist's point of view in her essay. Heathfield then defines abjection as an 'in-between space' between objects without clear borders, from which he perceptively observes that Baker's earlier work *enacted* states of physical abjection whereas her later shows *narrate* them, while 'the onstage falls of your body are cleaner and more classically comedic'. At this point Baker firmly switches the subject to maths and prime numbers.

The word 'abjection' comes from the Latin word *abjectus* meaning cast off or rejected. To this was added the sense of cast down, low in regard, despicable, and beyond that the meaning of being degraded and humiliated. Julia Kristeva's essay on abjection, *Powers of Horror* – first published in French in 1980 and in translation in 1982 – has influenced a generation of cultural critics. In the essay, Kristeva proposes a new understanding of 'abjection', one that departs quite radically from the received dictionary definition. Within abjection, she writes, looms a violent, dark, revolt of being: desire is sickened, it rejects. The abject is banished, but constantly beseeches; it is separate and loathsome: 'Not me. Not that. But not nothing either.' Kristeva's first example is food loathing – 'perhaps the most elementary and most archaic form of abjection'. She conjures up the moment in which a child gags at milk with a skin on it; in expelling it the child also expels itself: 'I spit: I spit *myself* out. I abject *myself* within the same motion through which "I" claim to establish *myself*.' Smartly, Kristeva moves on to corpses, which '*show me* what I permanently thrust aside in order to live'. The corpse, 'most sickening of wastes, is a border that has encroached upon everything'. It is 'death infecting life', it is abject. Abjection, she argues, is caused by what disturbs identity, system, order.

Further, when Baker used the word 'strays' in the interview, she chose Kristeva's exact term, and *straying* is different from getting bearings, belonging, refusing. In addition, for Kristeva, 'laughing is a way of placing or displacing abjection'. We've only got to page eight of *Powers of Horror* and there are plenty of points already

How To Shop (1993), LIFT, London. 'Obedience'.
Below: *Spitting Mad* (1996). Video grab.

to explain why performance studies critics see the application of Kristeva's idea of abjection to Baker's work. Later, we encounter the 'desirable and terrifying, nourishing and murderous, fascinating and abject inside of the maternal body' (Kristeva, 1980: 54). Kristeva sees much religious activity as an attempt to manage the problems of waste, and the threat to the integrity of the body that corporeal waste presents; frequently this involves defining the female as the source of pollution. The 'ritualisation of defilement' tends to separate the sexes and give power over women to men (1980: 70). Geraldine Harris discusses the religious dimension of abjection in some detail in her discussion of *How to Shop*. Not all substances that challenge the borders of the body are polluting, according to Kristeva: tears, and sperm, for instance, are not. The two important types of pollutants are those to do with excretion and menstruation. Excrement is aligned with decay, disease, death and challenges the ego with non-existence. Menstrual blood threatens the identity of each sex in the face of sexual difference (1980: 71). Orality, the mouth, stands at the boundary of the self's 'clean and proper body'. Food is always 'liable to defile'. Food becomes abject when it is at the boundary between nature and culture, between the human and the non-human. Food is also, according to Kristeva, 'the oral object (the abject) that sets up archaic relationships between the human being and the other, the mother, who wields a power that is as vital as it is fierce' (1980: 75–6).

Bobby Baker certainly comes across as someone who transgresses the requirement that children not play with their food. But how important is the element of 'abjection' in her work? Let us take some examples, where audiences are certainly uncomfortable with what she does with food. The tin of anchovies she put in her mouth in *How to Shop* is one. It is a mortification of the self, it is masochistic, it silences the woman on stage, who can only mumble indistinctly through it, but it's not clear that this is abjection in the Kristevan sense. The chocolate bath in *Take a Peek!* is another example. It has been said this is abject – the chocolate representing excrement, which Baker is wallowing in. But two of our audience member contributors – Lisa Jardine and Nigel Slater no less – experienced this moment as the completely triumphant conclusion of the show. In *Cook Dems* three coloured sauces are splattered, with the one over the face creating much discomfort for the audience – but Baker is doing the splattering, eerily only interested in the aesthetic effects of it. The person abjected is the stripping young man in the blue swimming trunks – he has to keep his mouth shut and breathe through his nose. Baker does frequently stage an 'abject' moment, in which she messes herself up, covers herself with food, humiliates herself in some way, but usually this is the penultimate moment of a show, shortly to be redeemed with a celebration, often to music, often with dancing.

One reason why the still photograph of *Displaying the Sunday Dinner* (shown on p. 119) comes across as 'abject' is because there is no possible movement out of it. The meat breasts trigger one form of revulsion and the feet stuck in the crumble and custard trigger another, and both seem abject to me, in the Kristevan sense. Hovering close by this territory is the enigmatic short film *Spitting Mad*, where Baker calmly considers the aesthetic properties and potential of various foodstuffs, as spat out.

However, in the majority of Baker's works, where there is a dynamic movement and structure, she is in control of the representation of abjection, and its function is to underscore the power of the redemptive moment that is to follow. Without sounding too Pollyanna-ish, she wants the audience to leave feeling uplifted rather than degraded, and in this she succeeds: the abjection is always trumped. Furthermore, and this point is often overlooked in focusing on the dramatic side of the performance, the moments of abjection are often the gestures, the strategies, that actually produce the final visual artwork. One *Table Occasion* is described by Adrian Heathfield (in his introduction to *Risk in Intimacy*) as ending, after many a transgressive 'spillage', with Baker wearing 'the soiled remainder of the evening's labour as the sum image of the piece' in a 'dense moment of marred transcendence'. But this 'soiled remainder' is also a striking visual image, its structured patterns of colour turning a white tablecloth into an impression of a tie-dyed textile. Baker's movements, slopping the food around the place settings at the table, are indeed transgressive – but for the image to emerge successfully at the end they have to be skilful rather than disorderly.

3 THE ARMATURE OF REASON

At the same time as deciding to go public on her mental health status, Bobby Baker has in recent years become increasingly interested in her 1976 work *An Edible Family in a Mobile Home*, and in linking this and her large show planned for 2008/9, *A Model Family*. The *Edible Family* is described in some detail in her 'Chronicle', along with her subsequent realisation that the family had been her own family of origin and that the baby was herself. In the photographic images we can see how shocking the event was, how much the hint of cannibalism must have inflected, for the person who lived out the duration of the show, the cheerful violence of the temporary visitors. The family figures were constructed from cake, supported on a metal structure, in sculpture-makers' terms an armature.* All except one, that is: 'The baby was made of solid coconut cake and was unique in having no armature.' The baby had no bones, no bodily defence against disintegration, and – unlike the other family members – retained nothing of its shape

*'Rigid framework, usually of metal, made by a sculptor as a foundation or "skeleton" to which clay or another mouldable substance is applied' (Ehresmann, 1979: 7).

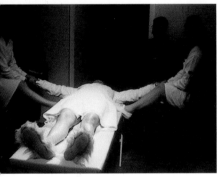

Top: *An Edible Family in a Mobile Home*
(1976). Stepney, London.
'Baby'. Coconut cake, butter and royal
icing sugar, food colouring, baby's cot.
Below: *Take a Peek!* (1995).
LIFT, Royal Festival Hall, London.
'Acrobat'.

after it had been eaten.

In retrospect, the *Edible Family* associated, at this early stage, a note of serious mental distress with Baker's work. This is qualitatively different from the vulnerabilities and ambiguities of her performance work, which have often been rather patronisingly referred to in the vocabulary of batty, barmy, dippy, daft, eccentric and so on. *Drawing on a Mother's Experience* refers to Baker's experience of moderate postnatal depression, but it is not centre stage. With *Take a Peek!* (1995), the third of the *Daily Life* quintet, we enter a world of much darker mood. The threat of incarceration is there, the coercion of the straitjacket is there. For much of the show, until the bold ending, the usual balance in Baker's work, between the high and the low, is thrown off, since Baker's body houses and expresses a damaged and threatened existence, and the young bodies of the assistants are given the counterpart. These two assistants are cheerful, bossy and explicitly sadistic at moments, and their gymnastic abuse of Baker's body in the carnivalesque hospital scene is startling. *Take a Peek!* is the performance that elicited Marina Warner's formulation of the submerged 'reefs of pain' under the surface of daily life, and her idea of the rebel in the joker.

The joker, the fool, is the one who is allowed to speak the truth by virtue of their low-power position at court. Foucault suggests, in *Madness and Civilisation*, that in the early modern period there was a mutually respectful dialogue between reason and unreason (Foucault, 1961). Polonius, thinking that Hamlet is mad, says, 'How pregnant sometimes his replies are! A happiness that often madness hits on, which reason and sanity could not so prosperously be delivered of' (Act 2, scene 2: 208-11). But now we have no time for extremes of emotion, no understanding of the driving irrationalities of love, jealousy or revenge, and we have no respect for the apt truths uttered by the mad. A watertight boundary has to be drawn between sanity and insanity, and the latter pathologised, stripped of its unreasonable truth and turned into nothing but illness. For Foucault, psychiatry is built on the forcible separation of reason and unreason; it is nothing but a 'monologue of reason' about unreason.

To conclude *Madness and Civilisation*, Foucault turns to the overpowering of reason through violence in de Sade, and to the possibility of recovering tragic experience through art in the work of Goya. In the contemporary world, Foucault notes 'the frequency ... of works of art that explode out of madness', but insists that we cannot reduce or conflate the two. Speaking of Van Gogh, Nietzsche and Artaud he insists that their work and their madness were in opposition: madness interrupts the work but is not to be confused with it. The work of art is not simply a matter of 'the features of pathology'; it engages with the world's time and 'masters it', so that 'by the madness which interrupts it, a work of art opens a void, a moment of silence, a question without answer, provokes a breach without reconciliation where the world is forced to question itself' (Foucault, 1961: 288).

These ideas may seem unduly portentous when set against the subtleties of Baker's *Daily Life* performances, but will come into their own when we come to speak of the drawings and paintings that Baker has been making, until recently, privately. As she says to Heathfield, 'It might seem like the ideas and images come out of being completely barking, but they don't actually – they come out

Diary Drawing 512 (2004). 'Week 43, 18 October. Getting unhinged – full rehearsal to team.'

of a refusal to succumb to that.' Meanwhile, these lighter shows suddenly got heavier with *Box Story*, in which the tragedy of her father's early and sudden death was carefully inserted – carefully, in the sense that the emotions it triggered were managed, in order to reduce the pain felt by the audience. With the end of the *Daily Life* series, Baker has focused her work more extensively on issues to do with her experiences with mental illness. She explains in the 'Chronicle' that she decided early on that her artwork would be about her own experiences, and consequently this is the outcome. Here we can usefully see *How to Live* and the *Diary Drawings* exhibition as two sides of the same coin – the one continuing her public style of negotiating difficult material (as Warner puts it, her humour makes it bearable for us to see), and the other revealing the level of her personal suffering.

In 2006, Bobby Baker responded positively to an invitation from Daniel Hinchcliffe, of the Institute for Interdisciplinary Arts at the University of Bath, to exhibit her drawings. As a contribution to Mental Health Week in March that year, Baker agreed to curate an exhibition of photographs, by Andrew Whittuck, of selected pages from her sketchbooks: *Diary Drawings*. These images record and reflect on her experiences since 1997 within the mental health system; they were specifically chosen for this educational (and agitational) purpose and are not necessarily typical of her work. Griselda Pollock, a distinguished art theorist who had previously written about, and for, Baker's performance work, was bowled over when she saw the exhibition at a subsequent conference at Bath on the subject of 'Trauma, Art and Representation' – at both Baker's skill and power in drawing and watercolour, and her courage in exposing her own psychic trauma. Griselda wrote to Bobby to thank her for making public 'brilliant and important work' that gives a visual form to the internal landscape of psychic suffering in a world 'hopelessly unable' to help or even recognise it. We asked Pollock to reflect further, for this book, on the significance of the exhibition, and we are delighted to print this new essay here.

Pollock comments on the courage required to choose to exhibit these images of the 'suffering soul', and draws out the political implications of their criticism of some aspects of psychoanalytic psychotherapy and the British institutional mental healthcare system. Also, however, she emphasises the *artist* at work in these extreme circumstances and shows that Baker's aesthetic project is very different from, and goes far beyond, using art to catalogue symptoms (the point that Foucault had also made). Using the work of the theorist and artist Bracha Ettinger, Pollock develops an interpretation of Baker's art in *matrixial* terms – relating to the archaic forms of the pre-birth world where recognising the intersubjectivity between selves unknown to each other points us towards a new understanding of compassion. Moving away from the traditional patriarchal themes of psychoanalytic criticism, and rendering the boundaries of the self both fragile and interactional, Griselda Pollock develops a fascinating and moving interpretation of Bobby Baker's art and work.

It might be helpful to clarify where Baker stands on the politics of this, as there are several issues at stake. The first is the clinical practice of psychoanalysis. In relation to the image of 'My Psychotherapist', Pollock suggests that there is a brutality in analytic therapy that only the very robust can cope with. Baker herself criticises psychoanalysis in the recent interview with Heathfield, on the grounds that it is both elitist and secretive; also relevant is the fact that she underwent several years of analytic therapy, during which her mental state deteriorated sharply. Baker is quite critical of some, though certainly not all, psychoanalytic practice, although it is not an issue on which she has a public position. Second, there are the institutions of the British mental healthcare system, of which Baker has experience. Here, her criticisms

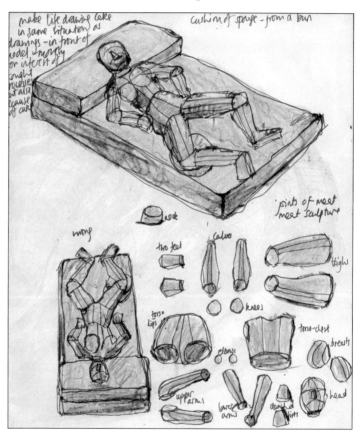

Drawing in sketchbook (1972). 'Cushion of sponge – from a bun. Make life drawing cake in same situation as drawings – in front of model – mostly for interest of thought processes but also because of cake.'

are more public. She has come to believe that mental health is the last great battle of human rights, and that discrimination against people with any history of mental health problems is the last great form of discrimination. There is a general cultural stigmatisation of mental illness, and the proper economic and social resources needed to care for mentally ill people are simply not made available. This general social disregard for the mentally ill is the context of the failings of the mental healthcare system. Writing in the *Guardian* (4 October, 2006) to defend the humour of *How to Live*, she expressed concern about 'the stigmatised, profoundly serious issue of mental illness and the provision for its care', and referred to 'the abuse of human rights in acute psychiatric hospitals' as well as the assumptions of 'insensitive professionals'. This is a campaign that she shares with many within these systems: she talks about 'extraordinary practitioners' fighting in the NHS to improve the situation. To balance the images shown in the *Diary Drawings* exhibition, this book includes drawings where a more positive side of these mental healthcare practitioners is shown.

It is in some of her visual artwork that the extent of Baker's mental disruption is shown. Her own self is fragmented, constantly doubled, and rendered with horrific images of bodily violence and disintegration. The word 'suffering' surfaces as Bobby Baker's own definition of psychosis in the Heathfield interview: 'Psychosis is really metaphor – a metaphor for extreme suffering.' For Griselda Pollock, the language that comes to mind is of 'the suffering soul', and the deep trauma of archaic matrixial wounding. The baby with no armature has no framework on which to build a bodily and psychic integrity, and the moments of psychosis, perhaps we might say madness as one form of 'unreason', are incursions into that profound vulnerability. Although Baker's violently psychotic images date from her recent periods of illness, some of the iconography is much older. Thinking about her own question, as a student, of 'what the cakes represent', I was struck by the preparatory drawings for her Goldsmiths show, *The Life Room*, in 1974. Here the figure of a woman is assembled from what one can only call 'joints' of cake, and the butchering reference is made clear on the page. A body such as this is not a coherent whole, which is then cut up and eaten in the performance, shocking as that was with the baby in *Edible Family;* this figure of a woman is already jointed, already fragmented, before it has been created in the form of art.

Bobby Baker's drawings of her experiences in the mental health system, in her fifties, reframe her student insistence on the importance of context. She wanted the cakes to work in an 'art context', for them to be seen differently. Her images of mental illness, as ever presented with humour, also function in a specific context. They are made bearable for the viewer by being lifted out of the simply biographical, and rendered as artworks to be examined. What has not changed, in a personal psychic landscape with much doubling and splitting, is her absolutely *single*-minded commitment to making artwork. Back in 1973 she wrote in her journal: 'Intentions. 30/11/73. I am sure that in the future I will continue my work because I sincerely feel that it is the only way in which I can live. If at any time these feelings should change I hope that I shall have the integrity to admit this to myself.' That has not been necessary. In late 2006 she talked to Adrian Heathfield about her increased confidence in her artistic judgement and her work being a process in which she was completely bound up: 'I can't see it ending while I'm alive.'

Opposite: *Box Story* (2004). BITE, The Pit, Barbican, London. Assorted foodstuffs, assorted boxes.

A Historical Artist

BOBBY BAKER

THE TALE OF THE EARLY YEARS

1950 born Sidcup, Kent.
Mother part-time PE teacher, campaigner for sheltered housing for elderly people, magistrate.
Father Company secretary for The Royal Exchange Assurance Company.
Sister eight years older.
Brother two years older.

Home Life 1950–66

Childhood shoes Clarks sandals with the toes cut out for extra growth, jellies and wellies.
Childhood outfits Aertex shirts, shorts and jumpers. Dresses made by my mother, worn under sufferance.
Selected childhood experiences
• Adopting my baby nickname 'Bobby' permanently when I realised that a boy's name was more fitting with my personal sense of status.
• Putting on shows on the landing upstairs with the small, select (but paying) audience sitting at the bottom looking up at us – an inversion of the traditional theatrical 'raked seating'.
• Teaching our dachshund Rudi (who thought he was a wolfhound) to jump special dachshund gymkhana courses and sing duets with me.
• Sitting next to my father every Sunday in church and absorbing his intense peace, faith and love.
Teenage shoes Flip-flops, patent leather sling-backs.
Teenage outfits Corduroy jeans and jumpers, snazzy dresses and coats

Opposite page:
Perpetuity in Icing (1978).
ICA, London. Cotton sheeting, icing sugar, food colouring.

23

Top : *L Baker 11 Embroidered plant* (1961). Canvas, embroidery threads. Below: *Life drawing of schoolgirl* (1964). Paper, pencil.

made from Butterick patterns.

Selected teenage experiences

• Being the only female member of the Bromley branch of the Dusty Springfield Fan Club.

• Protesting against golf etiquette by playing in bare feet.

Education 1954–66

Shoes Clarks sandals and lace ups, Clarks slip-ons.

Outfits Harris tweed coats, blazers with badges, felt hats, Panama hats, tunics, blouses and ties, bloomers, v-neck jumpers, striped summer dresses with cardigans, cloaks lined with house colours, pleated gym shorts, tennis dresses and shoes, lacrosse boots, gym shoes, brown Sunday dresses with optional lace collars, and on and on and on....

Selected Experiences

• Having one of my paintings exhibited in the main hall and the 'big girls' laughing at me because I'd painted it raining and sunny at the same time (but secretly knowing I was right).

• Managing to hold a fistful of jelly for the whole of break-time after lunch without spilling a drop, despite no one else taking any interest in, or being impressed by, this feat of skill and endurance.

• Loving Art with Mrs Burgess and being taught traditional, accurate life-drawing techniques using eye, out-stretched hand and pencil, constant measuring, and techniques such as 'swinging an ellipse'.

• Discovering with shock that I understood what she meant when, aged 14, I made a scarily accurate drawing of our 'life model' – an 11-year old girl in sports gear.

• Our form winning the annual drama prize for a production of *Androcles and the Lion* (with me as the Lion).

Schools West Lodge Preparatory School, Sidcup; Farrington's School for Girls, Chislehurst, Kent.

Qualifications/achievements (11 Plus – Fail); 'O'-levels 9 A-C; Under 15 Lacrosse and Tennis teams; Annual Art prizes.

Home life 1966–68

Shoes Desert boots, any old high-street shoes.

Outfits Jeans, rugby shirts, any old Bromley High Street, Millets and 'boutique' clothes.

Selected Experiences

• Performing being 'alright' after the death of my father by drowning in the summer holidays.

• Cooking, shopping and cleaning.

• Trying to protect others from the embarrassment of death, particularly sudden untimely death.

• Repeatedly rereading Jane Austen novels.

Education 1966–68

Schools Chislehurst and Sidcup Grammar School for Girls, Sidcup Art School evening classes.

Shoes 'Sensible' shoes or bare feet.

Outfits Pleated skirt, blouse and tie, Butterick home-made dresses in pale blue house colour, gabardine mac, blazer with badge, beret.

Selected Experiences

• Feeling mortified to realise I was a middle-class 'snob' and wondering how to change.

• Discovering that sarcasm was not an effective or comprehensible means of communicating the desire for friendship with others.

• Hating Art at the Grammar School, particularly appliqué.

• LOVING life drawing at Sidcup Art School.

• Making friends with the Art teachers Keith and Fred and going on painting expeditions.

• Featuring in the *Bromley Evening Argus* after being photographed on one of these 'outings' painting the Brighton Royal Pavilion. The headline was 'Great-niece of Queen's Art Teacher Hits the Big Time!'

• Learning to do really strong, exuberant life drawings.

• Discovering wild collage techniques.

• Being told I was a 'real' artist by my grandmother when she saw one of my drawings, just before she died.

Qualifications 'A'-levels – English C, History E, Art E.

Life 1968–72

Shoes Flip-flops, desert boots, platform boots, home-dyed baseball boots, scruffy hippy shoes.

Outfits Kensington Market hippy, Millets, jumble sale fur coats, battered old Harris tweed school coats, home-made crushed velvet suits, Dorothy Perkins and Etam glamour.

Selected Experiences

• Leading a Jekyll and Hyde existence between Bromley and St Martins – my transformation happening on the train every morning in front of frightened office workers as I smoked roll-ups with liquorice paper (to look like drugs).

• Finding that the process of making chocolate mousse made life more bearable.

Education 1968–72

St Martins School of Art; Pre-diploma and Diploma in Fine Art – Painting.

Shoes as above.

Outfits as above.

Selected Experiences

• Stopping by at the National Gallery most mornings, after my commute from Bromley to Charing Cross, to copy Cézanne's *Les Grandes Baigneuses*.

• Taking a whole term to finish a collage of a tomato as I was using the wrapping paper from the Tate and Lyle sugar cubes from my daily cups of tea.

• Realising that all the vague ideas in my head could never fit into any art forms I saw about me.

Top: *Painting in grounds of the Royal Pavilion* (1967). Brighton, UK. (Photograph *Bromley Evening Argus.*) Below: *Life Drawing* (1967). Sidcup Art School, Kent. Paper, ink, chalk.

• Reading and rereading essays and novels by Virginia Woolf.
• Spending two terms with my very own life model drawing all day every day, and being able to draw well from then on, despite only having produced one good drawing.
• Doing all the work for my Diploma show in the Easter holidays – paintings of my teddies and shoes (as there was no money or space for models in Bromley).
Qualifications Pre-Diploma and Diploma in Fine Art – Painting 2.1

Education October 1973–June 1974
Goldsmiths College, London: Art Teacher's Certificate
Key Decisions made during this period
Using food as a medium
I had made this decision in 1972 (see *Baseball Boot Cake* in the 'Chronicle' section, pp. 28–9), when I made a cake and 'the heavens opened and a new thought shone into my brain – I'd made a Work of Art, a sculpture'. A lot of cake-making had gone on prior to Goldsmiths.
Making work based on 'myself'
In the first week at Goldsmiths we had to exhibit our work or give a slide show. I chose to show slides of my cake 'artworks'. I was optimistic and excited by my discoveries and delighted by my work, but on witnessing the more traditional work of other students I became anxious as to how it would be perceived. I showed my slides and I cracked a few self-deprecating jokes and everyone laughed extravagantly. I remember being surrounded afterwards by well-wishers saying 'You're *so* funny, your work is *so* funny, *so* weird, you made me laugh *so* much, you're a hoot.'
I went into a toilet and wept. I could not believe I could clown around about work that I felt was serious and new, even though it made me laugh with pleasure. I felt quite tortured on the train journey back to Anerley, but then I had another Damascene bolt of inspiration that has fundamentally informed my work ever since.

Teddy Bear (1972).
Bromley, Kent.
Oil painting on canvas.

I realised that it was impossible to squeeze myself into this 'mould' of the artist. I could not *make* myself work like others no matter how much other work inspired me. I could not *be* like other artists; I could only be myself. Therefore my work could only focus on my own internal world, personality, opinions, concerns and experiences. I could not personally make work about things with which I was unfamiliar. Other people could, would, should do that but not me. It was another profoundly liberating experience. I realised that the work I made was not necessarily going to be of interest to others, but that was not initially a matter of great concern. As long as I made the work *from myself, for myself,* and if it then communicated my passionate concerns to others it was a transformative bonus.
Humour
Although I knew that laughing at life was part of me, it was not until I made *The Life Room* (see pp. 32–3) that I accepted it as a valuable method of communication. It has taken me years, and the observations of critical theorists including feminists like Marina Warner, to realise why humour is

such an important part of the 'package' that is my work and an effective way of conveying complex and sometimes subversive ideas.

Integrity

As part of the course at Goldsmiths, the art historian Barbara Reise delivered a series of seminars that significantly informed the way I've aspired to make work since. She proposed a recipe of the essential ingredients for 'The Perfect Work of Art'. Until preparing for this book, I had misremembered that she suggested there were six ingredients, the most important of which was *integrity*. On consulting my sketchbook in 2006, I discovered a list of five ingredients under the heading 'Abstract Linguistic Structure'; validity, relevance, coherence, elegance and change, with no mention of integrity! The notion must have come from her; I would not have conceived of such an ingredient myself, as it was her definition of integrity that was so startling and inspiring. The meaning I took from her is best summarised in this dictionary quote 'The condition of having no part or element wanting – unbroken state – material wholeness, completeness,

Meringue Lady on her own.
Meringue Lady with her husband,
daughter and son (1976).
Meringue, icing sugar, food colour.

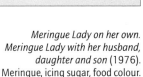

entirely.' I was thrilled at the idea that one could persist in the almost impossible task of trying to capture a *complete* set of ideas in one whole artwork. I felt that I had observed it in work that I loved; for instance in art such as Oldenburg's sculpture, Lichtenstein's paintings, Tinguely's 'events' or the writing of Woolf and Austen. To aspire to such an ambition using a transient encounter with cake left me breathless with joy.

Teaching

I'm sorry to say that I was uninterested in learning to teach, although impressed by those who could do it. I spent a great deal of my time making my own work and, surprisingly, I was allowed to submit *The Life Room* as my thesis. After a disastrous experience at the London Nautical School for Boys, when I fled the classroom for good after failing to control a papier-mâché fight, I was fortunate to do my teaching practice at an adult education institute in Wandsworth run by Mike Cutts. Although this institute subsequently employed me, I think it was due to my general enthusiasm for chatting to people and tackling storage problems rather than any aptitude for teaching.

CHRONICLE OF SELECTED ARTWORKS 1972–2007

Top: *Alley Cat* (1972).
Rose Alley, London.
Emulsion paint, paint stainers
on concrete render.
Below: *Rose Café Mural* (1972).
Gloss paint on brick.

1972

Title *Alley Cat.*
Shoes Painting shoes.
Duration July–August.
Location Rose Alley, South Bank, London (just about where the National Theatre car park is now).
Description Sam Wanamaker, who was holding annual summer Shakespeare seasons in a tent on a derelict site next to the Hayward Gallery in order to raise funding and publicity for his Globe Theatre project, commissioned several graduates to paint murals in the surrounding streets. I painted a sequence of twelve images of a giant cat, based on the Muybridge photographs, gradually transforming, in a painterly way, as it started to run down the street. I also painted the front of the Rose Café as a favour to the owner in exchange for free bacon sandwiches.
Artist's intentions and opinion I was very muddled as to why I joined the project, did what I did and what the point of it all was. Everyone else seemed to be able to justify his or her work and intentions. When it was finished I privately felt it was rather successful, indeed beautiful, and appeared to 'fit the brief'.
Remaining evidence The whole site, buildings, streets and all were ultimately knocked down for the National Theatre development.

Title *Baseball Boot Cake.*
Shoes Bare feet.
Duration 21 October (kept for eight weeks after, until it rotted).
Location Kitchen in a semi-derelict butcher's shop in Anerley, South London.
Description A cake in the shape of a baseball boot made out of a Madeira cake carved into the rough shape of a life-size boot, decorated with icing sugar and placed on my grandmother's cake plate.
Artist's intentions and opinion Leaving St Martins had been a relief, despite the fact I'd had some fun. I felt my ideas didn't fit in with the art I saw or the gallery scene. But I didn't know what my ideas were – they wafted around out of sight, like fleeting glimpses of butterflies – multi-coloured, in perpetual motion, three-dimensional, complex. My experience with mural painting and a commission for Knebworth House to paint a series of banners for its Banqueting Hall were dissatisfying.

I had decided to be a businesswoman instead and was successfully selling home-dyed baseball boots by mail order in *Private Eye.* It was too boring, though, and I started to make cakes for fun. Not for any occasions – just for the pleasure of it. The first ones were of my favourite ashtray (my father's) – a miniature armchair. In the middle of one night I made a baseball boot cake. I was particularly satisfied with it and sat looking at it for a long time. Suddenly it was like the heavens opened and a new thought shone into my brain – I'd made a Work of Art, a sculpture of equal status to Anthony Caro's epic and huge metal sculptures. For a long time I just laughed with delight at the sheer irreverence of this decision to name such a pathetic, poorly crafted object 'A Work of Art of Great Significance'. But I knew at the same moment that it was a pivotal turning point for me as an artist – I had discovered my own language, material, form – something that began to echo my fleeting thinking.

Remaining evidence The cake sat around for eight weeks till dust and the smell forced me to throw it out. The photo (see p. 5), plus sketchbook pages are all that exists. The title under the first drawing of the cake is 'Start Go. Ready Steady. Bang'.

Title *Cake Christmas Dinner.*
Shoes Silver knee-high platform boots.
Duration December, one evening at a Christmas party.
Location A studio, St Martins School of Art, London.
Description I made an entire life-size Christmas Dinner out of cake – nine items.
Artist's intentions and opinion I hoped that displaying my edible artworks in a more public setting would overcome the wasted food problem. The first guests (art students in a festive spirit) said, 'Wow, man, that's cool,' but the cakes had soon been eaten in handfuls or trodden into the floor and danced on.

Cake Christmas Dinner drawings (1972). Felt-tip pen, paper.

Remaining evidence Some photos, drawings in sketchbooks.

1973
Title *Birthday Tea Party*.
Shoes Green tap shoes.
Duration 28 October.
Location Sitting room, Anerley, South London.
Description Variety of cakes, meringues and jellies.
Artist's intentions and opinion The baseball boot cake not being eaten and my Christmas Dinner cakes being overwhelmed by a drunken horde bothered me. I decided to have a tea party to display my cakes. I wanted people to go away having enjoyed them aesthetically but carrying them in their stomachs. The party was a flop. I think people were overcome by the efforts I'd gone to and didn't want to 'spoil' the display. The setting was too social, but with no precedent (or alcohol), so no one knew how to behave.
Remaining evidence The photo on p. 99 plus drawings in sketchbooks.

Title *Princess Anne's Wedding Day.*
Shoes Pale pink plastic 'loafers' with weird small clumpy heels.
Duration 10.30am–1.30pm, 15 November.
Location St Martins School of Art, London.
Description A friend of mine from St Martins, Tony Hayward, had introduced me to a couple he described as 'performance artists', Keith and Marie. He invited me to join in a performance they were giving at St Martins to celebrate Princess Anne's wedding day. I'm the same age as Princess Anne, so it was decided I could be an alternative her. I wore a favourite long red velvet coat and pink swimming cap and we wafted around the foyer of St Martins and Charing Cross Road with a great deal of kitsch detritus around and about.
Artist's intentions and opinion It seemed a marvellously auspicious occasion on which to become a 'performance artist', as I had grown up with my brother and I being the same age as Charles and Anne and had a vague fascination and increasing horror at their fate. I was extremely glad to be scuffling about in Charing Cross Road and not bedecked in white in Westminster Abbey.
Remaining evidence None.

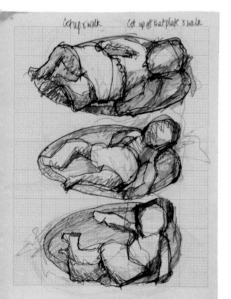

Baby Cake drawings (1973). 'Get up and walk. Get up off that plate and walk.' Felt-tip pen, graph paper.

Title *Baby Cake.*
Shoes As above.
Duration 25 November.
Location Oval House, South London.
Description Keith and Marie were doing a performance in the café at this radical alternative Art Centre. They suggested I present one of my cakes. I had made life-size babies on a meat platter before this and chose to take one of these. I carved the Baby Cake up and served it to people in the café. I wasn't sure what to wear, so opted for an old ball gown of my mother's covered with hand-made paper roses safety-pinned on, a maid's cap and had clown-like make up.
Artist's intentions and opinion I wanted the chance to see what people made of the cake in a more formal setting (if you could call our performance formal in any sense!). I was irritated by how shocked people were at the sight of me chopping up the baby, and their gasp of horror at the first cut, since to me it seemed an appropriate and interesting image to associate with Christmas.
Remaining evidence One photo and drawings.

Title *Xmas Pudding Party Sculpture.*
Shoes As above.
Duration 21–22 December, 60 minutes.
Location Oval House, South London.
Description *Meringue Ladies World Tour I and II.* I was accompanied by a bunch of Meringue Ladies who I handed out to people. I wore a rudimentary hand-made Meringue Lady dress and swimming cap, to try to look like them. I also made miniature peppermint cream Christmas dinners as 'boxed sweet' gifts.

Artist's intentions and opinion I loved the Meringue Ladies, whom I'd been making for a while. I thought they were a powerful, cheering and amusing bunch to perform with. As a group they form an image of strong women. Also it was easy, with my piping nozzle, to alter the mood of the crowd from happiness through to fury by adjusting their mouths. I was entertained by the idea of going on a world tour with them (Nottingham is the furthest we've gone, even after 35 years).

Remaining evidence Drawings in sketch books and the plaster moulds that were used to make the peppermint creams.

1974

Titles *1st Life Room, Street Performances, Head Cake.*
Shoes As above.
Duration Throughout January.
Locations St Martins School of Art; Trafalgar Square; Speakers' Corner; Troubadour Club – all London.
Description Generally I wore the favourite velvet coat. There was a lot of standing around being stared at. I was often working alongside other 'performance artists' and musicians including Roland Miller and Shirley Cameron, Keith and Marie, Rob Conn, Ian Hinchliffe, Lol Coxhill and others.
Artist's intentions and opinion Everything seemed possible and worth a shot. In hindsight I am pleased that I did things without knowing why. There seems to be an ever-increasing pressure to explain, contextualise, theorise every piece of work that one makes. I stand by the necessity and value of investigating vague notions. It is by walking into a cloud that one can sometimes come out the other side with vivid understanding. If an artist doesn't *make* anything, how can you *learn* anything?
Remaining evidence A few photos and drawings.

Title *Sweet and Sour.*
Shoes As above.
Duration 2 April, 7–8pm.
Location St Martins School of Art Lecture Hall, London.
Description I made 50 'boxed' marzipan roses to send out to people as invitations. There was a pre-recorded 'voice-over' of 'Billy's Dead and Gone to Glory' by George R. Sims. I performed a sort of cookery demonstration with a mobile kitchen involving sweet and sour pork balls, crystallised roses, rosé wine, etc. I fed the audience as part of the show.
Artist's intentions and opinion This was a more carefully considered piece involving a lot of preparation. It was meant as a commentary on the pros and cons of sentimentality. I wasn't very happy with it, as it seemed too pre-planned and slightly cloying.
Remaining evidence Drawings and a few stray 'boxed' marzipan roses.

Title *Meringue Ladies World Tour III.*
Shoes As above.
Duration 14 May, 30 minutes.
Location Oval House, South London.

Description I danced on the meringues and crushed them, for the first time.
Artist's intentions and opinion I think my intentions were to shock, express brutality and transience. Also it's a very pleasant experience to walk on a meringue. They sort of pop.
Remaining evidence None.

Title *The Life Room.*
Shoes As above.
Duration 10 June, 7–8.30
Location M&B Motors Exhibition Space, Goldsmiths College, London.
Description I lined the entire circumference of the space (approximately. 20 metres by 10 metres) with 27 floor-to-ceiling paintings on paper (made of sheets of newspaper pasted together) of a huge naked woman transforming stage by stage from a cake to the tree of life. In the centre of the space, on a mattress covered in a sheet, was a life-size naked 'life model' made of iced sponge cake. I had my mobile kitchen set up at one end, where I knelt and proceeded through a series of cooking processes with a variety of ingredients. Keith and Marie were performing something else down the far end of the space. At the end of the performance I cut up the cake and fed it to the audience.

The Life Room (1974).
Post show exhibition,
Goldsmiths College, London.
Newsprint, powder paint, cotton sheet,
chocolate cake, icing sugar.

Artist's intentions and opinion I was trying to pull a lot of ideas and working processes together to form an integral whole. On my terms it didn't succeed, but I learned a lot. The audience seemed to like it but it felt muddled to me. I have two pleasurable memories. The first was that Lindsay Kemp passed through the space before the performance and shuddered with horror at the sight of so many naked women. The second was squashing a tomato with a wooden meat hammer. The performance seemed to be dragging and I really didn't know what the hell I was doing. I didn't have the courage to speak much in those days, but I suddenly got an idea which I couldn't resist. I said 'You know what, I'm going to squash this bloody tomato with this hammer.' The gale of laughter from the audience as I pounded the tomato to a pulp led me to begin to trust more in hunches and humour. It certainly cheered us all up and dispelled the 1970s reverence for experimental art events.

Remaining evidence Photos and drawings.

Title *Meringue Ladies World Tour IV.*
Shoes As above.
Duration November, 15 minutes.
Location Oval House, South London.
Description I was without a home at that stage, so staying with friends in Putney. I planned a Meringue Lady Dance but didn't start making the meringues till late on the evening before the show. I discovered I didn't have my trusty Meriwhite catering egg substitute that I made meringues with in those days to save time, so instead I used all the eggs I could find at that time of night. I cooked all night and produced about 60 meringues. I laid them out with pride, in rows, on the sitting-room floor to show to my friends. When they appeared in the morning, their huge Irish red setter dog bounded in and 'hoovered' up 40 meringues, row by row, before we could stop him.
Artist's intentions and opinion General bewilderment and amusement. I really didn't care much in those days what happened, as long as I actually appeared and tried something.
Remaining evidence None.

1975

Title *To Bring a Sheep to Consciousness We Must Eat It. Therefore to Bring Virginia Woolf to Consciousness We Must Eat Her.*
Shoes Coffee coloured slip-ons with beige piping.
Duration Three weeks.
Location New Contemporaries, Camden Arts Centre, London.
Description I 'gate-crashed' the exhibition by proposing an edible artwork for the opening. My aim was to make a contemplative tribute to Virginia Woolf, using what a friend of mine told me was a Sufi proverb as part of the title. I made a life-size figure out of special human-shaped bookshelves seated on a chair. Small significant ornaments were glued to the shelves. I remember that there was a china bird on the top shelf, forming the centre of Virginia's head. Around this armature I then attempted to model a cake figure out of 1,080 buns and then to decorate it with marzipan. I served visitors to the private view with slices of buns gradually revealing the bookshelves and ornaments.
Artist's intentions and opinion This was meant as a development of the life models I'd made before and a reflection on Virginia Woolf, consumption, life cycles, the food chain, etc. Due to chaotic planning (I had no home

Virginia Woolf cake in preparation (1975). Camden Arts Centre, London. Buns, butter icing, wood, shelving, ornaments, plastic and metal chair on Persian rug.

at the time) and lack of sculpting experience, she ended up more like the Incredible Hulk. I was so disappointed with this piece that I abandoned her there in the foyer. Gallery curators kept on trying to contact me to collect the remains at the end of the exhibition, but I couldn't face going back and I therefore lost all the ornaments, including a Persian rug belonging to my grandmother.

Remaining evidence Lots of photos and drawings. I'd met Andrew Whittuck by then, and he helped in many practical ways as well as taking photographs of my work for the first time. (My possessions were scattered around the flats of various friends, so I asked Andrew to buy me a mixing bowl, bun tins and a wooden spoon to use in making the 1,080 buns in his studio. He came back with my first Kenwood Chef – a generous, and pragmatic, gesture.)

Below right: *Meringue Ladies World Tour V* (1975). St Martins, London. Meringues, icing sugar, newsprint, powder paint.
Below left: *Meringue Ladies World Tour VI* (1975). Garage Gallery, London. Meringues, icing sugar, newsprint, powder paint.

Title *Princess Anne's Second Wedding Anniversary.*
Shoes Platform high-heel grey and white fake snakeskin strap shoes.
Duration 15 November, 30 minutes.
Location St Martins School of Art, London.
Description This was *Meringue Ladies World Tour V*. They formed the bridesmaids whom I danced on to the tune of 'The Chapel of Love'. Marie accompanied me.

Artist's intentions and opinion To have fun, squash some bridesmaids, mark Princess Anne's progress and my own after two years of performance.
Remaining evidence A few photos.

Title *Meringue Ladies World Tour VI.*
Shoes As above.
Duration 30 minutes.
Locations Garage Gallery, Covent Garden (*Spare Rib* Benefit).
Description 'A Meringue Lady Dance'. I used the 'Tree of Life' paintings to form an installation.

Artist's intentions and opinion This was more organised, better planned and documented. I still didn't have the confidence to speak much, but I used music more effectively and felt pleased with the atmosphere I managed to create.

Remaining evidence Photographs.

Title *Performance Art Collective Christmas Party.*
Shoes Green suede high heels.
Duration A December evening.
Location Institute of Contemporary Arts (ICA), London.
Description I belonged to the Performance Art Collective which used to meet up at the ICA café. Sally Potter headed it up. Rose English was a member, too. We sat about planning letters to the Arts Council and newspapers. Ted Little, radical and controversial Director of the ICA, was the host. I made a *Hot Bauble Christmas Tree.* Guests could help themselves to hot Christmas puddings dangling from the tree.
Artist's intentions and opinion This party was our best event and was well attended. We enjoyed ourselves and it fostered a fleeting sense of community. Ted Little invited me to do a show at the ICA the following year. I fell over with surprise and pleasure.
Remaining evidence Photographs.

1976

Title *An Edible Family in a Mobile Home.*
Shoes The coffee/beige piping shoes mentioned above painted with pale pink gloss paint.
Duration One week.
Location 13 Conder Street, Stepney, London.
Description By now I lived in a prefab provided by Acme Housing Association for artists in the East End. I decided to make a life-size

Invitation for An Edible Family in a Mobile Home (1976), London. Cardboard box, foil carton, icing sugar, B&W photograph.

edible family and open the house to the public for one week. I applied, successfully, to the Arts Council for funding (£570).

My preparations were very thorough. I built a shed in the back garden to house a chemical toilet and then disinfected and sealed off the toilet indoors. I moved in with Andrew to vacate the prefab (and never moved out again). I 'papered' all the surfaces of the interior of the house with newsprint or magazines appropriate to the family member inhabiting each room. This included everything – furniture, curtains, floors, ceilings, walls, etc. I then 'iced' each room in fitting styles. I made all the armatures for the family figures and prepared and froze the cake in advance, before

Above: left to right
An Edible Family in a Mobile Home (1976), Stepney, London. 'Father': Fruitcake, butter icing, food colour, chicken wire, fabric birds, armchair, newsprint. 'Mother': stool with wheels, dressmaker's dummy, tablecloth, cardboard, Perspex, fablon, gloss paint, teapot, rubber spout, iced buns, sandwiches, fruit. 'Daughter': chicken wire frame, gloss paint, garden string, meringues, food colour, newsprint, icing.

assembling the whole family for three days before the opening. I invited as many people as I could think of. The invitations were hand-made and posted out in specially made cardboard boxes. I informed all the local press. The coverage was extensive.

There were five members of the family – mother, father, teenage daughter, son and baby. The hall had a visitors' book and was 'papered' in *The Times*. All the photographs were 'iced' out.

The teenage daughter was in the room to the right of the front door (which was actually her parents' bedroom). She was made of a hanging basket of chicken wire, painted pale pink and suspended with garden string from the ceiling, filled with pale pink meringues. The surfaces of the room were 'papered' with teenage magazines and iced with pale blue images of her dancing in a wild naked frenzy. She listened to pop music from an old-fashioned radio.

The son was in the bathroom/toilet to the left of the front door. He was made of pale pink painted chicken wire twisted into a plant-like shape and was covered in garibaldi biscuits cut into leaf shapes stuck on with icing sugar. He was 'planted' in chocolate cake water in the bath. The surfaces of the room were 'papered' with comics and 'iced' with a bower of leaves and twigs. He listened to a Roberts radio.

The father sat in a chair in the living room at the end of the hall. He was made of pale pink painted chicken wire shaped like a man slumped in a chair watching TV. He was hollow but small hand-made birds swooped around inside him. He was covered in a thin layer of fruitcake and 'iced' in pastel-coloured butter icing. The surfaces of the room were 'papered' with tabloid newspapers. The contours of all the figures in the photographs were iced in pale pink.

The baby lay in a cot at the end of the living room. The baby was made of solid coconut cake and was unique within the family in having

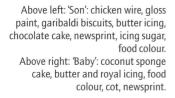

Above left: 'Son': chicken wire, gloss paint, garibaldi biscuits, butter icing, chocolate cake, newsprint, icing sugar, food colour.
Above right: 'Baby': coconut sponge cake, butter and royal icing, food colour, cot, newsprint.

no armature. She was 'iced' in pale pink icing with white rosettes for her nappy. Her cot was 'papered' with baby magazines and iced with dots. She listened to a small Swiss clockwork cuckoo clock, placed in the corner of her cot.

The mother was the only mobile member of the family. She moved around the house but mostly stayed in the kitchen. She was made of a teapot head, a dressmaker's dummy torso (with three cafeteria-style compartments inserted) and a stool on wheels dressed with a tablecloth skirt. All her body surfaces and skirt were painted in pale pink gloss. The surfaces of the kitchen were 'papered' in women's magazines. All the features of the photographs of women were 'iced out' with white rosettes. Her teapot head was constantly filled with fresh tea and her compartments were freshly stocked with fruit, sandwiches and iced buns. She had no entertainment provided for her.

For the first time I decided to dispense with the problem of deciding what to wear, apart from the Meringue Lady outfit, by making the decision that from then on in performances not involving the meringues I would always adopt more neutral garb, in the form of a woman's overall. On this occasion it was pale pink nylon and I wore a catering hat. I liked the fact that it was neutral and yet deeply complex in the ways in which it could be read. Also it was my conscious female riposte to Joseph Beuys's macho fishing waistcoat and hat. I wore my shoddy, humble female work outfit with equal pride.

The event was very well attended, both by a London-wide audience but also by large numbers of local people, especially, as the week went on, from local children as word spread that there was free cake. My manner was calm, polite, hostess-like and sedate. With everyone who attended, I offered them a cup of tea from the mother's head or other soft drinks. They were initially offered cake cut by me, but gradually, as the family disintegrated, people helped themselves, the children in handfuls stuffed into their mouths. The mother's compartments were freshly filled every day. I had programmed some performances by other artists in the garden at the back throughout the week.

Artist's intentions and opinion This was my most ambitious artwork to date and was the culmination of work I'd done before and all my thinking. I was extremely satisfied with it except for one issue I'll raise below. I was quite clear that opening my home to the public in this way resolved the problems of the 'art scene' being remote from a wider audience – in some ways, exclusive to a particular band of like-minded people. I liked the 'band' I was in by then, but I wanted to make work that was far more accessible. I had read about Oldenburg's *Store* and wanted to 'domesticate' it. The title, the form, the marketing (although I didn't know that word then) were secure and complete.

What bothered me all the way through making the piece was *why* I was making each figure in the way I did – *why* birds inside the father, *why* the mother mobile, *why* the baby so defenceless and lacking in a strong interior 'skeleton/armature' and so on? I was terrified that people would question me about these decisions and struggled to explain them to myself. But I could not come up with answers and the deadlines were tight, so I had to proceed using my hunches (I was not familiar with the word 'intuition' then). What seems to me astonishing is that *no one* asked me those questions then, and seldom do now. People go away and make their own judgments, talk about their own families, intellectual debates and so on.

But when the show was over, *I* realised why I'd made the figures in the way I did and it was a profound shock to me, although validating my decision to base the work on 'myself'. I realised that I had unconsciously recreated my 'family of origin' – my childhood view of family life. It was a bleak view at that stage of my life. The saddest thing was what became of the baby by the end of the week. All the others survived: either transformed with hidden beautiful secrets revealed as with the father (although only his skeleton remaining, the flesh gone); fresh, resilient, relentlessly present, as with the mother; or plundered but still intact, as with the daughter and son. The baby, however, was butchered, and then gone with just a pile of crumbs remaining. A horrifying image to me then, as now, since I am the baby of our family, and that was truly how I felt at the time.

One conceptual thing that really bothered me was the durational aspect of the show. A lot of people came at the beginning and saw the

YOU'LL have to be very quick if you want to meet Bobby Baker's family — they're disappearing fast!
Visitors to Bobby's house in Conder Street, Stepney, are invited in to have a chat, a cup of tea . . . and a bite at her mum, dad and kids.
No, this isn't a new cannibalistic sect in the East End, but an artistic project that really takes the cake.
Bobby's sweet family are made of cake, fruit, jam, icing, meringue — a current craze, you might say.
"The project is all part of my work as an artist," says Bobby, 25. "I received a grant from the Arts Council, and it cost me about £150 to make the family."
It took Bobby three months to get the framework built. "I started cooking on Friday — and have worked virtually non-stop on it since so that the family would be fresh."

Crumbs! Bobby's family takes the cake

An Edible Family in a Mobile Home (1976). Front page article in the *Express East Ender*, 25 March 1976.

'sugar bower' vision of family life. Truly at the beginning the house glittered and sparkled in a representation of perfect, spotless, sugary-sweet family life. By the end of the week it was more like *The Texas Chain-Saw Massacre*. Some people saw the transformation, but most didn't. I've struggled to resolve that issue since, mostly by making work of a shorter span so that people can witness the complete cycle of transformation.

The other thing that was problematic was my absurd 'post-fine art' assumption that, in order to have integrity and total authorship, I must do every single thing myself. Andrew did help with papering the ceilings (he could do them without a ladder). Later on, in the 1990s, I overcame this absurd notion (I stuck *every single* Letraset letter on the invitation, etc.) and involved others such as administrators, designers and other significant collaborators. If Andrew hadn't been around, I would not have the wonderful photographic archive that I do. He was most interested, in those days, in black and white photography so the strongest, most considered images are those.

Remaining evidence Photographs, local press articles, the mother figure still stands in my studio. There were no reviews as no one from that branch of the 'art world' came, despite being invited.

Title *Life Piping*.
Shoes As above.
Duration May, all day.
Location Grantham Guildhall, Grantham.
Description I had a polythene sheet screen that I wheeled around and 'life-piped' the on-lookers. I also took the mother from *Edible Family* to serve out food.
Artist's intentions and opinion Just an experiment. It looked beautiful and fragile but was otherwise inconsequential. The mother was popular.
Remaining evidence A few photographs and, I dare say, some police reports in hidden files, as one performer was arrested for showing anatomical drawings.

Title *The Dinner Party*.
Shoes The ones painted with pink gloss paint.
Duration One hour.
Location ICA, London.
Description I conducted a dinner party whilst cooking a nine-course meal for the six guests. The guests were made of wire clothes dummies – neck to stomach only – painted pale pink. Their stomachs, into which I poured the various courses, were transparent plastic bags. The finale of the show was wrapping them into one cohesive group with cling-film.
Artist's intentions and opinion It was the first time I talked throughout a performance and adopted a more confident 'hostess/cookery demonstrator' persona. It was my first performance in a 'black box' space with lighting and with a beginning/middle/end. It was well received. I *quite* liked it.
Remaining evidence Photographs, the dummies.

Below: *The Dinner Party* (1976). ICA, London. Assorted furniture, cotton sheets, kitchen equipment, food, metal stands and display dummies, polythene bags.

Previous page: *Meringue Ladies Tour VIII* (1976), Birmingham, UK. Trolley, assorted crockery, meringues, icing sugar, food colour.

Title *Meringue Ladies World Tour VII.*
Shoes Army boots.
Duration 30 minutes.
Location Midland Group Gallery, Nottingham.
Description This was part of a day of events involving luminaries such as Jeff Nuttall. I appeared early in the day. I took my Meringue Lady troop, but this time accompanied by the daughters, husbands and sons. I had a flat-bed trolley covered in earth. The meringue men were arranged in battalions at one end. The women followed behind. I played marching tunes and tramped all over the meringues. They gradually stuck to the soles of my huge army boots until I was walking way off the ground on squashed lumps of muddy meringues.
Artist's intentions and opinion It was intended as a commentary on war and brutality. I'd had technical problems making the men. Their fat legs and khaki food colouring made them soggy, hence the fact they stuck to each other rather than splintering into shrapnel-like shards. Unwittingly, the image I created was more shocking than I'd anticipated.
Remaining evidence Photos of the meringue family.

Title *Meringue Ladies World Tour VIII.*
Shoes Platform high-heel grey and white fake snakeskin strap shoes.
Duration All day.
Location Birmingham Festival of Performance Art.
Description I danced around with my meringue troop as before in and amongst barren spaces in Birmingham city centre. My meringues trundled around on a trolley. There were a lot of other performers roaming the streets. At one point, many came together in a central space, forming an extraordinary configuration of performers and witnesses who generally chose not to 'witness' each other. Amongst the performers were Keith and Marie, Reindeer Werk, and Welfare State.
Artist's intentions and opinion Experimentation, observation of audiences and performing in public spaces. I was dispirited by the lack of engagement with the majority of passers-by, but enjoyed the empty spaces and freedom.
Remaining evidence Photographs.

1977

Title *Mastering the Art of Piping.*
Shoes High-heeled backless, embroidered.
Duration 19 July–9 August.
Location Food Art, Kettle's Yard Gallery, Cambridge.
Description This consisted of 18 pictures made of icing sugar approximately 50cm × 30cm. They were inspired by a chapter entitled 'Figure and Art Piping' in *The Modern Baker, Confectioner and Caterer* (Kirkland, 1912). The images followed the instructions in the chapter as to how to produce a 'veritable sugar picture … piped from life'. The writer, a master confectioner, states: 'We may find subjects for our paper cornets everywhere around us – on the river, in the street, the park, the country

lane, and even the zoological gardens.' I then brought the concept up to date, finishing with an image of a hand pouring blue food colouring on Carl Andre's Tate bricks as a gesture against the public outcry at the time against 'wasting the rate payer's money'. Titles include '1 The Initial Inspiration'; '4 Animal Outlines'; '7 Grouping the Deer'; '11 Life-Piping'; '14 Dada-Piping'; '16 Pop-Art Piping'; '18 The Last Gesture'.

Artist's intentions and opinion I was struck by the passion of this pompous confectioner for drawing, and wanted to draw parallels with the current commercial art world. I wanted to make something intensely beautiful but ephemeral; a commentary both on art and the desire to both create and possess beauty. I also just loved making things out of sugar and adored most of the artworks I copied. Technically it was extremely difficult.

Remaining evidence A few of the pictures still exist, but the food colouring has faded. It was also included in 'Sucre d'Art' at The Louvre in Paris and came back with lick marks.

Title *Elitist Jam.*
Shoes Coffee coloured slip-ons with beige piping.
Duration 45 minutes.
Location Acme Gallery, Covent Garden, London.
Description I made a series of pots of jam that the audience were goaded into buying. Some was Elitist Jam and some was Normal Jam. When a person did not offer to buy the jam, I urged him or her to throw money at me as payment for my performance. A few coppers fell at my feet.
Artist's intentions and opinion This again was a commentary on the art world and capitalism, and was fuelled by my anger and a degree of ignorance on my part. Also most of the audience agreed with me, so it

Mastering the Art of Piping (1977). Kettles Yard, Cambridge. Left: '4 Animal Outlines'. Right: '16 Pop-Art Piping'. Wood, canvas, icing sugar, food colour.

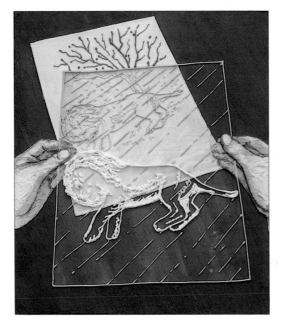

was a bit unfair to taunt them. Rose English was doing a performance upstairs in the same series where she just ran round and round the room jumping occasionally. I preferred the simplicity and mystery of that.
Remaining evidence One jar of Elitist Jam.

Title *To Demonstrate the Effect of the Popular Press upon an Artwork.*
Shoes Coffee coloured slip-ons with beige piping.
Duration 30 minutes.
Location Butler's Wharf, London.
Description This was another cookery demonstration held in this space run by an artist group named X6 Dance Collective. It was in a huge warehouse given over to artists' workshops. I had a long table laid out with a Baby Belling cooker with hob and assorted ingredients. I laid a tablecloth on the floor in front of the cooking table. The audience stood and watched. I heated up a noxious huge jam pan full of cheap food, like tins of soup, mushy peas, packet foods, fizzy drinks, etc. I put dog food in, which was a big mistake as it made me worry that I might throw up. Whilst it was bubbling away, I laid out a beautiful small iced cake in the middle of the tablecloth, which I nominated to be the artwork. Visitors then came in the form of bags of crisps bobbing about interestedly, school parties of cup cakes, all sorts of food packaged or otherwise representing the audience, but staying in their packets and enjoying the spectacle in an intelligent, observant way. I then demonstrated the effect of the bubbling popular press upon the artwork by pouring it over the whole tablecloth, artwork, audience and all.
Artist's intentions and opinion I was worried about the waste of food, good or bad, but it made my point dramatically. I decided never to work with dog food again. The demonstration was very well received. I have repeated it several times since.
Remaining evidence Photographs.

1978

Title *Art Supermarket, Perpetuity in Icing,* exhibition of Andrew Whittuck's black and white photos of *An Edible Family in a Mobile Home* and *Mastering the Art of Piping.*
Shoes Various.
Duration One month.
Location The foyer and entrance corridor of the ICA, London.
Description The main commission was the *Art Supermarket* and *Perpetuity in Icing*. The exhibition and Andrew's photographs accompanied this to form a sort of 'retrospective'. The *Supermarket* was an installation consisting of an L-shaped length of shelves approximately 10 metres by 3 metres. The shelves were stocked with around 3,000 artworks all made by me. They were all fabricated out of packaging materials and sugar and were commentaries on art language and aesthetics. There was a check-out point with a cash register and baskets where people could buy the artworks. The economics were that each artwork cost 10p but the slogan was 'The More You Buy The More You Pay', that is, if you bought

To Demonstrate the Effect of the Popular Press upon an Artwork (1977). Butler's Wharf, London. Table, cotton sheets, assorted kitchen equipment and food, tablecloth.

15 artworks it would cost you £3, not £1.50. The point was that the larger the image you purchased the more you destroyed the artwork and exponentially the more it cost you.

Perpetuity in Icing consisted of me laying out a huge circular cloth and then pouring different coloured cups of icing sugar on it to represent the various stages of my life. When the cloth was heavy with sugar, I climbed under it, stood up and cut a little hole so that my head popped out. I referred to another proverb quoted to me by my Sufi friend that 'In order to understand something you must stand under it'. I then attempted to leave the room but the cloth was so heavy I could hardly move.

Artist's intentions and opinion Some people liked *Art Supermarket* but I thought it a failure. The idea didn't work as people only bought small numbers of the artworks and the image didn't get destroyed – that is, the audience saw through the joke and their desire to purchase was not great enough; and, most importantly I broke my rule of the problems with durational work – the show lasted for ten days and few witnessed any

Above left: *Perpetuity in Icing* (1978). ICA, London. Cotton sheeting, icing sugar, food colouring.
Above right: *Art Supermarket* (1978). ICA, London. Wooden shelving, assorted packaging material, icing sugar, food colouring.

transformation taking place. But it is by failure that one learns most, so it was worth doing.

Perpetuity in Icing was more successful and was a precursor to later work such as *Drawing on a Mother's Experience* and *Table Occasion No. 4*. I was too anxious to speak as much as I'd intended to and the reverent feminist audience only seemed to find it moving and didn't appreciate my sense of humour. It *did* form a stunning image, but it *was* also hilarious when I couldn't move out of the room as I was so weighed down by sugar.

Remaining evidence Photographs and a terrible review by Caroline Tisdall in the *Guardian* that left me unable to work for a year. Since then I've always made the point of introducing myself as a woman. She only saw the *Art Supermarket* out of the whole show and assumed I was a man.

1979

Title *Packed Lunch.*
Shoes Everyday shoes.
Duration 45 minutes.
Locations Hayward Annual, Hayward Gallery, London; National Exhibition Centre, Birmingham; Old Mill Arts Centre, Loughborough.
Description I devised and prepared a packed lunch for the audiences. Andrew photographed the preparation – 80 slides in all. The meal consisted of a hard-boiled egg, dyed pink for women, blue for men; a hand-made brown bread roll filled with Flora Margarine; a small bag of crudités; a small tub of aïoli; a piece of fruit. The audiences sat at long tables and were served by me. They ate their meals watching a slide show with me 'lecturing' them on my skill, experience and consideration for their well-being in the preparation of these meals. I pointed out, for instance, the staggering beauty and strength of my hands as I crushed garlic into the mayonnaise.
Artist's intentions and opinion After the ICA show I thought I'd never have the confidence to work again. Helen Chadwick, who curated this part of the exhibition, persuaded me to take part. I was extremely grateful that she did and was happy with this show, especially when it was put on in Birmingham. The Hayward presented the usual problem I have encountered when performing in art galleries in that people tend to be rather cowed and silent due to the reverent anxious atmosphere. I preferred the passers-by who came to the National Exhibition Centre in Birmingham, who were more voluble and spontaneously appreciative or critically engaged. The response was extremely positive. I felt it was a culmination of all I'd learned from making my previous work; I spoke; it was complex but accessible on different levels; it was political; there was a profound and subtle transformation within the show; it had, dare I say it, integrity?!
Collaborator Andrew Whittuck
Remaining evidence Photographs. One review.

1980

Title *My Cooking Competes.*
Shoes Platform high-heel grey and white fake snakeskin strap shoes.
Duration 40 minutes.
Locations About Time, ICA, London; Arnolfini, Bristol.
Description This show was commissioned while I was pregnant with my first baby. She was six months old when I did the show. Andrew photographed, in the classic style of food photography at that time, nine meals that I typically prepared at that stage of my life, ranging from a baby's meal to a dinner party for six guests. The photographs were hung in a row, in a typical gallery style and setting. There was a long table in front covered with white cloths and the actual meals. Each meal had a small framed description in front of it, in the style of a village fête. A rosette was resting against each frame. I walked from one end of the display to the other quietly describing the meals one by one and my feelings about them

Packed Lunch (1979). Hayward Gallery, London. Projected transparency.

– from boredom, to anxiety, to pleasure. At the end of each description I awarded myself a rosette and pinned it to my overall so that ultimately I was bedecked with prizes.

Artist's intentions and opinion I wanted to encapsulate and critique my experience as a young mother at the time; my ambivalence about my role; my boredom and frustration; my loss of significant status; my pride. It succeeded on those terms.

Collaborator Andrew Whittuck.

Remaining evidence Photographs, the drawings, review (see p. 158–9).

Below left: My Cooking Competes (1980). ICA, London. Framed photographs, assorted food, cutlery, crockery.
Below right: My Cooking Competes (1980). ICA, London. 'Breakfast for Guests'. Colour print.

1980–1988 Interlude in work as artist

Birth of daughter 1980.
Birth of son 1983.

Reasons After *Packed Lunch* I had felt like taking a short break from making work. The experience of presenting this piece in an art setting in contrast to a booth within The Homes Show at the National Exhibition Centre in Birmingham made me want to pause for thought. Birmingham Arts Lab had been given a spare stand at this exhibition, so artworks were shown alongside kitchen gadget stalls, show homes and the like. The 'punters' were people who'd come for a day out and seemed to be in a fresh and 'up for anything' mood, especially free food. They responded to the work on many levels, ranging from perceiving the irony to taking it as a straightforward celebration of daily life. I loved the openness and unfettered intelligence that was evident without 'art anxiety' getting in the way. I felt I'd come up with a format for communicating with which I was happy. I adopted this model in *My Cooking Competes*. I was grateful and supported by the response, but felt I was preaching to the converted, so I wasn't sure where I'd go next. I didn't realise that my break from making work would last eight years.

Drawing of New Year's Eve Dinner. Dorset. Sketch book, pencil, watercolour.

Also, I later realised, I found it extremely hard to see myself as an artist once I had children. I lost my sense of 'self' and status alarmingly quickly. It was hard enough to find the confidence to do another sort of

job, let alone make my own work. It was only in 1985 when I realised that there was no precedent within my family history for women doing what they *wanted* once they had children, as opposed to their *duty,* that I was able to consciously give myself permission to change that and start planning a show again.

Paid employment After a tentative start I worked for Andrew as a photographic stylist. He had a very active career as a food photographer, working on glossy magazines, cookery books and in advertising. My role was to get the props and sometimes to paint backgrounds. I really loved it, working in a creative team with interesting skilled people from a range of disciplines. We did books with writers such as Robert Carrier, Keith Floyd, Antonio Carluccio and Claudia Roden. We got to try out all the amazing food. One of the bits I loved best was zapping around London in my car to prop houses and shops with time to think. Ultimately I progressed to working on commercials. It started my passion for the skill and imagination in adverts, which I often like more than TV programmes. I found it fascinating, but eventually the stress of coping with huge budgets and the lure of making my own work again led to a change.

An exception 1983–4 Diary of 'a timed drawing a day' for one year. I did these drawings when I was a full-time mother. It was a creative and amusing outlet.

1988

Title *Drawing on a Mother's Experience.*
Shoes Pale pink wedge heels with special anti-scuff driving feature.
Duration Approximately 50 minutes.
First locations ICA, London; Bluecoat Gallery, Liverpool; National Review of Live Art, Third Eye Centre, Glasgow.
Description I appear from a corner as far distant from the audience as possible, carrying two heavily laden large John Lewis carrier bags. I wear a white 'cross-over' overall and tiptoe around the entire circumference of the performance space, glancing anxiously from under my fringe at the audience while giggling nervously. I then put down the bags at the back of the space, step forward and introduce myself confidently.

I proceed to lay out a polythene sheet on the floor and then a white double bed sheet on top, rushing around, talking all the time, checking I've got it all straight and tidy. I lay out the contents of the two bags in a row behind the plastic sheet, finishing with reeling out an extension cable from the wall, plugging in a Kenwood Chefette (electric hand whisk) and checking it works. I then work my way through the ingredients and kitchen equipment, telling the story attached to each set while 'drawing' the food on to the sheet using a variety of techniques like dribbling, rolling, jumping and splattering. I sprinkle the final ingredient, two bags of strong white baking flour, over the entire drawing through a sieve, thereby obliterating the entire image. Finally, lying down at one edge of the sheet, I roll myself up in it 'like a Swiss-roll', struggle to my feet wearing the sheet and smothered in food, do a little dance to 'My Baby Just Cares for Me' sung by Nina Simone to celebrate the whole thing and exit with the bags and polythene sheet, leaving a faint trail and whiff of food behind.

Artist's reflections I only intended to do this show once, really to make sense of the first eight years of motherhood before moving on. I felt very strongly that the importance of the mother's role, indeed parenting as a whole, was shockingly undervalued. It seemed to me to be one of the most important jobs to accomplish successfully for the benefit of humankind, and yet it is accorded scant status in many cultures. It was the best thing that had happened to us, and yet it was so isolating, bewildering, boring, frustrating and joyful at the same time.

I decided to build on my experience of using my own true stories in *Packed Lunch* and *My Cooking Competes,* blending this with a commentary on domesticity, motherhood and the role of the artist. The first time I did this piece was at a 'Platform' showcase 'audition' for the National Review of Live Art curated by Nikki Millican and held every year in Glasgow. Lois Keidan, then Performance Programmer at the ICA, encouraged me to submit a piece of work. I'd never rehearsed anything before, but, having learned caution as a mother and the necessity to think ahead, I tried the show out the night before in Andrew's studio in Clerkenwell. I remember muttering the stories, as I was anxious the security guard might hear and think I'd gone mad. The whole experience was strange and embarrassing after such a long gap. I was completely taken aback by how besmirched in food I was and had to sit on the draining board, trying to clean up before going home.

For the showcase I had prepared meticulously to the extent of taking a packed lunch. As I surreptitiously ate it before my show, I ruefully realised that I was a generation older than my fellow performers.

The positive response was a pleasant surprise and bookings started to roll in straight away. Initially it seemed odd to repeat myself again and again, but I developed a passion for this repetition. I had found a subtly subversive political voice that communicated my anger in a bearable way. **Remaining evidence** Numerous video records, part of DVD 'boxed' set, photographs, reviews, essays, etc. plus the box of props and the overall.

1989

Title *Chocolate Money.*
Shoes Platform high-heel grey and white fake snakeskin strap shoes.
Duration 35 minutes.
Locations ICA, London; Mayfest, Third Eye Centre, Glasgow.
Description This piece started as a ten-minute showcase at the ICA in London. I got asked to extend it into a 50-minute piece for Mayfest. I decided to turn it into a musical. The show was about the dangers of greed. The central image was of hoarding chocolate coins and putting them on a chair, as a sort of bank, and then sitting on them to hide the wealth. The plan was that when I sat on the coins the chocolate would melt and I'd stand up to reveal a chocolate bottom. Unfortunately, that didn't work so I had to stuff camping pocket warmers down my pants to assist in the melting process. The resulting dollop of melted chocolate was suitably shocking. I don't remember the musical, other than the fact that

Opposite and above:
Drawing on a Mother's Experience
(1988). ICA, London.
Polythene sheet, cotton sheet, assorted food, kitchen equipment.

I pre-recorded all the songs myself. The main one consisted of me singing 'chocolate' in eight different languages.

Artist's reflections I was having another pop at capitalism but again it was not a success. I should have realised this when the chocolate coins didn't melt naturally. If an image doesn't work straightforwardly, it indicates that it is flawed. Some images are hard to achieve technically so it's really down to intuition again about what that means in each situation. The 10-minute piece worked in London but alarm bells should have sounded when I was asked to extend it for Glasgow. Where and why I got the idea of a musical I don't know. I'm not known for my musical gifts. I'd rather draw a veil over the show, which, after a lot of work, was only 35-minutes long. It was terrible and most of the audience walked out. I learned a great deal from it painfully, particularly to trust my hunches and stay humble.

Remaining evidence Some photos and a sympathetic review or two.

Title *Packed Supper.*
Shoes As above.
Duration 30 minutes.
Location ICA, London.
Description I prepared several 'classes' of fish suppers, all consisting of fish and bread packed neatly into sealed foil cartons. They ranged from high class (smoked salmon sandwiches made with best salmon and bread) to lowest class (fish paste sandwiches made with margarine and cheap white bread). There were very few high-class suppers with the majority being low-class. I served the audience of around 200 with their suppers randomly so they had no choice what class they ended up as. I gave a lecture, illustrated with photos, about each class of meal so that people could see what they were *not* getting. At the end I stood in silence gazing up to heaven while they ate and we listened to 'Laudate Dominum' sung by Aled Jones.

Artist's reflections This obviously was a reflection on the parable of the loaves and fishes but with human elitism thrown in. The main problem was that people wouldn't stop muttering with irritation if they got a low-class meal. I felt it was a somewhat crude attempt to engage again in the 'injustice within society' debate, although amusing. The revelation of true human nature was interesting, but the finale felt a bit simplistically cloying. It was a ridiculous amount of work preparing all those meals.

Remaining evidence Some photos.

1989 touring
Drawing on a Mother's Experience (DOME), Chocolate Money, Packed Supper.
The Third Eye Centre, Glasgow; ICA, London; The Leadmill, Sheffield; Chapter Arts Centre, Nottingham Contemporary Archives Festival; Open Hand Studios, Reading; Southampton Performance Week; Serpentine Gallery, London; The Green Room, Manchester; Leeds City Art Gallery; Harris Museum and Art Gallery, Preston; Phoenix Art Centre, Leicester.

1990

Title *Cook Dems.*
Shoes White plastic kitchen Birkenstock clogs.
Duration Varying from 20 minutes to 70 minutes.
Location First commissioned by the Third Eye Centre, for Glasgow, City of Culture.
Description I appear in a cleared empty space, in any environment from a community centre, women's refuge, shopping centre to a theatre. I

Cook Dems (2000). Jacksons Lane
Arts Centre, London.
Assorted kitchen furniture,
equipment and food.

introduce myself and explain that I'm going to do a cookery demonstration
and that the first thing I'll show is how one can set up a kitchen from
scratch, wherever one is. I rush in and out of the space with: four white
trestles; two white laminated work surfaces; two or three white wire
trolleys on wheels with three trays full of equipment and food in each.
Finally I carry on a large Brother Hi-Speed Combination Cooker, setting it
on the back table and plugging it into a white extension cable that I unreel
from the side of the space. I set the clock on the cooker. I draw attention
to the pristine symmetry, the clean white theme of my clothes (including
a caterer's white hat and white tights) and all the equipment, so that I
can check on the hygiene and cleanliness of my working environment. I
then proceed to go through either one, or a combination of two or three
separate cookery demonstrations. The title of each section is introduced
and its title displayed on a Perspex recipe board on top of the cooker. I
explain that the titles, like *Cook Dems*, are abbreviations, as it adds 'that
special professional touch'.

Dou

For this I use my trusty Kenwood Chef. I draw attention to the fact that
my Brother Cooker and my food processor are male, which comforts me
and gives me support. I kiss and stroke them occasionally. I make a batch
of bread dough using the brute power of the Chef. I set the dough aside
to rise, and then, using 'one I prepared earlier', I 'knock the dough back'
(a term for kneading the dough) using my own considerable strength. I
make three items out of the dough, all to be worn so as to make one feel
better. I make *Baked Antlers* 'to increase one's status', a *Breast Pizza* 'to
protect one against criticism' and a *Bread Ball Skirt* 'to add that touch
of glamour'. I finish this performance (if there is more than one section
this one is always the last) by donning the entire outfit and dancing to
schmaltzy show finale music while I demonstrate how it is as easy to
remove a kitchen as it is to set one up. This dance involves much twirling
and skipping as I remove, over-enthusiastically, the kitchen piece by piece
in time to the music.

Sauci

This section, if included, always starts the demonstration. When I have
finished setting up the kitchen, I also fetch a white chair which I place
to the left-hand side of the space. I say that I need 'one more bit', leave
the space and reappear leading a man wearing only a pair of blue
Speedo swimming trunks. I tell him to sit on the chair. Throughout the
demonstration he remains expressionless, silent and docile. Before I
start the recipe I draw attention to the fact that I have a blue theme in
my kitchen and point out a few details like the kitchen cloth to wipe
the surfaces and the man's Speedos. There are three sauces that I
demonstrate: chocolate – made in the oven; fresh raspberry couli;
custard ready-made in a carton. I taste the sauces by dipping in my
finger repeatedly and licking my lips. I then explain that I'd like to show a
'serving suggestion' for the sauces. I instruct the man to stand on a sheet
of newspaper 'to avoid mess' and then paint him with the three sauces
covering him from head to toe. I make him turn around and about so that

I can reach the back and also I run back and forth so I can check my work through squinted eyes 'in an artist's way'. I comment on my artistic skill, mark-making, etc. Finally, after admiring my work, although apologising, as it is not British to openly praise one's own achievements, I go up to the man and we have a passionate embrace. I jump back, overcome with embarrassment, revealing that I am covered in sauce, and comment that I have made a mono-print of my work. At the end of this section I instruct the man to leave, clear up frantically and rush out of the space for a moment to put on a clean overall.

Patiss

I make a batch of choux pastry, using a hotplate. Then, in a piping bag, I pipe a baby out on to an oiled baking tray. This is then baked in the cooker. While it is cooking I prepare one of the trolleys, lining the top tray with a doily. When the patisserie baby is cooked I fill it with cream and pipe on chocolate features and a cream nappy.

Finally I place the baby on to the doily in the trolley, remove my overall and clogs, revealing a lacy petticoat, and push my baby in its pram around the space, crooning at it and walking like a proud mother in high heels. When I reach the centre near the audience I pick the baby up, cradle it lovingly and then wolf it down, eating its head first.

Artist's reflections The day after the *Chocolate Money* debâcle Nikki Millican, for the Third Eye Centre (now named Centre for Contemporary Arts) supportively commissioned a new piece for the City of Culture programme. *Cook Dems* was what I thought of. I wanted to tour it to a wide range of venues in the Strathclyde region – that elusive 'community' that I'd encountered so positively with *Edible Family* and *Packed Lunch*.

We advertised it in a regional community network newsletter and bookings rolled in from an amazing range of places. I decided to just do *Dou*. We fixed two separate weeks' touring, within Glasgow and right out as far as the western coast. It seems incredible now that I accomplished that first week. I drove to Glasgow with Andrew's estate car loaded inside and on top with the kitchen. I had a helpful assistant from the Third Eye who accompanied me throughout the week. The show went down well but the stress and exhaustion were enormous.

When I came back to London I told my closest friend Pol (Polona Baloh Brown) about it and she offered to come along for the second week to help. I accepted immediately, as I found it so hard performing alone without feedback from someone familiar with my work and aims. Pol had seen the first 'showcase' at the Covent Garden Festival and so understood and sympathised with the aims of the piece. That first week together is one of my happiest work memories. It was the beginning of many years of Pol and I touring, and then working collaboratively together on shows. We remember many hilarious events. The work surfaces warped in all the rain, and once we got blown over as we carried a surface into a community centre in a gust of Scottish wind.

One morning we arrived at a windswept estate overlooking the Clyde on the edge of Greenock to find the designated Centre empty except for a cheerful community worker who had booked us for her 'sewing group

Diary Drawing 604.
Week 32, August 7 2006.
'Lovely Pol'.

ladies'. None of them had turned up but she was a doughty soul and set off around the estate to 'round them up'. Pol and I earnestly hid the show kitchen in various cupboards and I changed into my outfit in the toilet. A bunch of grumpy, damp women arrived with brisk remonstrations from the group leader that 'It'll do you ladies good on this wet morning and these two ladies have come all the way from London to teach us to cook some useful things'. The next ten minutes were an example of many I've had since – where I confront a bunch of astonished people (on this occasion they obviously thought they were in for a regular cookery demonstration) and am at the same time astonished that I've engineered such a bizarre situation. We are all probably of the opinion that either I'm mad or we're communally dreaming but, importantly, none of us knows how to exit gracefully so we just battle on. In this instance, as with most, there comes a moment when people stop trying to make sense of what's going on and just get into the swing of things. This was a particularly joyful occasion – my dream success event. They all chipped in and bantered all the way through. Their gritty, bawdy wit and appreciation of the innuendo was far greater than mine, so they took the whole concept miles further. When I did my final dance they all joined in and we shrieked with laughter together at the need for most women, and a lot of men, to wear a pair of baked antlers and just laugh, laugh, laugh.

Pol worked with me on the development of subsequent sections. Initially I hardly allowed her to do a thing, or say a word. She was very patient. It is a subtle, sensitive process – this collaboration about which she has useful views.

1990 touring
DOME, Cook Dems.
Southampton Women's Week; About Diverse Women in Time, Preston; Portobello Contemporary Art Festival, London; Women in Theatre Festival, Boston, USA; Theatre Museum, Covent Garden Festival; Hull Time Based Arts; The Junction, Cambridge; Richard Demarco Gallery, Edinburgh Festival.

Cook Dems has proved to be endlessly flexible, portable, accessible and adaptable. I've done it in venues ranging from tiny to huge theatres, international festivals, Cairo Opera House (with half the female audience veiled), in the huge Customs House overlooking Sydney Harbour, the BBC Radio 4 Woman's Hour recording studio, private houses, etc.
Remaining evidence Videos, part of DVD 'boxed' set, photographs, reviews, essays, box of kitchen equipment, trolleys, some Baked Antlers, a few dried-out Breast Pizzas and a Bread Ball Skirt.

1991

Title *Kitchen Show* (this became *Daily Life Series Part 1*).
Shoes Pale pink slip-on wedge-heeled 'house-shoes'.
Duration 70 minutes.
First location My own home in Holloway, North London, London International Festival of Theatre (LIFT) '91.
Description This show only takes place in working kitchens, the first time being my own. The audience are greeted by ushers and escorted to benches facing towards the area where cooking takes place. I appear from as unexpected a place as possible (my laundry room in my home) and greet the audience. I explain that I am going to show one dozen actions that take place on a regular basis in my own kitchen. The first is to immediately offer them all a hot drink, as I feel anxious when guests first arrive until I have given them one, preferably tea or coffee. I serve

the audience with drinks and a Nice biscuit (I have assistance if there are more than 20 people). I talk all the way through the show explaining my reasons and thoughts. While everyone has a drink I demonstrate with one or two guests a particularly important action, that of stirring in the milk and sugar myself, as a sign of extra care and hospitality, 'chinking' the spoon on the edge of the cup to tap off drips.

I mark this action by bandaging my hand into the necessary grip needed to hold a teaspoon firmly. I pause for a moment holding my hand up to show it bandaged in this way.

The show proceeds through the dozen actions. There is a story and reason for the importance of including each particular action. Each action is then marked 'about my person' and each sequence is completed by a pause. (All the actions are recorded on pp. 164–72). I add one extra action and mark, a 13th – to make my 'Baker's dozen': 'Showing all the marks whilst standing on a cake stand placed on a coffee table and showing this image to the public'.

With this final action I slowly swivel around on the cake stand while a piece of piano music is played by my daughter and a friend (live in London, a recording on tour). Occasionally I do a bit of high up dusting whilst I twirl around on my cake pedestal.

Artist's reflections The idea for this show was initiated while I was peeling carrots. I admired my technique enormously. I spent a great deal of my time doing mundane tasks and I entertained myself, while doing them, by having imaginary conversations with famous men where I described my skill, dexterity and endurance and they were always suitably fascinated and impressed. One day this did not seem sufficient recognition, so I suddenly decided that an international satellite link should be set up where my live actions would be beamed around the world to crowds of cheering spectators. I had to sit down for laughing and delight at such an idea. When I'd calmed down and reality set in, it struck me that the next best thing would be to open my kitchen to the public and display a set of live actions. Judith Knight of Artsadmin immediately contacted Rose Fenton and Lucy Neal at the London International Festival of Theatre (LIFT) who agreed to commission the show.

I discussed the ideas over a period of time with Pol. I wanted there to be a swirling set of actions culminating in a final pose. The idea for a dozen actions seemed to perfectly echo the mundanity of my choice, plus I loved the notion of a 'Baker's dozen' allowing me to add the public 'showing' of the marks. There are many layers of thinking in the show, the reference to stigmata being one of them.

It was obvious that there would be small audiences and the theme was grandiosity so I thought a film and book was fitting. I liked the idea of there being a life after the live shows – a 'packaging' of the actions – so that they could be popped into Jiffy bags and easily dispatched around the world. We made the 20-minute video, directed by Carole Lamond and the book designed by Lewis Nicholson with photographs by Andrew, with a commissioned piece of writing by Griselda Pollock. It was an enormous amount of work to produce them before the show launched.

We toured the show so extensively that the book sold out quite quickly, whereas the video really now *is* the show and it's circulated so far and wide, possibly initially because it was included in the Grey Suit Video for Art and Literature series edited by Anthony Howell. The reason is to do with the economics of producing work. Books without a publisher and sales outlet are generally impossible to reprint, whereas video, and now DVDs, can be reproduced in small batches at low cost and trickled out over a period of time.

Pol and I weren't sure how this show would work in other people's kitchens. Our Arts Council funding stipulated that we must tour, so we had to give it a shot. We discovered, as we have with subsequent shows that have been possible to tour, that we end up preferring the adaptation. It was the added oddness, the twist on the original thinking, that gave a new perspective on my 'North London kitchen' when I reproduced these actions in other private spaces in Britain and abroad.

Kitchen Show (1991). LIFT, London.

The press response to this show has been extraordinary. For instance, when I appeared at the Adelaide Festival, Australia and Sydney National Theatre in 1992, I did 26 performances in 5 weeks and 29 press interviews, many on television both local and national. I enjoy that sort of press attention (when it's jolly; I've been mauled by the Australian press in more recent years), as it means I can reach such a wide audience. For instance I demonstrated 'how to throw a ripe pear against a distant wall in fits of intense rage' to a live studio audience plus three million viewers on a popular day-time chat show (see below, pp.161–2). It was a great success in the studio, eliciting roars of laughter, and I was mobbed thereafter in the street with people saying they'd taken to hurling pears around and felt 'Bloody marvellous, thank you, Bobby.'

Remaining evidence A few copies of the book, the video, part of a DVD 'boxed' set, photographs, many recordings, press interviews, TV footage, reviews, essays.

1991 touring
DOME, Kitchen Show, Cook Dems.
Contemporary Archives Festival, Nottingham; Arnolfini, Bristol; Prema Arts Centre, Uley, Gloucester; Venn Street Arts Centre, Kirkless; Walsall Museum and Art Gallery; Carlisle Museum; Brewery Arts Centre, Kendal; Brighton Festival; Utrecht Festival, Holland; Angell Town Festival, Brixton, London; Portobello Contemporary Art Festival, London; Traverse Theatre, Edinburgh Festival; Douai Festival, France; Dublin Festival, Éire.

1993
Title *How To Shop (Daily Life Series Part 2)*.
Shoes White fake patent leather kitten-heel sling-backs (embroidery on toe).
Duration 70 minutes.
First location LIFT '93.
Description This show takes the form of a lecture on the art of supermarket shopping. In LIFT it was performed in Tuke Hall, Regent's College, which was originally one of the first women's universities. It is a multi-media show involving film, both live and pre-recorded, a lighting design, two fellow performers both 'planted' in the audience, a lectern, a piano and a hoist for flying.

At the start of the show I enter and introduce myself from the lectern, stressing that I am an 'Expert Shopper'. I wear my usual overall but with tarty shoes, a gold ankle chain and bare legs. At the beginning I adopt a

1992 touring
Cook Dems, DOME, Kitchen Show.
Theatre 140, Brussels, Belgium; ICA, London; Cirencester; Colchester; Boulevard den Bosch, Holland; Galway Festival, Éire; Harbourfront World Stage Festival, Toronto, Canada; Theater a/d Werf, Utrecht, Holland; Old Museum Arts Centre, Belfast; Brighton Festival, Brighton Pavilion; Museum of Modern Art, Sydney; Adelaide Festival, Australia; Greenwich City Gallery, London.

How to Shop (1993). LIFT, London.

serious tone and quote a sociological treatise to back up my theories on the significance of shopping in our culture. I say that I understand that most of the current audience might not understand my level of learning so I have decided to address 'the lowest common denominator'. I give a practical illustration, accompanied by slides, of a range of 'trolley techniques'. I then proceed to explain that I am going to teach 'how to shop' for a range of spiritual values in any supermarket and that my inspiration is drawn from Bunyan's *The Pilgrim's Progress*.

I teach seven spiritual values, stressing firmly that you have to acquire them one by one in this exact order so as to really 'own' them. These are 'Humility' (a bunch of parsley), 'Obedience' (a tin of anchovies), 'Patience' (a block of shaving soap and brush), 'Joy' (a toffee apple on a stick), 'Courage' (a glass jar filled with oil), 'Compassion' (a glass of red wine) and 'Love' (a basket of garlic croutons). I explain that one cannot simply purchase these items to acquire virtue but must *transform* them in special ways. I then go through each virtue with scenes involving my two fellow performers, filmed sequences, piano-playing, dancing and cooking.

I make a pretty little bundle of parsley tied with a white ribbon. This demonstration, as with others, is filmed live from a camera suspended above the stage and projected on to a screen. I search for a man in the audience to demonstrate this on and my planted male performer volunteers and swaggers on to the stage. I throw him the bouquet, and when he catches it he instantly becomes meek and humble and leaves the stage displaying his gratitude. With 'Compassion', there is an animated film sequence where I 'morph' into a bottle opener, stand on the edge of a giant glass of red wine and leap in and swim naked Busby Berkeley style. For 'Love' I fry the garlic croutons and, accompanied by my assistants,

How to Shop (1993). LIFT, London.

distribute them to audience members in the style of a communion service.

These demonstrations are followed by a slide sequence of me paying for my shopping. The checkout assistant hands me two free gifts — one a cardboard halo and the other a folded up piece of polythene. I display surprise and pleasure and am seen leaving the supermarket in a blaze of sunlight.

On stage I produce this carrier bag with 'How To Shop' printed on it. I put on the halo and then discover the folded polythene, which turns out to be a giant version of the carrier bag. A chanting Christian choir is heard while I take off my shoes, place them and my shopping into the giant bag

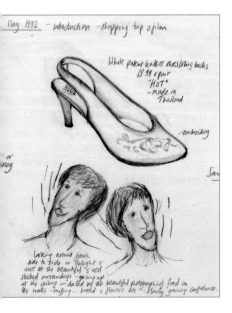

Above: *How to Shop* (1993).
Part of a sequence of five story board
drawings done in 1992.
Opposite: *A Useful Body of Herbs*
(1994). Preparatory drawing and 'Herb
Woman' sculpture, Chelsea Physic
Garden, London.

1993 touring
How To Shop, Cook Dems, DOME.
Pegasus Theatre, Oxford; Arnolfini,
Bristol; NOW '93, Nottingham; Warwick
Arts Centre; OctoberFest, Derry,
N. Ireland; Cairo International Theatre
Festival, Egypt; Kirin Festival of Arts,
Cambridge; Theater der Welt, Munich;
Museum of Contemporary Art, Sydney;
Canberra Comedy Summit;
South Bank Centre, London.

and then climb in myself. My two assistants come on to the sides of the stage, and a hook on a chain slowly descends until it is above my head. I am attached to this (I am wearing a harness under my overall) and am raised high above the stage where, after dropping the carrier bag, I adopt angelic poses in front of beautiful cloud and rainbow lighting effects accompanied by holy music. The music stops. The lights return to normal and I am brought down to the stage with a bump in a state of flustered embarrassment.

Artist's reflections The idea for making *The Daily Life Series*, a *Domestic Quintet* of shows around the everyday routines of life, came from the wealth of ideas unleashed by *Kitchen Show* and its success. The series was, in part, in response to the tradition for Important Trilogies and the like to be produced by Famous People. I liked the idea of framing my ideas in such a grandiose way to highlight this absurdity. I set myself the rule, for arbitrary reasons, that each title would have three syllables, and that each show would be structured around a numbered sequence of events.

I also decided that, with each show, as with *Kitchen Show*, there would be another version of it to assist in the dissemination of the ideas. For this show we produced a set of eight cards with text on one side and photos representing a virtue on the other. These cards proved to be a great success and are now in various collections as artworks in their own right.

The process for making this show was the most complex I had attempted. Pol and I had by then developed an effective way to collaborate, but in order to include others I adopted methods like writing a crude 'script' and drawing 'story boards', recommended by Carole Lemond to help her in making the specially shot films. These techniques proved useful in communicating images to the team and have been developed in subsequent shows.

I was pleased with the show, but have always felt it was flawed in sections and in need of more brutal editing. The most rewarding elements for me were the films by Carole and starting to work with a skilled production team led by Steve Wald, along with the cards. It is a great pleasure to work with a team of like-minded people in contrast to thinking so much on my own. We learned a great deal from touring this show so extensively. It attracted a similar amount of press interest to *Kitchen Show*, but this time – irritatingly – journalists wanted to talk endlessly about their own 'trolley techniques'!

Remaining evidence Video, photographs, sets of cards, reviews, essays, part of DVD 'boxed set'.

1994

Title *A Useful Body of Herbs*.
Shoes Gardening.
Location Chelsea Physic Garden, London.
Duration One summer weekend, four shows of 30 minutes each per day.
Description A small marquee was erected on a lawn in this beautiful and historic herb garden in Chelsea. Inside the tent a herb garden growing in a wooden planter made in the form of a life-sized woman's body was

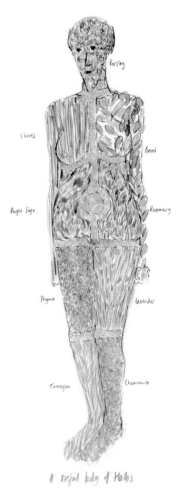

A useful body of Herbs

displayed on a 'village fête' type table.

Parties of 30 visitors at a time were met by me and escorted to a spot next to the marquee, where I gave them a brief introduction to the garden and my ideas. They were then led into the tent and I lectured them on the nine types of herbs growing in the Herb Woman, describing how I had picked these particular herbs as they were all historically used by herbalists to deal with, 'control and contain', or treat women's ailments.

At the end, trays of small samples of all the herbs in the form of drinks, ointments, and edible or medicinal samples were brought in for the visitors to test out.

Artist's reflections This show was done as a form of research for *Take*

a Peek! Pol and I were particularly interested to see how easy it was to lead a group of people and instruct them in a variety of tasks. In the event I found it remarkably straightforward to manage the group. I was astonished how easy it was to lead them and they mostly did exactly as I asked them.

It was a satisfyingly complete small piece of work, but I felt it lacked a real 'edge'. In the introduction and during my talk I expressed my feelings of wilting boredom (at that stage of my life) with gardening. I have always regretted this crass utterance in the face of such a natural and gently nurtured harmonious garden that brings relief and joy to others. Also the Herb Woman had a touch of the Incredible Hulk about her.

1994 touring
DOME, Kitchen Show, Cook Dems, How To Shop.
International Festival of the Arts, Wellington, New Zealand; Traverse Theatre, Edinburgh; British Studies Seminar, Helsinki, Finland; Centre for Performance Research, Cardiff; Mayfest, Mitchell Theatre, Glasgow; Kanonhallen, Copenhagen; Cankarjev Dom, Ljubljana, Slovenia.

1995

Title *Take A Peek! (Daily Life Series Part 3).*
Shoes Pink fluffy slippers.
Duration 50 minutes.
Locations LIFT '95, South Bank Centre, London; Arnolfini, Bristol.
Description This show took place in an installation especially designed by architects Fraser, Brown, McKenna for a terrace at the rear of the

Royal Festival Hall, with a view to it being reconfigured in other settings. It consisted of a series of booths, corridors, stands, towers and seating areas, all spotlessly white, constructed so that audiences of 30 at a time were led around this labyrinth from space to space through curtains and gaps, sometimes revisiting earlier spaces that had been reconfigured, and occasionally revealed, as a group, to passers-by on parallel terraces.

The show is devised as a funfair with nine attractions. Its co-existing theme is of a visit to a Health Centre where all the exhibits refer indirectly to a woman's experience of the healthcare system. I am the patient and my two assistants are funfair/healthcare workers.

Audiences are met by me wearing nine overalls, one on top of the next and ranging from size 10 to size 26, with bare legs and slippers. I lead

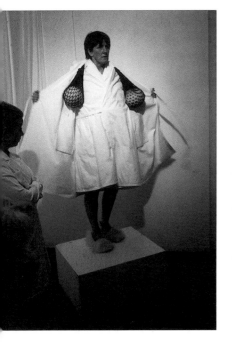

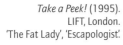

Take a Peek! (1995).
LIFT, London.
'The Fat Lady', 'Escapologist'.

them, without speaking, through the foyers and escort them into a small waiting area, where they must sit close to each other on benches.

I leave through some curtains and the audience are left alone for some time. My two assistants then beckon them into a small adjoining area, where I am exhibited as The Fat Lady. My assistants, throughout this and all following sequences, adopt a hectoring, fairground tone of banter, cajoling the audience to enjoy themselves and peek at me, the patient on display. In each sequence I remove an overall. In this, the first, a 'pair of lovely juicy melons' are revealed hanging around my neck in string carrier bags.

The 'attractions' are as follows:

1 The Fat Lady – two melons around my neck.
2 Nut Shy – three hazel nuts.
3 House of Horror – jar of juicy bottled plums.

4   Fortune Teller – glass jug of water.
5   Show Girls – a sharp kitchen knife.
6   Drinks Stall – Guinness frozen into ice cubes.
7   Acrobat – a white towel.
8   Escapologist – glass of water.
9   Lucky Dip – a bath full of chocolate custard and 'hundreds and thousands'.

In the final sequence, I stand behind the bath and remove my last overall so that I am naked. I climb into the custard and 'bathe' Busby Berkely style accompanied by music by k.d. lang and then Annie Lennox's version of 'Keep Young and Beautiful'. When I emerge covered in custard, I am sprinkled by my assistants with hundreds and thousands and exit

Take a Peek! (1995).
LIFT, London.
'House of Horror', 'Lucky Dip'.

1995 touring
DOME, Kitchen Show, How To Shop.
Colchester Arts Centre; Salisbury Festival; Stamford Arts Centre; Union Chapel, London; SPIEL.ART, Munich, Germany; City of Women Festival, Ljubljana, Slovenia.

wrapped in a baby's blanket.

Artist's reflections This was an extremely happy working collaboration and is a favourite show of ours. It required an extraordinarily generous gift of time from collaborators, such as the architects who worked so carefully to create an environment for such a complex, surreal set of scenes. We did three shows a day and a large team of volunteers were hard stretched to maintain all the technical and stage-management requirements. It was particularly enjoyable to perform alongside Sîan Stevenson and Tamzin Griffin.

We could only afford to tour it to the Arnolfini in Bristol. I realised early in conception of the idea that anything to do with women's bodies was so taboo that subtlety and cunning, and a surreal approach, would be necessary to evoke images and provoke complex responses.

Remaining evidence Video, photographs, poster, reviews, essays, part of DVD 'boxed set'.

1996

Title *Spitting Mad.* Expanding Pictures – a BBC2 and ACE Commission, Euphoria Films. Executive producer: Keith Alexander.
Shoes Invisible.
Duration 9-minute film.
Location London.
Description This was made with film director Margaret Williams. It is shot in an interior space which references both an artist's studio and a domestic setting. I make a series of images on white oblong cloths taken from my laundry cupboard. The images are all created using food with a variety of techniques, which all involve the food entering and exiting my mouth on to the 'canvas'. Whilst I create these images I converse about my artistic processes and decisions with satisfaction. The culmination of this sequence is me filling my mouth to brimming point with ketchup (my head held back with my mouth wide open to achieve maximum capacity) and then spitting it all on to the final cloth. The next shot shows a washing line full of drying food 'paintings'. I select two and fix them on to sticks at one end, forming flags. The final shot shows me on a barge cruising past the Houses of Parliament using the flags to convey a semaphore message spelling out 'PROVIDE BETTER FEEDING'.
Artist's reflections This was part of a series of six commissioned films and has been one of the few times that 'performance' or 'live' artists have been able to collaborate with experienced directors. The precedent for this was the tradition for dance films. It's the closest I've got to working with something like the advertising film process that I'd so loved being part of as a stylist. I love this film, its shock quality, constrained anger, subtlety and vulgarity. I did, as on many occasions in my life, get rather worn out by how patronising people in 'respectable' professions can be to someone like myself.
Remaining evidence the film.

Title *Game Fair.*
Shoes As inconspicuous as possible.
Duration Two months, one day a week.
Locations Brecknock and Robert Blair Primary Schools, Camden, London and Goodinge Community Centre, London.
Description This work was intended as a research project held in local primary schools with Year 5 pupils to inform us about creating *Grown-Up School.* With each school we held an event to introduce ourselves to the pupils. At Robert Blair School I made a 40cm × 60cm plain shallow cake with a rudimentary cake house. The children decorated the house with icing and marzipan trees, foliage, wildlife, people, vegetable garden and toys. In the afternoon we held a party, with treasure hunt and quiz followed by eating the cake. At Brecknock I made a chicken-wire cake figure which the children decorated with multi-coloured hand-made biscuits, followed by another party.

We then carried out a series of workshops where teams of children

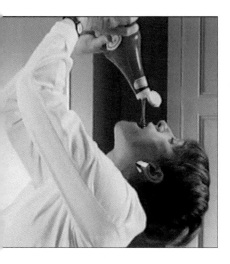

Spitting Mad (1996).
Holloway, London.

1996 touring
Kitchen Show, DOME.
Salisbury Festival; Welt in Basel Festival;
Pittsburgh University, Kansas; PS122,
New York; Performing Arts Chicago,
Chicago; On the Boards, Seattle.

invented games. The final event was when all the games were staged at a mini festival followed by a feast.

Artist's reflections This is an example of other exploratory research projects that inform the making of major shows. It was a joy to work with the children and staff. It was ambitious, but we all seemed to have a very good time.

Remaining evidence A few photos.

1997

Title *Escaping Gravity*.

Shoes As 'sane' as possible.

Duration A week-long two-hour daily workshop producing a 5-minute video.

Location Ashworth High Security Hospital, Liverpool.

Description This was a commission for an artist's residency from the Foundation for Art & Creative Technology (FACT) at the Bluecoat Gallery and the Artists Co-ordinator at Ashworth. The aim was to produce a short video that would be shown in the Video Positive Festival. I undertook the residency with Sîan Stevenson (who had been one of the performers in *Take a Peek!*) The aim was to enable some of the female patients – who were a minority of approximately 60 in a largely male community of 600 – to have their own specially tailored arts project.

We ran workshops around food that included making things out of it and enjoying it. This led to making a life-size food collage of a female figure. This process was filmed from above so that no one's face could be seen, only outstretched hands arranging sweets, sugar, etc. All the ingredients used to make this woman were sweet, which had been a communal decision. On the last day, as a group including all the staff members, we made a 'live' dancing picture out of food on a sheet on the floor. The video footage of the sugar woman was edited and the final version was accompanied by a soundtrack of me humming the nursery rhyme 'Sugar and Spice and all things nice, that's what little girls are made of'.

Artist's reflections I undertook this residency at the beginning of my time as a patient at Pine Street Day Centre (a mental health centre in Clerkenwell, London). The Art Education Head at Ashworth was an inspirational, dedicated woman keen to provide a special programme for the small female community within the hospital, who were literally beleaguered and fenced off within such an overwhelmingly male community. It was hard to gain the permission of the clinical team, who were concerned for the safety of the patients and ourselves. It was as though we were all dangerous, monstrous. They agreed as long as Sîan and I did not discuss patients' sentences or personal issues and focused on art alone. If they had known my diagnosis, they would, I'm sure, never have agreed to the project.

The workshops proved to be such a success with both patients and staff alike that we got oversubscribed, which led to difficulties achieving our goal for the video. The setting was like a prisoner-of-war camp and the

constraints imposed by the security guards were stifling. We managed a good rapport with both patients and staff, though, particularly since one patient was deaf and Sîan does 'signing', so they had long conversations which the staff could not monitor. That way we learned everyone's stories and formed a closer, satisfyingly illicit bond with the women. The video was not a total success, largely due to the practical constraints.
Remaining evidence The video.

Table Occasion No. 4 (1998).
Purcell Room, London.

Title *Table Occasions*.
Shoes Best shoes.
Duration Anything from 5 to 25 minutes.
First location LIFT '97 Festival Launch, Australian Embassy, London.
Description These are shows that are designed and created specifically to fit particular occasions. The original idea was that there would be *18 Table Occasions*.

I always appear, with a rucksack-style 'cool bag' on my back (painted with pale pink gloss), walking on two chairs by holding onto their backs. I arrive at a table and step on to it. I introduce myself in the usual way, explain that this is a *Table Occasion* and that there are strict rules to these 'occasions': 'there must be a table, two chairs, my travelling cool bag, an occasion, and, of course me ... oh and best shoes'. I get a pair of gold and silver high-heeled shoes (jumble sale) out of the rucksack and put them on, teetering about so as not to fall off the table. I explain that 'the strictest rule is that *I must not walk on the floor*'. I finally explain that the POINT of this all is to do something entirely new each time to celebrate the 'specialness' of the event.
Some examples
• *Table Occasion No. 1:* I appeared on two chairs in the huge hall at the Australian Embassy following the speeches to launch LIFT '97 and stood on an enormous banqueting table. I created a special pudding to represent the Festival including lots of juicy fruits, liquor, sugar and delicious things piled high into a special bowl. I then lifted a step ladder on to the table. I took a jug full of cream, to represent the audiences, and climbed to the top of the ladder. I poured this cream into the bowl below, from a great height, to represent the fusion of art events and witnesses in a festival. Fruit, juice and cream splattered everywhere and the audience were invited to join me in licking the bowl clean.
• *Table Occasion No. 4:* staged as part of the British Festival of Visual Theatre at the Purcell Room, South Bank Centre, London. I stated that there was nothing particularly special about the occasion apart from the fact that we all would never be together again. I demonstrated what I'd normally be doing at home on Saturday night; namely, entertaining guests to a dinner party. I restaged this meal with imaginary guests by laying out a tablecloth, cutlery and glasses from my rucksack, walking around on top of it all. A rope was thrown out from backstage and I hauled on a trolley laden with crockery and dishes full of food. I re-enacted the meal, talking all the time to my invisible guests and expressing my feelings. As the meal progressed I became increasingly slapdash and seemingly drunk, chucking

the food into people's dishes. I then sat on the front edge of the table drinking wine and swinging my legs, saying that I needed to understand what the point of all these meals was. I mentioned my friend's Sufi proverb that 'In order to understand something one must stand under it.' I explained that the *point* of rules is that they are broken and then I walked on the floor. I climbed under the tablecloth so that dishes, food and all were spilled over the cloth and floor. I stood up and cut a hole so that my head popped out, did a dance to the Gypsy Kings displaying my beautiful new garment and exited wearing the tablecloth.

• *Table Occasion No. 6:* Similar to *No. 1* but I made a trifle where the layers of ingredients represented different elements of the festival (Salisbury), such as: the staff – sponge cake; funding – sherry; marketing – roasted almonds. Finally I showed how a festival should be celebrated by plunging my face into the bowl and displaying my beaming, smothered face consuming the trifle with great pleasure.

Artist's reflections Fortunately my somewhat muddled and incomplete application to the Arts Council for *Grown-Up School* (then entitled *Jelly Game*) had been rejected. Development of this show was held up by my ill-health, so it was a relief to have longer to work on it. By this time we had obtained modest Fixed Term Funding from the Arts Council and had set up Daily Life Ltd. In order to fulfil my funding obligations, I had to come up with shows to fill the time until the next LIFT in '97. *Table Occasions* was the result. They were great to do, and have carried on way beyond the original planned 18. I got a bit sick of the rules after a while, so openly broke them whenever possible. *Table Occasion No. 4* proved to be a big hit so I've done variations of it countless times, often as a double bill with *Cook Dems*. I 'cheat' about the numbering as I've lost count and so No. 4 is either 19 or 23 as they are favourite numbers of mine (being primes).

Remaining evidence Photos, videos, one forming part of the'boxed' set.

1997 touring
DOME, Kitchen Show, Table Occasions 1–6.
Leicester New Works Festival; Board Member's House, London; Purcell Room, South Bank Centre, London; 'Shattered Anatomies' book launch, Arnolfini, Bristol; Hanover Industry Fair, Tanz und Theaterburo; University of Essex/Minories Gallery/Colchester Arts Centre; Brecknock School, London.

1998 touring
Table Occasions Nos 6–10.
Salisbury Festival (press) Launch, Salisbury; Schouwburg's 10th Anniversary, Rotterdam; UK EU Presidency Launch, Künstlerhaus, Munich; Arts Council Party, London; National Review of Live Art, Glasgow.
Cook Dems, How To Shop.
Cafe Teatret, Copenhagen; Purcell Room, South Bank Centre.

Guest Professorship
Giessen University, Germany.

1999

Title *Grown-Up School (Daily Life Series Part 4).*

Shoes Knee-high heeled pale pink lace-up boots.

Duration Workshops over six months to produce pupils' book, show length 60 minutes.

Location LIFT '99, Brecknock Primary School, London.

Description This was a project in two sections and was entirely site-specific and unrepeatable. The first part of the project was for Pol and me to work with Mark Storor – as part of LIFT's education programme directed by Tony Fegan – to produce a book documenting the 60 Year 5 pupils' creation of their ideal school for 'grown-ups' to attend. These workshops led to the devising of ideal School Buildings, Uniforms, Barriers to Learning, a Dream Room, The Curriculum, Playground Language, Punishment, Rewards and the Staff (the children themselves). Artwork by the children, plus their words and photographs by Andrew were incorporated into a book designed by Jacqueline Palmer.

The second part of the project was a show created by me (in collaboration with Pol) where the children, in groups of three monitors at a time, assisted me in teaching 30 adults per show.

The audience members arrived at the school and congregated in the playground during break while pupils swarmed around them. When the bell rang they were escorted by the child monitors through the corridors of the school, past infant classes, to a classroom where I awaited them. They sat in children's chairs at child-size tables. I told them a story, based on my own childhood experience, of three characters called The Berries. There was Big Berry, Bad Berry and Baby Berry. Rudi the dog was also a heroic character in the story, which involved a journey to a park, violent battles, narrow escapes, etc. The audience members were required to make their own 'berries' consisting of two strawberries joined with cocktail sticks. All these little figures were then placed on a central table as a group. The audience also had to make cardboard outfits for themselves. The monitors instructed them and assisted throughout the show. The finale of the show was when the three monitors sat around the central table for their 'tea'. I served them milk and they ate their way through the Berry figures. Gentle soothing music played as the audience were escorted out of the classroom, having been handed a printed exercise-book style version of the story, illustrated with my drawings.

Artist's reflections This show took four years to develop instead of the two I'd planned. It was a complex piece and difficult, as it was viewing evil within the context of childhood. It had to be managed very sensitively. The children's project was inspiringly and skilfully facilitated by Mark Storor and was particularly well received by the school and participants. Staff commented that the children who shone were those who were normally disengaged. The material generated for the book revealed the participants' sophisticated, realistic but optimistic view of the world of adults. In the book, one of the children says, 'It's like they are in prison, a prison for adults, we showed them how to get out. We unlocked the door, I suppose we need to show them how to do it for themselves.'

My show in the classroom was quiet, strange and subtle and unlike anything I've done before or since. I don't know quite what I think of it although I am pleased with many aspects of it. The one major problem was that I wrote the Berry story and learned it off by heart in order to 'tell' it. I know now that I work best when I am free to ad-lib and adapt what I say as I go along, within a firm structure. This way of delivering the story was somewhat restrictive. People generally left the classroom in silence, sometimes in tears.

Remaining evidence Video, photographs, reviews, book written by the children, Berry story book, part of DVD 'boxed set'.

Diary Drawing (1999).
'Day 268, Monday 22 March.
Big. Bad. Baby.'
LIFT, Camden, London.

Title *To Bring a Sheep to Consciousness We Must Eat It. Therefore, to Bring the Staff of the New Art Gallery in Walsall to Consciousness We Must Eat Them.*
Shoes Silver 'trainers' with a heel.
Duration An afternoon.
Location Walsall Shopping Centre.
Description This was a commission as part of a series held in Walsall to

foster public interest in the run-up to the launch of the New Art Gallery, Walsall. Andrew photographed the staff of the gallery in a group. I made iced biscuits in the shape of the group which were packaged in cake boxes with the photographic image and title on the lid. On a Saturday afternoon in the middle of Walsall Shopping Centre, which adjoins the gallery site, Sîan and I set up a smart mobile café and served tea, coffee and the biscuits to shoppers. If they were unwilling to sit down for a while (which most were), we gave away the boxes for them to eat at home.
Artist's reflections This was a variation on my Virginia Woolf show in 1975. I was pleased with it, particularly as it proved popular with shoppers. I've no idea how they responded to the idea – they were too busy eating (or too polite to admit to confusion) but they loved our caring service and free food and drink is always a guaranteed hit.
Remaining evidence A few boxes and photographs of the event.

1999 touring
Kitchen Show, DOME,
Table Occasions Nos 11–18.
Sesc Festival, Brazil; Sala Cuarta, Madrid, Spain; Artsadmin 20th Dinner Celebration, London; Newlyn Art Gallery; University Theatre, Essex; Home 2, Camberwell, London; Church House, Westminster, London; Moving Parts Festival, MAC, Birmingham; Stamford Arts Centre, Lincolnshire; Pandora Festival, Vienna.

The Woman Who Mistook Her Mouth for a Pocket (2000). Holloway, London.

2000
Title *The Woman Who Mistook Her Mouth for a Pocket.*
Shoes Silver 'trainers' with a heel.
Duration 15 minutes.
Location Art in Sacred Spaces, St Luke's Church, Holloway, London.
Description This piece was devised as a one-off sermon to take place during a Sunday-morning service in this busy church, of which I am a member of the congregation. It was part of a series of art events and exhibitions held in churches and other sacred spaces.

I selected the hymns and prayers, with advice from Dave Tomlinson and Fraser Dyer, to reflect an old-fashioned 'hell and damnation, repent ye sinners' theme not remotely typical of this parish.

My 'sermon' was built on this theme. I confessed, in lively story style, to six actual 'sins' like petty theft, lying, making abusive gestures at other drivers, etc. After each tale I smeared part of my overall with a foodstuff generally resistant to 'stubborn stains'. I then demonstrated how these stains could be 'washed clean'. I put on a pale blue towelling beach-style garment (a bit like monastic garb) and removed the stained overall. I then cut this up with a pair of scissors and demonstrated, in a style similar to TV adverts, using various Stain Devils (special stain-removing products) to get rid of the marks. Finally I removed my towelling garb to reveal another 'cleansed' pure white, skimpy overall made of a patchwork of sewn-together fragments. To celebrate my redemption I danced rapturously up and down the aisle to an ABBA track.
Artist's reflections This festival attracted a lot of press interest due to the likes of Tracey Emin and Damien Hirst being part of the programme. It was pretty light-weight and fun to do. The church was packed to brimming with the regular congregation plus art punters. I was surprised how difficult the art lot found being in church, although I *had* contrived a rather dour service to contrast with my sermon. My stories of 'sins' produced gales of laughter and the many children of the parish seemed to love the shocking mess and wild dancing.
Remaining evidence Photographs, a video.

Title *Pull Yourself Together.*
Shoes Red lace up Campers.
Duration 6 hours.
Location Central London.
Description The event was part of the performance series 'Small Acts at the Millennium', which was conceived by Tim Etchells and curated and produced by a consortium of Tim Etchells and Verity Leigh of Forced Entertainment, Lois Keidan, Adrian Heathfield and Hugo Glendinning. In

this series, a range of artists created small artworks in relation to the new millennium.

This 'act' was done as part of Mental Health Action Week sponsored by the Mental Health Foundation. Special banners were made to fit the sides and back of a large flat bed open truck. The ones on the side spelled PULL YOURSELF TOGETHER in red letters and the one on the back spelled IN AID OF MENTAL HEALTH ACTION WEEK.

A car seat was bolted onto the back end of the truck and I belted myself into this. Steve Wald then drove me round Central London while

I yelled at passers by to 'Pull yourselves together', 'Get a grip', 'Buck up now', 'Cheer up, darling, put a smile on your face', etc.

Artist's reflections This was the first time I'd made a piece of work specifically around mental illness and, delightfully, without any food being involved for a change. A good way to start the millennium. It was initially terrifying as I had no idea how people would respond, but as the day went on I became more confident. It was delightful to bawl these insults – of which I've been at the receiving end so much of my life –

Pull Yourself Together (2000). Trafalgar Square, London. Photograph by Hugo Glendinning.

at crowds of people with such irreverence. The response was almost universally cheerful, but it was great to watch people laugh but then read the sign on the back as we moved away and then stand for a moment clearly thinking. The only annoying thing was that we could not get permission to drive round Parliament Square. One thing I particularly like about this piece is that it communicates well to people simply as an idea.

Remaining evidence Photographs, an essay by Clare Allan in *Small Acts: Performance, the Millennium and the Marking of Time*.

Houseworkhouse (2000).
'Grab' from website.

2000 touring
Table Occasion No.19,
DOME, Cook Dems.
Jacksons Lane Theatre, London;
Artist in Residence for *Time Out*,
Year of the Artist.

Title *Houseworkhouse.*
Shoes Silver 'trainers' with a heel.
Duration 6 months to make; exists as long as we keep paying the provider.
Location www.bobbybakersdailylife.com
Description This is a 'virtual' house containing a collection of 'actions'.
The actions are animated and the site has an accompanying sound-track.
Six of my own actions are featured.

The actions were collected from a group of older people from two community projects. We ran a series of workshops. Andrew photographed our house and I did a series of drawings based on these of different spaces within our house. Deborah May then created the 'house', inserting the actions within appropriate rooms. It is possible to 'scroll' through the house selecting numbered spots which, when clicked, reveal animations and sounds of each collected action. These animated 'gifs' are accompanied by text written by Clare Allan.

Artist's reflections My interest in the internet had been growing and it seemed a good idea to apply for money to get 'trained' and produce a website with an artwork as part of it as a result. Deborah agreed to join me. What actually happened, since she is extremely patient and skilled with technology, animation and film-making, was that she got trained, while I sat and watched, managing to put up 'firewalls' against any unnecessary computer language.

My concept was to expand my own interest in the minutiae of life by our creating a 'virtual' house/museum to contain other people's. We were both pleased with the result but expected it to have a short life. The fact that it can potentially last as long as we pay the annual charge to the provider is a pleasant surprise. It has lasted, is still viewed widely and has featured in architectural studies and been 'Pick of the Week' on a variety of sites. Some of the participants found it informative and enjoyable. The tea-party launch in an internet café was a great success with all.

Remaining evidence Website, *Monographias 30 Casa House* – a chapter.

2001

Title *Box Story (Daily Life Series Part 5).*
Shoes Blue satin stilettos decorated with sparkling jewels on the toes.
Duration 60 minutes.
First location St Luke's Church, Holloway, London. Commissioned by LIFT '01 in association with Warwick Arts Centre.
Description This show initially took place in this church. Special raked seating was installed in the church for the duration of the show (two weeks) so that the audience could see clearly. A choir of nine singers accompanied the show. The music was composed by Jocelyn Pook.

I enter from the vestry behind the altar, struggling to carry an enormous cardboard box which appears to be very heavy. I drop the box (revealed to be quite light) and introduce myself. I point out that the most important feature of the show is … my shoes. I do a special walk to show them off and delineate the performance space. I ponder whether I dare open the box to reveal its contents, but of course I do. I tip out ten packets, boxes of foodstuffs and household products. I take one box at a time and tell a true story from my life connected to the contents of the box. All these stories are misfortunes – some insignificant, some catastrophic – sequenced in the correct chronological order. At the end of each story I draw part of a 'map' of the world onto the floor. The choir sing accompanying commentaries on my actions throughout.

When all the boxes are empty I contemplate with despair the world that I have created. While the choir sing the words from the packaging of the boxes I sweep up the entire map, hurl it into the cardboard box using a dustpan and brush, throw in the empty boxes and then finally climb into the box myself. Two members of the choir seal me into my 'coffin' while they continue singing.

A noise is heard that the audience cannot initially locate the source of: me sawing a large hole in the back of the box. I then cut three holes in the front of the box and manage, by much wriggling around, to stand up, triumphantly wearing the box. I do a celebratory dance and exit back out

Box Story (2001).
LIFT, Holloway, London.

to the vestry as the music ends on a crescendo.

Artist's reflections This was an intentional revisiting of the model used in *Perpetuity in Icing* and *Drawing on a Mother's Experience*. I found it very frustrating, as I thought up the beginning and ending of this show right after *Kitchen Show*. It became unbearable at times to wade through the other shows till I could get on with this one. It felt good from the start and is one of my favourite shows. It is not the sort of show that one can repeat often, though, as it is so personal.

I had become a big fan of Jocelyn's music over the years. Our working process was tentative initially, but Pol, Jocelyn and I came to communicate in a very relaxed way. It was the first time I'd had commissioned music. Working with the choir was a constant delight as I love live music, and particularly loved this music.

We were concerned how the show would function in theatres on tour (without the image on the stained glass window behind the altar that the map refers to) but, as in other cases, we generally prefer the 'virtual' choir version as it is more intimate and natural in tone.

One of the themes of the show is the myth of Pandora. While I was writing the first application I was a resident in a crisis house. The show is about misfortune and I felt overwhelmed with the bleakness of it all. One of the staff, Bill Briscombe, told me the bit of the myth that I had forgotten – that Pandora finds Hope left in the box. Hope became my sharp knife to get out with. There are many layers to this piece. The ones I will stress are that I wore a blue overall to reference the Madonna. The map is the most crucial and central image.

Remaining evidence Video, photographs, booklet, reviews, essays, part of DVD 'boxed set'.

Above left to right:
Smashing Lunch (2001).
Royal Festival Hall, London.

Title *Shop Until Your Mind Goes Pop.*
Shoes Everyday.
Duration 15 minutes.
Location BBC Radio 4 *Woman's Hour* series.
Description This is an edited sound recording of an actual shopping trip where seeing certain items on the supermarket shelves trigger off memories for me. The three stories attached to these memories were recorded separately and edited into the trip as a sort of 'stream of consciousness'. At the end, as I queue at the check-out, I reflect on what stories lie hidden in fellow shoppers' trolleys.
Artist's reflections I got this commission due to Lucy Cash (formerly Baldwyn)'s promotion of my work. I gathered later that it was seen as a risk to try a performance artist. I am glad that it was well received and has led to further commissions. I really like making work for radio. It has such potential. I particularly like the fact that listeners contribute their own internal imagery to concepts and words.
Remaining evidence The recording.

2001 touring
Box Story, Cook Dems,
Table Occasion No. 20.
Warwick Arts Centre; Theatre 140,
Brussels; Arnolfini, Bristol.

2002
Title *Smashing Lunch.*
Shoes Red Campers.
Duration Friday–Sunday.
Location Royal Festival Hall, London, as part of Rescen's Nightwalking weekend.
Description I assembled a 1950s-style dining table and five chairs on the ballroom floor next to a barrier above the lower ground floor. The table was laid for a Sunday lunch consisting of: roast leg of lamb, roast potatoes, carrots, greens, gravy, mint sauce, trifle, jug of water. The crockery was blue Willow pattern with traditional cutlery and glasses.

On Friday evening, in front of an audience assembled at the start of this weekend event, I sat at the table with my arms crossed looking depressed and sullen for about 15 minutes. I then, suddenly and violently,

tipped the whole ensemble of furniture, crockery and food over the barrier on to a specially laid dining-room floor below. I then went downstairs and sat against the wall surveying the wreckage until everyone had 'got the hint' and wandered away. The following morning the area was cordoned off and I spent the whole of that day and the following morning sorting, repairing and reassembling a new transformed version of the original installation. I used a hammer, nails, masking tape and large quantities of glue to accomplish this massive repair. Things that were smashed beyond repair I sorted into polythene bags. On the Sunday, with the task complete, and at the appropriate time for a traditional family Sunday lunch, I re-enacted serving the food to an imaginary family while a small audience looked on.
Artist's reflections I liked this show more than pretty much anything else I've ever done, but it ran up against the same problem I've encountered before, in that so many people saw the beginning, but so few witnessed the mending process or the ending. Deborah May and I attempted, by creating daily updated posters, to inform visitors what had gone on before, but they could not really capture and communicate what had happened.

The utterly frail and bizarre re-creation of the meal and the transformation that took place seemed redemptive to me, in the best way, of the utter despair that underlay the commencement of the show. By the end of all that mending, I could barely stand due to the crouching pose I'd adopted, my hands were covered in cuts from broken glass and thick with glue, and yet I felt triumphant.

Remaining evidence Photographs and unedited video footage.

Title *Dainty Feeding.*
Shoes Ugly.
Duration Around 5 minutes per person.
Location Victoria and Albert Museum, late Friday, London.
Description This piece was devised for Sîan Stevenson to perform, initially at this event at the Victoria and Albert Museum in the foyer. Sîan, dressed in a white overall, sits on a chair with a stack of baby food jars containing fruit purée and some plastic teaspoons piled next to her. She invites passers by to sit on her lap and be spoon-fed like a baby. While she feeds them, she chats to them as though they are infants.
Artist's reflections This is the first time I've devised for another performer. It was commissioned by Laura Godfrey Isaacs, who curates 'home'. It was repeated in that venue. It seems to provoke a range of strong feelings in people. I would not have the courage to perform it myself. There are strange undertones to this idea.
Remaining evidence Photographs at home.

Title *Box Story.*
Shoes Blue spangly high heels.
Duration 50 minutes.
Location BBC Radio 4 afternoon play.
Description A specially reworked radio version of *Box Story*.
Artist's reflections This was the first time I worked with Marilyn Imrie and the team at Catherine Bailey Ltd. Although it was difficult to adapt an existing show, because they were so skilled it was a very positive and liberating experience. The response to this production was fantastic, and it was great to be reaching such a wide audience.

2002 touring
Box Story.
Minster Church of St Mary, Reading;
New Territories, NRLA, Glasgow;
Theatre Neumarkt, Zurich.

Remaining evidence A recording.

2003

Research for *How To Live* This was a period of research, funded by a Wellcome Trust Sciart Award, undertaken with Dr Richard Hallam, clinical psychologist, in preparation for *How to Live*. The research period culminated in a 'controlled experiment' held at Toynbee Studios. A full account of this research forms a chapter in *Experiment: Conversations in Art and Science* (see Baker and Hallam, 2003), published by the Wellcome Trust.

Title *Behave Yourself.*
Shoes Various.
Duration Five × 15-minute episodes played daily for one week.
Location BBC Radio 4 *Woman's Hour*.
Description This series was commissioned by the Drama Development Department at BBC Radio 4. The idea was based on the self-help movement.

I am dreading a work party on the Friday evening so I have sent off for a manual which arrives first thing on the Monday morning. This manual instructs me to carry out a series of tasks each day, based on the Labours of Hercules, to improve myself and my confidence. These tasks include a beauty makeover, a shopping trip for a new outfit, an exercise routine, etc.

On the Friday I attend the party with the manual in my bag. My nerves overcome me while speaking to an arrogant producer, so I try and leave the party quickly, but mistakenly find myself trapped in the stationery cupboard. I don't know how to exit without further embarrassment but see that there are trays of canapés waiting to be fetched by waiters. This inspires me to effect a quick and subtle transformation and I emerge from the cupboard, to gales of laughter and cheering, dressed as a Giant Canapé.

Artist's reflections This was a challenging piece to accomplish but I worked with Lucy Cash again and a great crew. I found most of the tasks genuinely difficult. The worst was shopping for clothes in Oxford Street, which we recorded with my daughter as herself. She found it as difficult as ever to get me to even pretend to try on clothes.

It's the only piece of my work that my mother has found funny, so it must be okay. We held a real party with guests like Franko B and Curious, who performed with great skill.

Remaining evidence A recording.

2003 touring
Box Story.
Theatre Arsenic, Lausanne; Chang Kai-Shek Cultural Centre, Taiwan.

How to Live. Preparatory drawing (2002). 'One pea all on its own'.

2004

Title *How To Live.*
Shoes Pale pink loafers – psychologist's shoes.
First dates/duration 5 and 6 November, 75 minutes.
Location Barbican Theatre, London.
Description The specially designed conference-style set of a huge back projection screen and flanking banners (with the *How to Live* logo projected on to them) lights up as I walk on stage. I strut around the stage, beaming at the audience, building an uncomfortable tension and expectation. I explain that the therapy is for everyone, whether they think they need it or not. During the pompous introduction my assistant Frank Bock appears to film me, producing a giant projection of my head. I lecture the audience, in order to 'contextualise' my treatment by, for example, explaining how to identify the difference between psychiatrists, psychoanalysts and psychologists by the type of shoes they wear; my inspiration from and preference for psychologists; examples of their research methodology and ideas for treating people with Cognitive Behavioural Therapy. As with the entire show, sequences of film and still

photographs illustrate my points. I then explain that I will teach the 11 skills with the help of one of my many patients. Frank brings on the *Ideal Treatment Room* to help us feel comfortable: a smart sofa, a flickering fire and a cosy light and rug.

Frank brings my patient on stage. It is a life-size garden pea dangling on a thin thread. I welcome it, talking to it throughout as if it were a real person, introduce it to the audience and treatment room. When the pea/patient becomes shy in front of so many people, we go to *Plan B* and

Above: *How To Live* (2004).
BITE, Barbican Theatre, London.
Opposite: *Bread and Butter* (2005).
Watercolour board, pencil, watercolour.

Frank brings on a model of the theatre and set that fits the pea. There is a scene, filmed by Frank so that the audience can see the tiny detail, where the pea sits on the sofa and meets a miniature puppet version of me. This model is then moved upstage out of the way so that the pea/patient can watch.

I then teach the 11 skills with the help of the pea/patient, Frank, filmed or animated sequences, photographs, stories and live sequences. As part of one sequence I dress up as a giant pea. The skills are:

1 Breath
2 Exercise
3 Assertiveness
4 Exposure
5 Mindfulness
6 Adult Pleasant Event Schedule
7 Acting Opposite to the Emotion
8 Chain Analysis
9 Validation
10 Interpersonal Effectiveness
11 Charm.

The finale is an astonishing feat of engineering in the form of 3,000 'peas' suspended on plastic thread which are lowered to approximately 1 metre above the stage, filling the entire stage. They are lit by a spectacular lighting sequence while they 'dance a Mexican Wave'. This whole section is accompanied by the verse sung by a pre-recorded choir.

Artist's reflections I initially thought up this idea to poke fun at the treatment that I was receiving and my frustration with the training material generated in the United States. I discovered the world of therapies, their inventors and websites. I wanted to create my own 'therapy' as a subversive commentary. Gradually, though, I grew to respect and become interested in this movement and so worked with Richard Hallam to research the subject in depth. He is a clinical psychologist, has been a practitioner in the NHS, a lecturer, with a background in social anthropology, so has contributed a great deal to my thinking.

Here are three quotes from collaborators:

'I would say that the pea rig is probably the most difficult thing I have ever made and certainly the most beautiful.' (Simon York, set builder and structural engineer)

'It's good working with collaborators who don't feel the need to prove everything all the time.' (Steve Wald, production manager)

'As a complete novice to the theatre, I was struck that a group of anarchic individuals could work so effectively together when they had a clear goal in view.' (Richard Hallam)

Remaining evidence Photographs, reviews, essays, part of DVD 'boxed set', a reworked radio version of *How To Live*, BBC Radio 4 afternoon play made with Marilyn Imrie and Catherine Bailey Ltd, with Jocelyn Pook as the pea.

2004 touring
Box Story.
The Pit, Barbican Centre, London;
Beijing, China.

2005 touring
Box Story.
National Review of Live Art, Perth.
How To Live.
International Festival of Arts and Ideas,
New Haven, Connecticut, USA.

2005

Fellowship I commence a three-year Arts and Humanities Research Council Creative Fellowship in the School of English and Drama, Queen Mary, University of London.

Title *Bread and Butter.*
Shoes Slip-ons with a large pink button on each one.
Duration One week.
Location My home, North London.
Description An exhibition of 30 especially painted watercolours all containing images of bread and butter, some still-lives with loaves and butter, but mostly ones of me wearing bread and butter or eating it.
Artist's reflections I did this show entirely to make some 'bread and butter'. I knew I loved painting and had a gap in earnings so thought this a witty and useful solution. It turned out to be one of the hardest things I've done. When I paint for myself I'm not anxious at all, but the thought of painting something to sell was paralysing.

It was a pleasure that people bought the paintings but I would not repeat this. I didn't make a lot of money and I never knew it was possible to invent so many 'displacement' activities.
Remaining evidence 30 framed pictures in assorted homes.

2006

Title *Diary Drawings*.

Shoes The uncomfortable ones with pink buttons.

Duration Touring indefinitely.

Locations ICIA, University of Bath; Queen Mary, University of London.

Description An exhibition of a selection of 30 of my collection of over 600 Diary Drawings spanning 10 years In the mental health system.

Artist's reflections I had not intended these drawings to be shown to anyone other than those close to me or to professionals. I started them on my first day at Pine Street Day Centre. They were a survival mechanism, a way of hanging on during such an alarming time, and they gave a focus to my time and experiences. They were a valuable way of processing and commenting on what I was going through and witnessed, thereby giving me some control when I felt so out of control.

I thought I'd be at the Day Centre for three weeks. I stayed there for five years, although increasingly part time. I'm still doing the drawings as, irritatingly, I've not been pronounced cured. I do them weekly now and they are a very important part of my life. Many of them now are about other things like work, friends, fleeting thoughts or joy.

Daniel Hinchcliffe of the University of Bath suggested the idea for an exhibition for Mental Health Week. As I would not consider exhibiting the actual books, he suggested Andrew photograph them. My daughter and I chose them carefully with the aim of communicating to students on this subject. We included none of the most shocking images and only a few cheerful ones (of which there are many these days). We included a few overtly critical ones.

The fact that they seem to communicate effectively what my experience of mental illness has been has encouraged me in plans to exhibit more. Mental distress is largely invisible and anything that increases knowledge seems worth a shot.

Remaining evidence Sketchbooks containing drawings; photographs and prints of a selection of these.

2007 and onwards

Shoes Black leather Birkenstock lace-ups. 'Cool' enough.

Projects in development *A Model Family*, *Geography Dog*, *Ballistic Buns* and *F.E.A.T*, *Shoeshopworkshop*, an exhibition of a larger collection of the *Diary Drawings*, a major project involving mental health 'service users' for the Olympics, a performing 'Peas' movement for Peace with fellow mental health campaigners.

Opposite page:
A Model Family: pilot (2007).
Queen Mary, University of London.
Cooking Mrs Beeton's invalid gruel with Sîan Stevenson in my great-great grandmother.
Sculpture: Charlie Whittuck.

2006 touring
How To Live.
Barbican Theatre, London; Gardner Arts Centre, Brighton.

2007 touring
How To Live.
Oxford Playhouse; ICIA Theatre, University of Bath; Nuffield Theatre, Lancaster; Clean Break, Norfolk Playhouse as part of Norfolk and Norwich Festival; Warwick Arts Centre as part of Fierce; Horsebridge Arts Centre, Whitstable; Queen Mary, University of London, Medical School; Bonkersfest, London; Artsadmin, London.

Part Two
The Work

IN THIS SECTION of the book we print a selection of the critical writing on Bobby Baker's work in general, as opposed to the focus on specific shows which animates Part Three. We start with Adrian Heathfield's much-quoted interview with Baker, 'Risk in Intimacy', which was published in 1999. Aisling Foster is one of several audience members who, having followed Baker's work since the early years, we asked to comment on Bobby Baker's work over a period of time. Next we reprint Marina Warner's essay on Baker's work, 'The Rebel at the Heart of the Joker', which has struck a chord with many readers. Originally commissioned by the Arts Council for the opening of *Take a Peek!* in 1995, the essay was expanded and published in this revised form in 1998. Next we have chosen a piece by Geraldine Harris and Elaine Aston, introducing Baker's work to a performance studies readership. Originally published under the title 'A Passionate Desire to Communicate', their essay discusses feminism and autobiography, Baker's stage persona, form and action, her care of the audience, issues of authorship and collaboration, and the question of authenticity and integrity. Helen Iball's essay on the complex meanings of food onstage, brings a theatre studies perspective to bear on Baker's work. Some of Baker's work is highly site and time specific, for example *Grown-Up School*, and consequently features rather lightly in this book, whilst much of it is extensively photographed and recorded. It thus cuts across the discussion of what in performance studies is debated between the 'ontological' model put forward by Peggy Phelan and the 'mediatised' concept of Philip Auslander. In a new twist on this debate, Elaine Aston looks at the patriarchal provenance of 'the archive' and the disruptive possibilities of Baker's work in that context. For this book we commissioned a second interview with Adrian Heathfield, in which in late 2006 he and Bobby discussed the significant changes her work has undergone in the intervening years. Finally, Roy Foster, another long-time follower of Baker's work, links her work – unexpectedly for some no doubt – to Irish literary modernism.

Opposite page:
Life-piping
(1976).
Grantham
Guildhall.
Polythene sheet,
icing sugar,
clothing rail, pink
gloss paint.

MICHÈLE BARRETT

81

Risk in Intimacy

ADRIAN HEATHFIELD

AN INTERVIEW WITH BOBBY BAKER

Reprinted from
Performance Research: On Cooking,
4 (1), Spring 1999.

Adrian Heathfield is a writer and
curator working on and in the scenes
of live art and performance. He edited
the books *Live: Art and Performance,
Small Acts* and the box publication
*Shattered Anatomies: Traces of the
Body in Performance*. He is Professor
of Performance and Visual Culture at
Roehampton University.

Opposite page:
An Edible Family in a Mobile Home
(1976). Stepney, London.
'Mother': stool with wheels,
dressmaker's dummy, tablecloth,
cardboard, Perspex, Fablon, gloss
paint, teapot, rubber spout, iced
buns, sandwiches, fruit.

The genre of female solo performance has seemed to turn around key American figures, such as Karen Finley, Holly Hughes and Annie Sprinkle, for whom a concern with issues of sex and sexuality has brought a ready assimilation into the tumult of argument on the nation's cultural politics and sexual morality. In comparison, British live artists have rarely suffered from the heat and indignities of full-scale censorious media, religious or party-political attention. Yet in Britain over the last twenty years Bobby Baker has developed a body of popular solo performance works that have come to occupy a complex, critical and resilient position within the cultural landscape. These works have explored, imaged and given voice to feminine experience against a culture in which it has been systematically blanked. As with Finley, Hughes and Sprinkle, her work has often been placed by writers within the formal conventions and political co-ordinates of feminist autobiographical performance. Here the artist is both the subject and object of the artwork, claiming a previously denied autonomy and agency, pressing disclosures of private experience into the public arena in order to speak of an identity overshadowed by patriarchal culture. For Baker this has led to critical attention around her use of the figure of the mother-as-artist, and its implicit valorisation of women's 'domestic' work.

However, as Claire MacDonald (1995) has noted, the identities presented in feminist autobiographical performance are rarely as stable as this sketch may suggest, and in fact it is often the security of identity itself that is called into question in these works. Baker's place within the category is somewhat unstable, since her work has often resisted sustained narrative exposures of the self in favour of other more elusive and formally innovative ploys. Baker's interest in food as an art material has underpinned all of her work. But as she states in the following interview, this concern is only one part of a wider project of exploring the everyday logics of women's practice, not simply to assert its unacknowledged creativity, but to mine its hidden sensuality and joy.

Baker's work, within and against the context of British sexual mores and class conventions, has always contained a delicate play with the fine arts of repression and sublimation. However, watching her *Table Occasion* at the South Bank Centre, what is most striking about this work is not its humorous use of social formality and restriction but the foundations of pain and fear upon which this playfulness is seen to rest. On this occasion Baker's performance is an attempt to stage a celebratory three-course meal; however, she has set herself arbitrary and limiting rules which govern the enactment. Standing in the centre of the table Baker serves her fare to a gathering of absent friends and family whose ghostly presence infiltrates her speech. As her serving progresses, the formal conventions which sustain the order of the meal are surpassed with increasing frequency by digressive anecdotes, intrusions of memory and returns of the repressed. Each transgression is marked by spillage, until in a final gesture Baker gets under the tablecloth, sending the dinnerware crashing to the floor, in order to wear the soiled remainder of the evening's labour as the sum image of the piece. In this dense moment of marred transcendence, Baker's work is emblematic of that of many feminist performance artists for whom the expression of contemporary feminine experience must, by necessity, negotiate instabilities of thought and identity and the physical conditions of excess and abjection.

Table Occasion No. 4 (1998). Purcell Room, London.

Adrian Heathfield You have spoken elsewhere about your approach to food as an artistic language, and within this you've not only been concerned with creating food objects, but with eating itself. The early works like *An Edible Family in a Mobile Home*, where the audience actually ate the artwork, seemed to employ the act of eating as a major structuring metaphor. Your use of this act now is much more occasional and selective; why is this, have you lost interest in its power?

Bobby Baker No, I think my use of it has just become more focused and controlled. Thinking back, I started by making cakes and established in my mind that they were sculptures. I didn't know what to do with them and the obvious thing was to feed them to people. So I had these tea parties which were a bit of a flop socially. I would spend hours making the cakes and the event and then people would be overwhelmed in a social setting to be presented with all this effort. That's when I put eating into a more formal setting of a performance. I have a strong interest in the formal structure of meals and, beyond this, in working with everyday routines. So at the Hayward Annual in 1979 I made *Packed Lunch* where the audience were served with a precisely made meal, and in *Kitchen Show* I made a very clear point of giving people tea and biscuits which I handed to them at the beginning of the piece. I'd say I have a selective fascination with the particular purposes of eating. But I'm interested in this as part of a way of moving people into different structures beyond the normal ways of presenting food, setting food on the table and feeding people.

A The use of eating in *Edible Family* seems much more destructive.

B Yes, though I think of the act of eating as 'absorbing'. With that specific piece I was thrilled at the prospect of the family disappearing; that the work would be lost and that it would be absorbed into other people's bodies. I am fascinated with the object becoming part of a body and then being shat out, the whole material cycle; so that you make a work of art which represents something and then it is physically transformed. But in later pieces I'm more interested in the complex physical associations attached to eating and feeding and the way in which they fit into our society's perceptions. I take delight in exploring and experimenting with the different processes and meanings of eating, and in connecting with an audience through them.

A When you do this you move into a very different world of reception for an audience, distinct from the cold experience of gallery viewing because the audience is engaged with something immediately sensual, and you're making that sensuality a dominant part of the meaningful exchange.

B Yes, I often attach other notions to that sensuality; say by referring to my role as a woman as a sort of provider or nourisher. In *How to Shop*, a very theatrical piece, there is a barrier between me and the audience, which I break through by serving little croutons with my two fellow performers. I actually put them either on to people's tongues or into the palms of their hands. So this is referring to my role as a woman but I am also complicating this by celebrating communion and becoming a priest. In that show I particularly like breaking through the theatrical barrier, walking out amongst the audience and touching them at the same time. But these are fleeting moments. They can't ever happen again. Like going around and actually kissing everybody on the lips. Kissing each member of the audience – the possibilities of that.

A So it's about getting people to savour a transient experience together?

B Yes, the sharing of those moments. I'm constantly looking at different ways of taking or highlighting moments like those, which I have privately all the time. I find my daily life a very exciting arena; the small actions, tastes, sights, observations, discoveries that are so thrilling. I want to take those experiences and enlarge and explore them, communicate them to other people in a variety of ways. Eating and cooking are involved in this, but really they are only part of a discovery of everyday life, they're not the central focus. I'm concerned with the many daily aspects of how we live, and how we express ourselves.

A The taking of those momentary experiences of sensuality, brilliance and wonder in the everyday also seems to be about valuing moments which are widely undervalued. Your work is very clearly part of a feminist project here, because that whole undervaluing of the everyday is very gendered. In this sense you're bringing to light areas of women's experience which are

seen as boring and mechanical, not proper work, and certainly not proper
to Art.

B Yes, but you know it's also about a connection to the sensuality of
infants; about carrying on the delight of children in their physicality,
playing with food and objects in a very fundamental way. We all have a
connection with those discoveries and I want to re-awaken that delight
which is lost or very formalised into society's obsession with cooking. I
am fascinated by the organisation of Ingredients into different shapes and
forms, the formality of cookery programmes, particularly the *Junior Chef*
ones, where you get 12- or 13-year-olds making these bizarre elaborate
meals. Little praline baskets full of home-made ice-cream, constructed and
decorated in the most intricate ways.

A It's a peculiar phenomenon.

B I can't understand it, having had children of my own, having watched
them at that age, the last thing in the whole world they would want to
do would be to spend hours gaining the skills to present food in that way.
It takes a very particular focus within a family to arrive at that degree of
expertise.

A I suppose making those pleasures part of the work is about reminding
people of what they've forgotten in their culturedness. Perhaps it's a way
of coming back to some of the elemental pleasures of relations between
things; between yourself and substances or objects. So it's not only about
revaluing those relations but also about allowing the audience to revel
in them, to play with them again, because they have been repressed
or sanitised. The junior chefs are learning how to tame and train their
pleasures into adult forms.

B It's a particularly British approach to cooking. It isn't simply about the
sensual delights of food or the visual pleasures, as you would get in Italian
or French cuisine. In this country we approach cooking as a form of *Come
Dancing*, where you learn cooking skills in order to present them with
a flourish. All those food programmes with people like Loyd Grossman
and Ainsley Harriott, they all do those little trills and dribbles at the end
that make the dish look supposedly more fabulous. It has all become so
formalised and twee. You can't really imagine getting in there and just
sticking your finger in.

A You're keen to draw attention to the social pretensions of cooking,
particularly class pretensions.

B Oh, they amuse me enormously, and I am constantly on the lookout
for fresh thrills in that area. I avidly read the packaging in supermarkets
for this. You see the way food is marketed for the *haute cuisine* approach
that we've supposedly adopted as a society. I love it all – I could spend
my whole life in a supermarket trolleying around and sifting through the
objects.

A The way you undermine the sense of complexity and sophistication
that goes along with the marketed versions of food and cookery is often
through returning to the nature of the materials. I am thinking about your
use of mess and excess, and particularly smearing.

B I recently did a piece for BBC Radio 4, a pastiche of perfect-body exercise regimes; how to exercise the obscure parts of your body that need stimulating. I made up a series of blancmanges from their packets and laid them out across the table in a row, each with different colours, but they were all wobbly, round, beautiful and glistening. I smacked them very very hard so that they splattered all over the kitchen. It was quite painful actually; it stung my palm. I systematically destroyed them all, but the point of this was supposed to have been to exercise the palm of my right hand. The blancmanges referred rather obviously to breasts. I was trying to get at the strange sexuality of those programmes. But the central contradiction was about doing something so infantile and so rude, making such a wonderful mess, but doing this so that people are aware that they cannot see it. They can only hear the objects smashing all over the kitchen floor and my shrieks of delight.

A With these excesses you often push your own body into compromised positions, so that there are images of self-ridicule. This is made more powerful by the fact that you seem initially to present a confidence and integrity, a very solid persona …

B *(Laughs)* I don't know about very solid.

A *(Laughs)* I mean in the sense of being very present, having a certain assurance. But then you do things which it is hard to do as a performer to make oneself look uncomfortable, fallible, or foolish.

B Yes. I've had a particular fascination over the last year or so with exploring embarrassment and humiliation and self-destruction. But I think it is a very powerful position to take to humble oneself. When, for instance, in *Take a Peek!* I've got nine overalls on, I am this immensely fat, embarrassed, silent person, who can hardly look anyone in the eye, who is systematically humiliated by my two assistants, turned into an object and exhibited. This exerts a huge control over the audience because they've become complicit in some sort of humiliation of me, so this is a two-way process, and the fact that I take that position so powerfully, is almost an abuse of the audience, since they are asked to take part in that relationship. It's something of an angry position to be in.

A So you are using the audience as a stand-in for society, in order to make apparent to them the forces which see you, or position you, in this way. Is this how you often think of the audience in your work?

B I think of their experience as being like a journey of exploration, and I am using all my intuition, skills and powers to take the audience on that journey in a way that is somehow safe, based on trust and not abusive. The piece I'm working on next year is quite the reverse of my interest in humiliation, where I will become the aggressor. It is far more difficult to move into that kind of relation between myself and the audience.

A What sort of format will that take?

B Well, it's a grown-up school. I am playing quite a complicated game. I have a group of people, an audience, who will be my class. I am the teacher and children are my assistants. The children are on my side and we teach these adults a lesson. Like most of my pieces at this state it's a collection of images and ideas, the way in which it will come together is not yet set. But I know there will be some very fine lines across which I

Take a Peek! (1995).
LIFT, Royal Festival Hall, London.
'The Fat Lady'.

cannot go. I'm interested in that, like in *Take a Peek!*, being near the edge all the time, the edge of taboo. In that show the edge was so much about the body, in this one it will be about aggression, violence and power. I'll have to tread a very delicate path.

A When I think about other performances that employ an aggressive relationship to their audience, or some kind of heightened physical risk for the performer, there is a question, which often undermines the aspirations of the work, around how powerful this kind of infringement actually is. Like La Fura Dels Baus, for instance, where one either has a sense of well-worn technique within the supposedly rough relations, or the meaninglessness of danger in and of itself, because it isn't tied to an enlightening idea.

B My interest in risk is quite different. I am sometimes working in very close proximity to small audiences, so that I'm actually capable of leaning over and touching their cheek and spooning strawberry jam into their eagerly opened mouths. The kind of transgression I am after is very slight, but nonetheless present. The danger is there in small gestures rather than large ones; the risk in intimacy, that's what interests me particularly in this next piece.

A This seems like a return to the privacy of earlier pieces like *Kitchen Show*, a move away from the grander public staging of shows like *How to Shop*. Do you see the theatricality and public scale of *How to Shop* as just one aesthetic strategy amongst others?

B *Take a Peek!*, the show that followed it, had an elaborate set with nine booths that the audience journeyed through, groups of thirty people at a time, but it created an intimate, private space in a public setting. I went back to having a close proximity between myself and the audience but in a more formal and public setting than that of my own home in *Kitchen Show*. The next show actually continues that intimacy, although it is once again in a real space, a classroom in a working primary school. The audience will have to wait by queuing up in the playground.

A In orderly lines?

B Yes, and they will be escorted by my monitors, my assistants, up to the classroom. It's about trying to find the best form and the best structure for examining whatever topic is at the heart of the journey. Each show informs the next one. Each piece has to discover its appropriate site. It is this flexibility that I like about my current series *Table Occasions*. It has a structure in that it is a series of eighteen performances, but they can take place in many different settings. The only constant is that they have to have a table and two chairs. I stand on the table and I walk on with the two chairs, since I'm not allowed to touch the floor. It's a set of really obscure, rather ridiculous rules that I've established in order to experiment with different ideas, in different places; so I could do one in a garden or in a theatre or in a hall or anywhere.

A You mentioned your use of rules and nearly all of your works foreground the idea that there are systems governing the performance. There is a strong sense of a need for order around symbols and actions.

B It's a constant searching for shape and pattern, an almost mathematical fascination with form, that you may be able to put ideas together in arrangements which you imagine, in a rather fantastical way, might become perfect. As if there is a perfect geometrical shape that you can strive for, or an order that corresponds with your thought, and yet in my work there's always an acknowledgement that this is an extremely crude ambition. All of the shows are part of a series or include serial numbers, but they are arbitrary. Just as in *Table Occasions*, the idea that I'm not allowed to walk on the floor is completely meaningless. It's a conceit and yet it's the fact that I'm organising or imposing a form on the event that is important. It's an observation about form. But it's also an acknowledgement that the piece could be perfect, that you might achieve in one show, when everything corresponds with that particular audience, a sort of ecstasy of perfection.

A They are always rules which you yourself are seen to impose.

B I'm playing with the fact that we have rules in life, built up over the years, we have rituals, just as in church services …

A But I don't think that these rules feel so institutional, they are seen to be self-generated. They are shown as part of the project of the performer in relationship to the goals of the performance. The rules enable you to create the work. But the little laws and systems which you set up are shown to fail you personally, to be inadequate. So the work created far exceeds the rules, and is in fact a product of the failure of the rules.

B I like that idea. It's like the relationship between a set of ingredients and a meal. I imagine a picnic lunch where you set a cloth in the middle of some arbitrary bit of countryside you've chosen. You have a set of people that you've invited, then you have all the food which you lay out, and you've made all these decisions about what goes into that meal or that outing. Then what you get is an experience, an event, which is beyond the sum of all those parts. That's what I'm interested in, that uniqueness, the specialness of that event. I find it delightful.

A So it is a pleasure derived from a loss of control for you as a performer; the pleasure of being exceeded by the thing you've set in motion.

B Yes, and yet, of course, having a rigorous control on all aspects of the way these shows are put together, even down to the marketing. So there is that kind of control, and yet as you say, arriving at a point in performance where all those things add up to a loss of control.

A You often end your pieces with very ambivalent moments. I'm thinking of *Drawing on a Mother's Experience*, where you wrap yourself in the food painting that it has taken the whole performance to create, and then foolishly attempt to do a dance for us. These are moments of pleasure and beauty but they are also marked by pain.

B I'm hoping, dreaming, aspiring to happiness and the perfect ending and yet knowing that it doesn't exist. Like the moment in *Take a Peek!* where I climb naked out of a bath of chocolate custard and I'm showered by hundreds and thousands that stick all over me. That ostensibly is a happy sight, arriving back inside a wonderful infantile bliss and yet actually it's a very disturbed and disturbing image, quite frightful in its association. I find that often people say that they laugh and cry at the same time in my work, which is, I suppose, my own experience of life. I haven't arrived at

Drawing on a Mother's Experience (1997). Greenbelt Festival, Deene Park, Lincolnshire. Cotton sheeting, plastic sheeting, assorted food stuffs.

the perfect ending yet.

A Griselda Pollock, in her piece on *Kitchen Show*, writes about your work as a way of bringing into presence the figure of the mother, which she says is marked by a 'culturally endorsed tedium'. But I'm wondering if that identity isn't in some senses also a straitjacket …

B Oh yes. Very boring.

A It forces you into particular corners; for instance, it may turn the relations that you stage towards nurturing or caring. It strikes me that the areas that you are now pushing into, the eroticism of food, and the idea of a more violent, oppressive or careless relation to an audience, are partly about resisting some of the problems of that identity.

B I think in the early stages of the experience of being a mother it is extremely difficult to be transgressive, because what you represent to your children is the superego, and you are constantly caught in that position, and that actuality. As I absorbed and worked through that position I was able to distance myself from the whole experience. It was once very much where I focused my attention, but now I think I've moved on. I don't want to denigrate it, because it is such a neglected area of experience, so ignored and so hidden. I was the first woman artist in my circle who had children, and before me, if women artists had children they tended to hide them.

A Or they stopped being artists.

B Yes, it was always a problem and I had assumed that this was getting easier for women, but I don't think that this is the case.

A Did you stop making work entirely when you had your kids?

B I did no public work for eight years. I was drawing constantly during that period, but it was impossible for me to make performance work.

A You stored ideas?

B Yes, which I'm still working through, so it wasn't wasted time in that sense. Only towards the end did it seem restrictive or frustrating. The process of establishing my work again was difficult. But I see that time as an exploration of life; discovering in order to assimilate, to move on to make work in the future.

A You've mined this part of your personal history well, but I'm wondering from what you have said about your work, if you are now inclined to examine your own childhood.

B Oh, very much so. This new work is really about that time and the process of socialization. It is also a way of dealing with the dark side of one's personality.

A Is it difficult to access that material?

B Yes, I blithely, innocently set myself on this course, that this was the subject that I was going to tackle next. It was a terrible shock to discover the impact it had on me, how risky it was. But it has been a very useful process to go through and very productive I think in the long run. It's just that I hadn't anticipated the risks and the dangers attached to that path. It's good to know about that material, but one discovers, well, one's nastiness.

A What comes back to you is not necessarily what you sought to know?

B Yes. I am just emerging from the experience of having revisited my infancy. Accessing that memory material involved becoming like a child, like a frightened child; imagining things that children can see and need parents to reassure them about. When you open the gates to that state you have to then reconstruct yourself and hope that at the end of the process you will have a well of knowledge and insight to inform the future. But it can be like walking along a path and thinking 'Yes, I want to go there' and not realising that in order to go there you would have to fall down the cliff and get quite badly damaged, before picking yourself up and moving on.

A Is there something corrective in this reliving of trauma to generate work, a sense in which you also do this in order to not repeat the injustices of your own childhood and to become a better parent?

B Perhaps, but the injustice comes out of ignorance. What you're constantly striving for is insight. Unfortunately the process of gaining insight involves self-collapse. You have to work very hard within your relationships at this in order to then be able to impart the information to your children. And it isn't like you've done it and then you can tell them. You're doing it all at the same time. As they're growing up you're growing up, because you continue to grow up throughout your life. It is also a two-way process; they're feeding back information on what they've observed of the way you live, and then you're feeding back your insights. It's quite different from the experience I had with my parents, where things were contained and set and there was no opportunity for movement. I had a steady and conservative upbringing but one that was shattered by the fact that my father died tragically when I was 15. This caused a lot of problems within the family and for me. Our lack of ability, and of society's, to cope with tragic death, or death in any way. Nobody really ever acknowledged what had happened. It emerged through a process of embarrassment. A terrible experience really, but I think quite commonly shared.

A Do you find that embarrassment repeated in the work?

B It was a fundamental part of my beginning in life – that's why I refer back to it with such anger and irony. The way I use it in my work is as a sort of fury at the restriction and cruelty of embarrassment, the damage it does to people's ability to communicate in an honest way. I haven't moved out of that interest yet. I still think it is a fundamental part of our society.

Comment

AISLING FOSTER

Opposite page:
Drawing on a Mother's Experience
(1991). Glasgow, Scotland.
Cotton sheeting, plastic sheeting,
assorted foodstuffs.

TRYING TO CONVEY a Bobby Baker work is like describing jazz. No matter how you tell it, you just had to be there. I have eaten her human family and filled a wire basket in her art supermarket and watched her boil the poisonous stew which was the effect of criticism on a work of art. In theatres, after a show, I have seen grown men weep and women unable to rise from their seats. Everything is contradictory and exciting: Bobby's extraordinary voice, that white coat, the food, her pain, our laughter. Yet unlike much performance art, she assumes her audience capable of taste and empathy and thought. We are somehow part of her celebration of life and the psyche, a detailing of what is ordinary and deeply private – all painstakingly selected, chopped up and cooked into devastating entertainment. The effect is of great satisfaction; then a hunger for more.

What is going on underneath all that?
and why are you wearing those stupid slippers?

Bobby Baker: The Rebel at the Heart of the Joker MARINA WARNER

This essay was commissioned by the Arts Council and published in *Art and Design: Photography in the Visual Arts* 1995: III–XIII; it was revised and expanded in Nicky Childs and Jeni Walwin (eds) (1998) *A Split Second of Paradise: New Performance and Live Art,* London: Rivers Oram Press. The 1998 version is reprinted here.

Marina Warner's most recent books are *Phantasmagoria: Spirit Visions, Metaphors, and Media* (Oxford, 2006) and *Signs and Wonders: Essays on Literature and Culture* (Chatto & Windus, 2004). She is currently writing a novel, and continuing research into forms of contemporary enchantment. She is Professor of Literature, Film, and Theatre Studies at the University of Essex.

'There are three things that are real: God, human folly and laughter. Since the first two pass our comprehension, we must do what we can with the third.'

Valmiki, quoted in the *Ramayana*

'Whatever you do, laugh and laugh and that'll stop him.'
Ingrid Bergman to Ann Todd about Hitchcock and his dirty jokes

IN A MOCK-HEROIC bow to the traditional housewife's ability to wash whiter than white, Bobby Baker opens her video *Spitting Mad* with a shot of herself pegging out dazzling laundry on the line. She then snuffs up the smell of it: unlike most advertisements for soap powder, her visuals put in play all the other, baser senses besides sight. Inside, smoothing out the dry cloths, now immaculately ironed into folded squares, she prepares to make paintings: the foods she will use as medium, all taken from the blazing end of the orange–red spectrum, stand on the table; she strokes bottles of wine and ketchup and checks the sell-by dates, bringing the viewer into touch and taste; then she stabs an orange incongruously straight through the core with a stiff index finger, and makes a little 'oops' sound.

The undertow of disturbance beneath the control and paragon

Opposite: Drawing from sketch book (1994). Watercolour paper, pencil, watercolour paint, aqua crayons.

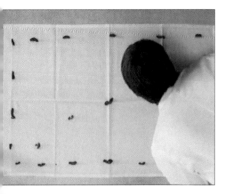

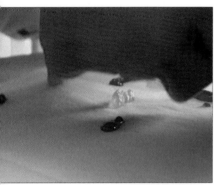

Spitting Mad (1996).
Holloway, London.
Video grabs.

of housewifely veneer, the sense of some impending wild loosening and dishevelment has already begun: but nothing will erupt and break surface to shatter the order Bobby Baker's performance establishes: it just feels as it might, any minute, and the tension is painful, gripping and eloquent.

In *Spitting Mad*, Bobby Baker applies – parodies? – craft techniques: tie-dye with orange pulp chewed and spat out again; she echoes artistic movements of the past, using red wine for an Abstract Expressionist splatter image; but she also works with her own body directly, without covert references, when she milks the ketchup bottle into her mouth, her head thrown back, and then spews it savagely on to the cloth – with that little nervous smile of women when they know they are not acting quite as expected of them.

The apologetic diminutive 'oops' at the beginning of the video is followed by similar noises – little 'oohs' and 'aahs' punctuate the marking of the cloths; while on the background tape, an arrangement by Steve Beresford of *Besami mucho*, the Brazilian *bossa nova*, plays languidly. The music adds 'Latin' sensuality, the captive's fantasy in the midst of kitchenware banality. But on closer hearing, it connects to Bobby Baker's exploration of the glories and the horror of oral gratification: on the soundtrack, a paean to kissing, on the table, biting, murmuring, chewing, upchucking, and spitting from the highly charged range of oral practices. Her scarlet and yellow effluvia of choice transform the shining laundry into receptacles of bodily pollution – with reminiscences of sanitary towels, nappies, hospital linen.

The film only lasts nine minutes, but it is richly woven, and climaxes with a stunning mock-heroic coda to the tune of the ride of the Valkyries, in which Bobby Baker has turned her artworks into semaphore flags and is seen sailing down the Thames, past the Houses of Parliament, Big Ben and the tower of Bankside. On the prow, like a living figurehead, still wearing her trademark stiff white overall, she signals grandly with emphatic eagerness; the image, mocking the portentous and the official, combining the comic and the poignant, the small things and the big issues, packs a strong political punch. The performance sets the artist's skewed and poignant homage to womanly skills, to domestic processes and cyclical necessities of sustenance, against the rigid towers and structures of masculine energy and authority. For her flags signal – to them at Westminster? to us? to herself? – 'Provide better feeding'.

The video was Bobby Baker's first film, commissioned by BBC2 and the Arts Council and created with Margaret Williams. She made it between two live performance pieces in the sequence of five that she has been working on since. *Take a Peek!*, the third in the series, was premiered at the LIFT festival in 1995; *Jelly Game* (later retitled *Grown-Up School*), the fourth and most recent, explores the urgent fears around children, definitions of innocence and the presence of violence. Bobby Baker will perform it in primary schools, and, in the same way as *Take a Peek!*, is constructed as a funfair with sideshows and booths, so *Jelly Game* follows a preconceived form of popular entertainment: in this case, the TV game show, in which the children in the audience will take part. In the aftermath of the Bulger murder and the Dunblane massacre, Bobby Baker began increasingly to notice the level of violent attacks reported daily on the radio, in the press. A typical news item would say, she notes on a drawing, 'A man has run amok with knives in a supermarket in Broadway Green.'

Drawing in sketchbook (1995). 'Help arriving? My own hand? Oh soft self-wounding pelican (Her legs aren't bad for 45!)'. Watercolour paper, pencil, watercolour paint, aqua crayons.

She's not (of course) a law-and-order tub-thumper; the harrowing preliminary drawings she has made to the performance piece reveal, as if through dreamwork, how terrified she is of murderous feelings she experiences. She shows herself spilling out of her own forearm while her open hand is bloodied and armed with a knife. 'It's important', she says, 'to be aware that you are a murderer, a fascist, that everything is within yourself.' Her view of endemic, individual aggression coincides with the argument of Gillian Rose, the philosopher, in her posthumous collection of essays, *Mourning Becomes the Law*, that fascism must be struggled with: 'to argue for silence ... the witness of "ineffability", that is non-representability, is to mystify something we dare not understand, because we fear that it may be all too understandable, all too continuous with what we are – human, all too human'. Fascism, writes Rose, but socially disseminated violence could be included here, retains its hold when it is not faced and challenged through representation (Rose, 1996: 43).

Working with schoolchildren in her local area of London, Bobby Baker has found 'they instantly picked up what *Jelly Game* is about. I went in with a bowl of fruit, and said, "Let's invent a game." One boy immediately grabbed an orange, and cried, "Boom, boom, it's a bomb, it's a hand grenade" – I felt I'd come home at last, they understood so well.' The artist spares no one from uneasiness: *Jelly Game* will show Bobby Baker, wearing pink jackboots, as the game show's host, and will implicate her, and ourselves, in both banality and evil.

Take a Peek!, Bobby Baker's preceding performance piece, began with a sequence of intense, personal coloured pencil drawings, self-portraits showing the artist in the form of one of those stiff Neolithic fertility figurines, arms by her sides, legs close together. But in her case her body was opening up, showing its bounty – and its poisons. In one drawing, her figure is divided into internal compartments, like a chemist's wall cabinet, and from under the flaps come unpredictable fluxes and oozings ('bodily emissions'). In another, the effigy has become a doll's house, with storeys of furniture and books which the artist has annotated: 'The desire for order – body and household possessions – neat and tidy –

Drawing in sketch book (1994). 'Thursday 17 Feb 94. Bodily Emissions'. Watercolour paper, pencil, watercolour paint, aqua crayons.

Top: Drawing in sketch book (1994).
'9.1.94 Lucky charms'.
Watercolour paper, pencil, watercolour
paint, aqua crayons.
Above: *How to Shop* (1993).
LIFT, Tuke Hall, Regents
Park, London.

PROPERLY LOOKED AFTER.' Other drawings show her head exploding with a burst of silver lucky charms, a breast fountaining with blood, and her body segmented into flowerbeds, 'growing useful herbs'. This woman is seeking to be of service: in one image it looks like one of those Egyptian corn effigies, which were planted with seed and placed in the grave to sprout. These private sketches strip away the comic play-acting which Bobby Baker uses to present herself in performance, and they reveal the work's roots in profound and painful self-exposure.

Two years before, in *How to Shop* (1993), Bobby Baker combined the idea of a management training lecture with a housewife's weekly supermarket experience; in *Take a Peek!*, she has taken up the question of women's bodies more directly than ever before, and spliced a woman's nameless ordeals in hospital and clinic with the shows and shies of a traditional fairground. Members of the public are hustled and bustled through in a series of nine moving tableaux and invited at each stage to participate in some way. The highly structured sequence was her most ambitious performance to date. *Take a Peek!*, first staged on the back terrace of the Royal Festival Hall, then toured the UK and abroad in a series of purpose-built spaces and booths designed by the architects Fraser, Brown, McKenna. Co-directed by the artist's longtime collaborator Polona Baloh Brown, it involved two other actors performing and dancing with her – at the LIFT festival Tamzin Griffin and Sîan Stevenson manipulated the artist/patient in their care with false bright smiles and muscly dispatch throughout. In the first booth, Bobby Baker was displayed, bundled up in nine of the starched cotton overalls that have become her signature costume: she's 'The Fat Lady', a freak on show; this corresponds to the 'Waiting Room' stage in the hospital narrative that pulses disturbingly under the whole piece. Explosions of entertainment and circus spectacular interrupt the exploration of the nameless female complaint, as the spectators – taking a peek – follow the artist through the 'Nut Shy', during which she's pelted with hazelnuts, then on through to the 'Show Girls' where she performs an acrobatic dance with the others to a hurdy-gurdy. She is making a spectacle of herself, as Charcot's patients were made to do during his lectures on hysteria in the Salpêtrière Hospital in Paris in the 1880s. (Freud owned a lithograph of one of these sessions, showing a young woman displayed in a contorted trance, and it is still hanging, above the famous couch, in the Freud Museum.) When Bobby Baker saw the images of herself grimacing, taken by Andrew Whittuck (her husband), she realised they caught the feeling of the photographs that Charcot had taken of his patients – most of whom were women – to illustrate the passions that surfaced in the hysterical condition (Showalter, 1985: 147–50).

The most distressing tableau involved the 'nurses' pirouetting as knife-throwers, with all the terrifying associations of reckless surgery; and the acrobatics scene which cunningly and horribly combined expert bed-making with a post-op anaesthetised body and strenuous circus tumbling.

Each phase of her journey through *Take a Peek!* is marked by a fresh, enigmatic, painfully absurd and peculiar sign of the body, as consuming and consumed – oversize melons in a string bag, kumquats swimming in a plastic bag, looking like fairground goldfish, bubble-pack ice cubes filled with Guinness, grass and dirt in a round jug. Each of these signs are again reproduced in photographs Andrew Whittuck has made to accompany the piece, which approach their odd subjects with the cold formal precision of the most highly skilled commercial food photography. The audience of *How to Shop* also came away with ironically glossy souvenirs: handsome postcards of items in that show's series of ordeals, like a bowl of croutons, labelled 'LOVE'.

When Bobby Baker was a student at St Martins, the contemporary artists she most liked were Claes Oldenburg and Roy Lichtenstein, and her interest in objects and food was partly shaped by Pop Art's approach. But her time at St Martins was also the period when Gilbert and George were first appearing as Living Sculptures and beginning to send round their mail-art pieces – traces of their breakfast that day, clippings from their hair. But while they have turned to two-dimensional imagery for the wall, however, Bobby Baker is continuing to use herself as subject and object at once, and to explore pathos and the absurd in daily life.

In 1972, when she first baked a cake – in the shape of a baseball boot – and carved it and iced it, Bobby Baker

Top: *How to Shop* (1993).
LIFT, London.
One of a set of eight cards: 'Love'.
Below: *Birthday Tea Party* (1973).
Anerley, South London.
Assorted cakes, meringues, jelly, fruit,
biscuits.

> looked at this object, and when I thought of carrying it into the college, as a *sculpture*, sitting on my grandmother's cake plate, it was as if the heavens opened and light fell on it – it was *so* funny and rebellious.

Later, Bobby Baker performed a tea party, offering cakes and meringues to invited friends, and there came a second vision, more painful, and more crucial to the subsequent course of her work:

> I made fun of myself, as I had often done in the past, and everyone laughed immoderately. I was utterly distraught. But then everything began to fit. It was quite the most extraordinary sensation. I had been turning myself inside out yearning to be other than myself, but I realised then in one instant that I had to go back into myself, use that and work with that and put it into my art – and that I could do that anywhere.

In that discomfort, when she was laughed at, in that clash between the audience's response and the earnest effusions of the caring

Above: *An Edible Family in a Mobile Home* (1976). 'Father': fruitcake, butter icing, food colour, chicken wire, fabric birds, armchair, newsprint.

tea-party giver, Bobby Baker's performance art is rooted. Through it she provides for others, both in reality and in mimicry in such performance pieces as *Drawing on a Mother's Experience* (1988) and *Kitchen Show* (1991). She could be called a hunger artist, working with her own cravings and the common needs of people for sustenance, for comfort, for nourishment, of which food is the chief sign and the chief embodiment in the real world.

The hungers Bobby Baker represents build on her own self-portrait, and the revelations she makes are so open they provoke embarrassment. Embarrassment, the emotion close to the intimacies of shame, also depends on arbitrary social codes: it is not one of the grand passions, the cardinal virtues or the seven deadly sins, but that does not make it less important, less acutely felt. In this, her use of embarrassment corresponds to her interest in working with the most mundane and overlooked daily tasks (cooking, shopping) and using everyday materials (packaging) and trinkets (a gold ankle chain). But the theatre of embarrassment in her hands turns out the lining of all these ordinary processes and stuffs and makes them raw and deep; she works with what is concealed in the domestic and the homely and the banal and exposes its complexity and its conflicts with humour and imagination and reefs of pain.

In the sequence of performance works, Bobby Baker avoids lulling the audience into a false sense of security through her comic self-parody; her art is planned to be raw, unsettling – even violent in its relationships between subject and the audience. She has defined the effective artistic works as those which

appear like the structure of a cell rushing through the air, so that you can still grasp it intuitively though all you can see are its blurred edges. This reflects the reality of experience, in which one can't really grasp what is going on.

Attending *Take a Peek!* as part of the audience should communicate this same feeling of rush and bewilderment, as the audience too are bundled about and asked to do this, to do that, without explanation; in *Jelly Game*, collaboration with the violent instructions, as in one of those blind tests of human aggressive responses, will inspire insights into one's own collusion and responsibility.

Though the illness or the disorder is never defined – never found? – in *Take a Peek!*, the piece communicates the female patient's predicament, as she is passed on from one investigation or examination to another, each stage appallingly transmogrified into fairground entertainments. Each time she is handed on, she sheds one more overall, as if approaching the anatomy theatre for the final operation. However, by a blissful reprieve, in the climax of the piece, she's undressed to take a blessed, easeful bath instead – chocolate custard. She emerges from this smeared and speckled all over with hundreds and thousands. So *Take a Peek!* ends in cel-

Below: *Take a Peek!* (1995).
LIFT, Royal Festival Hall, London.
'Lucky Dip'.
Bottom: *An Edible Family in a
Mobile Home* (1976).
'Father'. Fruitcake, butter icing, food
colour, chicken wire, fabric birds,
armchair, newsprint.
'Mother': stool with wheels,
dressmaker's dummy, tablecloth,
cardboard, Perspex, Fablon, gloss
paint, teapot, rubber spout, iced buns,
sandwiches, fruit.

ebration: in the spirit of look we have come through. The catharsis of its ending corresponds to the bittersweet triumphs which have brought others of Bobby Baker's performances to a reverberating conclusion: in *How to Shop*, for instance, she ascended into heaven on a hoist, a virtuous housewife who has done her job more than properly; in *Kitchen Show*, she tucked J-cloths into her shoes to give herself wings to fly, and then perched herself on a revolving cake stand, with the J-cloths still standing out stiffly from her heels, and memorably began to turn, like a clumsy, poignant, female Eros of the sink and the stove and the cooking spoon.

These narratives of feeding and being fed are highly ambiguous in their picture of home victories. For her first major piece, performed in 1976, *An Edible Family in a Mobile Home*, Bobby Baker made life-size figures out of cake worked on to chicken wire as if the dough were papier mâché, and set them out like figures in a doll's house, in rooms lined with newspapers and magazines: beauty pin-ups in the girl's bedroom where she was lying on the bed, reading, comics in the boy's room. The mother had a teapot for her head, from which Bobby Baker used to pour a cup for her visitors, as she was inviting them in to eat the family.

At the end of the installation of *An Edible Family*, when all that was left of the figures was a stain on the floor and a mass of twisted chicken wire, Bobby Baker realised, as she had not done before, how fundamentally transgressive she had been, how she had in effect made a model of her own brother and sister, mother and father and herself. The experience was distressing, but the work crystallised her approach: in the most normal scenes of everyday life, she would find disturbances. Her art's game of let's pretend reveals how much is truly pretence.

An Edible Family in a Mobile Home defined a powerful and recurrent theme in Bobby Baker's original art of performance: the piece was a profane communion, a family tea party in which the family was eaten, so that the most polite, indeed genteel, national ritual of friendship became an ogre's banquet. The artist who nearly twenty years ago made effigies of her own family out of cake can now present herself, at the close of *Take a Peek!*, emerging out of confusion and physical suffering into the blissful state of gratification, a childhood fantasy of pleasure and sweetness, fit for licking all over, good enough to eat.

This kind of an ending is again intertwined with the theme of communion in her work: it reflects the structure of a ritual like the Mass, which in its Protestant form does end with the ceremony of the Eucharist, the eating of the body and blood of Christ by the congregation. The Mass mirrors his passion, death and resurrection, in a ritual pattern which demands that sacrifice take place before rebirth and renewal can happen.

Bobby Baker's father was a Methodist, and she went to a Methodist school; her grandfather was so strict that when she made an aeroplane out of putty on a Sunday, and gave it to him, he pulped it with a scowl. On her mother's side, there are 'strings of vicars'. She is still a Christian, and owns up to it, an unusual act in itself for a contemporary artist. But its principles and discipline are intrinsic to her pieces. The abjection she records is bound up with the idea of suffering and humiliation as a resource; she inflicts mortifications on her own body, as in the horrific moment in *How to Shop* when she put a tin of anchovies in her mouth, under her cheeks, stretching her face from ear to ear in a ghastly mockery of a virtuous smile. She has said that she 'wants to share feelings of no worth, of being humiliated', and does not feel that by enacting them, she compounds them, but rather gives herself back power in the act of wilful imitation.

Among the violent preliminary drawings for *Jelly Game* is a bleeding wound, with a small flattened figure brandishing a knife emerging from it. She has captioned it 'Oh soft, self-wounding pelican' in a reference to the hymn which invokes the sacrificed Jesus as the mother bird who, according to the classical and medieval bestiaries, pierces her own breast with her beak in order to nourish her brood on her blood. For this reason, in medieval images of the crucifixion, a 'pelican in her piety', sitting on her nest, often appears at the apex of the cross. For Bobby Baker, the symbol moves closer at hand: to the simple maternal feeding and sustaining of family.

Cannibalism fascinated the Surrealists, as part of the outrageous transgressiveness they cultivated, and Bobby Baker's work also connects with the movement's aesthetics, in her attention to quotidian details, to discovering in everything and anything the quality of the marvellous – what André Breton called *le merveilleux banal*. The macabre feel of *An Edible Family*, and its burlesquing of gentility, is close, too, to Surrealist staging of street scenes and enigmatic incidents. They used dummies in combination with fabricated objects in order to mount a political attack against the hypocrisy of the guardians of culture and morality then in power. The word 'banal', with its etymological connection to the Greek word for 'work' and its sixteenth-century meaning of 'common' or 'communal', has been degraded to mean 'trite' or 'trivial', just as the ordinary work everyone must do has also fallen into disregard, if not contempt. This is especially marked recently with respect to the domestic routines of women and the daily business of mothering – the very territory Bobby Baker makes her own as an arena of art.

Another Surrealist artist, Meret Oppenheim, in several mordantly ironical mixed media objects, likewise explored the connections of the female body and food, of love and nourishment: for example, a pair of bridal shoes trussed and upturned on a dish, with butcher's paper frills around the heels (*Ma Gouvernante – My Nurse – Mein Kindermädchen*, 1936), and the bread roll in the shape

How to Shop (1993). Part of a sequence of five story board drawings done in 1992. 'Obedience – whole tin of anchovies – in my mouth'.

of a woman showing her vulva, laid on a chessboard as place mat, with knife and fork alongside ('*Bon Appétit, Marcel!*', 1966). But Bobby Baker did not merely invite eating in an eternal moment of suspended time; the family was eaten by her guests. This was uncanny, and comic, too, and it brilliantly realised theories of family conflict and the place of food, as simultaneously the symbol of care and love and the instrument of control and authority: 'I'll be Mother' means taking charge of the teapot.

Similarly, in one of the powerfully bizarre episodes of *How to Shop*, she made a baby out of shaving foam, in an appeal to male help and protection – and then destroyed it. The clash within the very core of the maternal role figures vividly in Bobby Baker's earlier performance piece, *Drawing on a Mother's Experience* (1988), where she is no longer the daughter but the mother, and is herself feeding and being consumed, physically and mentally. It is a most upsetting piece to watch, and a powerful one; it begins with Bobby Baker, bright and cheery, giving a pretty straight account of the birth of her two children and the first eight years of her life as a mother: there's nothing very dramatic recounted – except for the sudden successful delivery of her son, on the floor, at home – 'on the only rug I hadn't washed'. At each stage in the story, Bobby Baker remembers some item of food – the Guinness she drank to build up her strength, the fish pie her mother brought her – and produces them on stage from a shopping bag, and then uses them to draw (as the double entendre of the title promises) on a sheet she has spread on the floor. The result is a kind of mock Jackson Pollock, an action painting made of beer and blackberries and splattered fish pie. Then, at the very end, she rolls herself into the sticky, wet, dribbling mess and stands up and hops, stiffly, in a kind of celebration dance that she has survived.

Drawing on a Mother's Experience was performed in a church in Bobby Baker's part of North London the night I saw it. From preference, she would always perform in public spaces in ordinary daily use, like schools and churches and halls (she initially wanted *How to Shop* to take place in a supermarket), and says that her ideal would be to 'take a stool out into the street and stand up on it and do it' – rather in the manner of a lay preacher. She finds her material to hand, never in specialist shops or fancy, brand name boutiques; she is developing a vernacular at all levels – dramatic, visual, topographical – and is intentionally not hip like street jargon, or nostalgic like dirty realist drama dialect, but the particular urban language of the informal unofficial networks, of the usually disregarded working local community. *Kitchen Show* was patterned on a coffee morning among neighbours; she deliberately broke down the distinction between strangers in the street and family in the house, and it was shocking, in a pleasurable way, to be invited into Bobby Baker's own private kitchen to see her perform. She is interested in the ordinary stories people tell

Drawing on a Mother's Experience (1997). Greenbelt Festival, Lincolnshire. Cotton sheeting, plastic sheeting, assorted foodstuffs.

one another; in the exchanges that take place between strangers on a bus.

The audience in the church for *Drawing on a Mother's Experience* responded vividly, with cries and sighs, hoots and giggles, but as Bobby Baker worked towards the end, there was a hush and tears. The tragicomic atmosphere was under her complete command: she assumes a tone of stoical jollity in the way she tells her story, while her characteristic physical bashfulness adds to the excruciating vulnerability she communicates. We

Drawing on a Mother's Experience (1990). ICA, London. Cotton sheeting, plastic sheeting, assorted foodstuffs.

learn of what that body has been through, and though her body is on show in some way on the stage, it remains hidden at the same time, under her recurring uniform, the anonymous white overall, and through the conventional gestures she adopts. She says, 'In any place I wear an overall I become faceless and voiceless and I find the possibilities of that really interesting.'

The laughter she causes is not mirth; it is sadder, and deeper. It expresses recognition in both male and female spectators of the ordinary human mysteries of life and survival and all their accompanying difficulties she is representing; but it is very far from the kind of collusive laughter that protests provoke. Bobby Baker does not come on as a victim, asking for solidarity in her sufferings. Her re-enactment of her experience as a mother is matter-of-fact – no grievances are being aired, no self-pity. But she draws us into her anger at helplessness, and at the corresponding terrors of inadequacy, into understanding her confusion at all the demands and the tasks, and the incommunicability of trying to sustain life.

The Surrealist writer and artist Leonora Carrington said in an interview that for her painting was 'like making strawberry jam, really carefully, really well'; she cultivates 'dailyness' and its pleasures. Similarly, the undercurrent of unease in Bobby Baker's pieces rises up to a surface that must be rich in sensuous delights for her. Recalling *An Edible Family*, she talks of the figures' perfect prettiness at first, before they began to rot and to disintegrate (and be eaten); she remembers 'the irresistible sparkle of the sugar against the newsprint'. Her work is consistently concerned with pleasure, with the lively, connected responses of palate and eye, and inspires her to introduce sensuous surprises in every piece, which are frequently funny because they displace sexual engulfment and bliss. Even in the midst of recording the humiliations of the body, she will take a pause to admire – the dazzling purple of plums, the peachiness of some pale pink stuff. It brings to mind something the writer Colm Toibin composed about Egon Schiele, another self-portraitist with a taste for performance:

> Schiele was so brave in the way he let colour decorate his painting, in the way he would allow pure moments of delight to happen, revelling in the richness of the materials at his disposal so that his sense of mingled disgust and desire at the nature of the body is always mysterious and oddly comic.
>
> (Toibin, 1994: 121)

Partly, Bobby Baker 'guys' herself as a woman, with all the paradoxes that entails. When she was little, she wanted to be a boy, like so many girls brought up in the 1950s with the tomboys Jo in *Little Women* and George in the 'Famous Five' as role models. Her name was Lindsey (itself ambidextrous), but she chose Bobby, and stayed with it. Names are obviously important: in the game of Happy Families, there was Miss Bun, the baker's daughter, and Bobby hated her for being so round – and red-cheeked, such 'a diminished creature'. While taking up baking with a vengeance, Bobby Baker was turning on that fat and happy alter ego who was so supine in her lot.

The figures of women in her work often seem to belong in a game, too, a game of 'let's pretend' that she is playing. She conveys the strangeness of all the duties women are expected to fulfil, and her own ambiguous relationship to shopping and cooking and mothering and so forth put in question the naturalness of such activities for women at all. She pinpoints the springs of feelings

Cook Dems (2000). Jacksons Lane Theatre, London.

How to Shop (1993).
Part of a sequence of five story board
drawings done in 1992.
'all the shopping in the
bag + the book – the halo on'.

How to Shop (1993). LIFT, London.
One of a set of eight cards.

of worth, and destabilises them, as when, in *How to Shop*, she comments on how accomplished she feels when her trolley is filled with more bargains and healthier items than the next person in the queue. The uniform helps here too, as if she needs the costume to perform correctly in the task of being-a-wife-and-mother, but its anonymity and its ungainliness only bring out the imprisonment of gender expectations more vividly. She also seems to affect feminine mannerisms: she has a penchant for baby-pink slippers, slingbacks, even the overalls were to be pale, pale pink. She gives quick nervous little giggles after a phrase in order not to seem too assertive, and to cover up, without really succeeding, feelings of panic and tension. She purposefully adds flurry and fluster in her eagerness to communicate, dipping and nodding in a pantomime of social expectations from carers, mothers, homemakers. This is often excruciatingly funny too.

Rituals, sacred and domestic, are sometimes structured to include humour; the festivals of Greece and Rome accorded a hugely important role to comedy, in the raucous satyr plays, for example, which concluded the performance of tragedies, and in the Saturnalia, which survive in some form in carnival topsy-turvy. The Christian liturgy used to include the *risus paschalis*, or Easter laughter, which greeted the resurrection of Christ. Anthropologists have shown the link between the way rituals define identity and belonging, and the way jokes, for example, set borders between 'Us' and 'Them', or challenge adversity with laughter and confirm a sense of social solidarity. The court jester was allowed, in the guise of jokes, to tell the truth, as the Fool does in *King Lear*. Mary Douglas, the anthropologist, points out, 'The joke works only when it mirrors social forms; it exists by virtue of its congruence with the social structure' (Douglas, 1975: 106). She goes on to discuss the joker as a ritual purifier among the Kaguru, the Gogo and the Dogon and other African tribes, where a joker enjoys privileges of open speech others are forbidden, and can therefore cleanse the community. His modus operandi is different from the straightforward flouting of taboos, however:

> [The joker] has a firm hold on his own position in the structure and the disruptive comments he makes upon it are in a sense the comments of the social group upon itself ... he lightens for everyone the oppressiveness of social reality, demonstrates its arbitrariness by making light of formality in generality, and expresses the creative possibilities of the situation ... his jokes expose the inadequacy of realist structurings of experience and so release the pent-up power of the imagination.
>
> (Douglas, 1975: 106)

Douglas could have been writing about Bobby Baker; her use of the comic mode is interestingly related, given her taste for ritual structures. The women in her childhood – her grandmother and her mother – were given to laughing:

> they laughed at everything and anything which made me angry – great hysterical shrieks and hoots. My grandmother was a very, very frustrated woman – she used to throw things about, and cook very badly and say things, like 'Have a bun', and then throw it at you. But this wicked sense of humour was very, very liberating.

Derision was these older women's way of tackling the world. Freud wrote in a short essay on 'Humour' that laughing was a powerful means of self-assertion:

> The ego refuses to be distressed by the provocations of reality, to let itself be compelled to suffer. It insists that it cannot be affected by the traumas of the external world; it shows, in fact, that such traumas are no more than occasions for it to gain pleasure ... Humour is not resigned; it is rebellious. It signifies not only the triumph of the ego but also of the pleasure principle, which is able here to assert itself against the unkindness of the real circumstances.
>
> (Freud, 1928: 162–3)

The various comic modes on which Bobby Baker draws – stand-up patter, self-mockery and burlesque, clowning and pantomime – consist of different ways of acknowledging the state of abjection and making a virtue of it, which is a form of refusal, but not complete denial. Her crucial change is that her humour doesn't taunt or jeer at others, or like a comic, make the audience laugh at others' distress (the banana skin principle). She is the target of the laughter she provokes, but remains in control, however weak and vulnerable she presents herself to be. She said once that going into a local church gave her

> a terrible desire to fall about laughing, or stand up high and just shriek with laughter, because I find it so bizarre – and I have the same reaction in supermarkets. That is really one of the starting points of my work, that irreverence and rebellion and freedom.

Bobby Baker has turned her perception of her own vulnerabilities and folly and anger both as herself and as a woman into a brave show, a new way of fooling: like the jester, she tells the truth but seems to be making mock while she does it, so that we can bear what she makes us see.

Integrity: The Essential Ingredient

GERALDINE HARRIS
WITH ELAINE ASTON

An edited extract from 'A Passionate Desire to Communicate: Bobby Baker' in Aston and Harris *Performance, Practice and Process: Contemporary [Women]Practitioners*, (Palgrave Macmillan, 2007).

Geraldine (Gerry) Harris is Professor of Theatre Studies at Lancaster University, UK. Previous publications include *Staging Femininities* (1999), *Beyond Representation: The Politics and Aesthetics of Television Drama* (2006). With Elaine Aston she co-edited *Feminist Futures: Theatre, Performance, Theory* (2006) and co-wrote *Performance Practice and Process: Contemporary [Women] Practitioners*, (Palgrave Macmillan, 2007).

Opposite: *Table Occasion No 4* (1998). Purcell Room, London.

IF BOBBY'S WORK 'communicates' to a wider public than usual for 'experimental' performance this is because her focus on the objects and rituals of everyday life, the play of humour, and above all her famously 'endearingly eccentric' stage persona, render her work 'inclusive' and provide numerous points of identification. Yet, Bobby's shows are multifaceted and densely layered and her relationship with the audience is far more complex than might first appear. Even while she uses self-deprecation and self-parody to encourage laughter at her claims to knowledge and expertise on the basis of her years of experience of being a mother and a housewife (or a patient), she transforms everyday domestic items into highly evocative and aesthetically pleasing 'art objects', through the power of her *extraordinary* skill as an artist *and* a mother *and* a housewife (*and* a patient). Her 'endearing' persona then is deployed ironically to persuade the audience to question social and political assumptions about social roles and identity categories, but the 'discursive' is explored through the local, the specific and the material. In many shows she engages in actions which foreground the ways in which discourse acts on the body in a manner which can verge on the violent and masochistic, for instance forcing a tin of anchovies into her mouth in *How to Shop* or pouring a whole bottle of tomato sauce into her mouth in *Spitting Mad*. At these points it is not unusual for spectators to gag in sympathy, but such acts can also create a sense of unease or embarrassment at such excessive behaviour. Similarly, her shows frequently touch on serious, even distressing autobiographical material in ways that can give a discomforting sense of complicity in witnessing the public exposure of profoundly personal and painful experiences. In short, as the feminist critical response to her practice suggests, Bobby's work often manages to produce the *affect* she sought as an art student, that is the 'experience [of] an extra-ordinarily complex set of realities, associations' (Baldwyn, 1996: 38), not least in relation to the profoundly ambivalent, intellectual, emotional and physical experience of being gendered in our culture. The production of this affect, however, is a matter of aesthetics as well as politics, of 'art' as well as 'life'.

Hard work comes into this equation and it can take her years to develop a show. For instance, she says she started to think about the concept of the pea in *How to Live* between 10 and 15 years ago. This may be partly because as she indicated in an interview in the 1990s, Bobby is engaged in a 'constant searching for shape and pattern, an almost mathematical fascination with form, that you may be able to put ideas together in arrangements which you imagine, in a rather fantastical way might become perfect' (Heathfield, 1999: pp. 88–9 above). Integrity in all its meanings is a pre-eminent principle within Bobby's own process and practice and can be understood to include an understanding that a passionate desire to communicate important ideas involves a commitment to searching for the appropriate (if not perfect) form through which to express them. This sense of integrity and a concern for form counterbalances the deeply felt autobiographical and sometimes 'taboo breaking' or disturbing nature of her work, allowing her to engage with the audience in a way that moves between distance and identification, so as to take them on a journey that 'is somehow safe, based on trust and not abusive' (Heathfield, 1999: p. 87 above).

My Cooking Competes (1980).
ICA, London.
Framed photographs, assorted food, cutlery, crockery.

BOBBY'S STAGE PERSONA

As has often been noted, Bobby's stage persona is a matter of playing 'herself' but her style of achieving this is noticeably much 'rawer' than that of younger performance practitioners such as Leslie Hill from the group Curious in *Smoking Gun* and *On the Scent*. Bobby's style of delivery remains rooted in her origins in performance art of the 1970s and 1980s, with its emphasis on the position of the artist as 'author' rather than performer, a stance that was often part of an aggressive anti-theatricality. While certain 'themes' associated with this stance may have always informed Bobby's practice, as already suggested, in recent years she has been happy to embrace aspects of the theatrical. Indeed, in developing *How to Shop*, which was to be shown in larger venues than her previous works, Bobby went to well-known theatre voice coach Patsy Rodenburg to improve her vocal technique. She reports that after a couple of sessions Rodenburg dismissed her, saying, 'Honestly, Bobby, I'm just going to do more damage than good. Do it the way you do it. It's working.' Bobby's apparent lack of technique, reflected in a slight physical and vocal 'awkwardness' as a performer, works because it guarantees the 'ordinariness' of her persona in ways that invite trust and identification and 'authenticates' the shows' experiential and political content. Yet at the same time, as noted above, there is always a degree of self-parody and ironic self-reflexivity in this persona that implies an acknowledgment that she is playing a 'role'. This same contradiction emerges very clearly in one of the 'trademarks' of her stage persona, the white coat or overall, which she has worn throughout all her shows, except for *Box Story*, in which it was dyed blue. Discussing the white overall, she has said previously:

Kitchen Show (1991). LIFT, North London. Image from booklet.

> An important part of creating a performance is to decide how best to encompass a complex range of ideas within an appropriate form. I found it irritating to 'clutter' ideas with clothes. That carried too many associations. The white overall offered an inexhaustible range of associations to play with as well as a certain blankness.
>
> (Baldwyn, 1996: 44)

As exemplified by her use of a 'pea suit' in *How to Live,* in the course of a show this overall is occasionally cast off in favour of another more 'theatrical' costume, but only temporarily. More importantly, the overall is always 'personalised' through hair, make-up, shoes or jewellery, 'details' which she often draws attention to and which, thrown into relief by the blankness of the overall, become, as she indicates in *How to Live,* highly significant. Nevertheless, the formality of the white coat creates an impersonal distance, making space for introjection and projection on the part of the audience that goes *beyond* Bobby's specific identity and experiences due to its associations with social 'roles', as opposed to individuals. In various shows therefore, it can be said to have suggested the cookery demonstrator, the housewife, the (domestic) science lecturer, the patient and the psychotherapist.

THE CENTRALITY OF THE 'ACTION'

Bobby's 'almost mathematical concern for form' is especially evident in a tendency to structure her larger-scale shows around a particular number of 'actions', with, for instance, *Kitchen Show* being based around 13 actions; *How to Shop,* 7 actions; *Box Story,* 10; and *How to Live,* 11. Sometimes the number of actions is significant – for instance, in *Kitchen Show* 13 is a 'Baker's dozen'. However, in other shows the meaning of the number, if any, is

* Actually the nature of the imposition of form as a 'conceit' in Bobby's shows is evident in *How to Live*. While we have said that there are 11 actions in this show, Bobby includes two extra 'poses', an introductory one and a final summative one, so that in terms of Whittuck's photographs, this produces another 'Baker's dozen'. This has been done so that the first letter of the first word of the written text that accompanies each of these 'poses'/still photographs can together spell out the words 'Watch Yourself' in the manner of old-fashioned poetic 'conceits' and/or riddles.

Drawing on a Mother's Experience (1997). Greenbelt Festival, Deene Park, Lincolnshire. Cotton sheeting, plastic sheeting, assorted food stuffs.

less clear and Bobby has suggested that the rules she imposes on herself may be arbitrary – 'a conceit ... it's the fact that I'm organising or imposing a form on an event that is important' (Heathfield, 1999: see p. 90 above).*

These actions are sometimes 'attached' to autobiographical stories, which again tend to provoke a personal identification with Bobby and have often been the focus of critical attention. Yet, Bobby points out 'there's not always a story – I'm thinking of *Pull Yourself Together* (2000), which is entirely an action and there's no story. Shows that I really cherish don't necessarily have stories. The next piece I'm doing – a new website – I've got none of my stories in it. The live piece I'm working on is not going to have my story in it. So the story bit comes and goes.' For her the actions are at the core of both her work representing and expressing the overarching ideas or a 'concept around a particular detail or feeling about what it's important to try to open a debate about'. Using *Kitchen Show* as an example, she says, 'I got very angry and frustrated about the way these daily actions, these daily routines and rituals are not observed and cherished in our society. I could see how fundamentally complex they were and how they related to things like the butterfly effect in chaos theory, or the Blake thing – "the world in a grain of sand", the idea that the minutiae contains the enormous.' The concept of the show emerged from 'wandering about' thinking about this and more specifically during a moment when she had a fantasy of having 'a world satellite link' to her washing a carrot, an 'action' that featured in the show.

Usually once the action is completed, it is represented by a 'mark' made on (or through) her own body and Bobby then 'make[s] a pose, just for a moment, for a fraction so that people can observe the mark. It's an essential part of the performance because it gives people that moment to reflect on what's happening' (Baldwyn, 1996: 43). While the 'pose' occurs live in *Kitchen Show*, in other large-scale shows it is sometimes also shown in the form of slides of still photographs taken by Whittuck. The pose, and its doubling in the still photographs, then interrupts the flow of the live performance and are intended to promote reflection on the ideas Bobby is 'passionately attempting to communicate'. As such, the 'actions', their marking and the posing can be said to function like the Brechtian notion of *gestus*, a gesture which materialises the social and political 'gist' of the scene or section or of the whole. At the same time, these strategies and devices reflect Bobby's earlier positioning within the 'live art' part of the performance continuum, which (is still) often focused on 'body art', human sculpture and 'actions', rather than narrative, whether 'fragmented' or otherwise. Similarly, the manner in which Whittuck's photographs are *part* of the shows and also available separately as 'documentation', which in turn might be perceived as self-contained 'performances' in another medium, is in accord with performance *art* practice.

As all of this suggests, it is possible to identify certain formal and thematic continuities across the body of Bobby's work but her search for the 'appropriate' form for each piece has led her to employ an enormous variety of media, stagings and performance techniques. As noted, she has worked in film, radio, drawing and websites and her live shows have incorporated pre-recorded and live-feed video, computer animation, still photographs and specially composed music. Across various shows she has engaged in lip-synching, dancing, theatrical 'flying', slapstick and all sorts of contortions, gymnastics, attaching things to her body, strapping herself to the back of vans, etc. In a fashion similar to, but pre-dating, Curious's work, she has frequently experimented with the use of smell and taste in her work* and although this is seldom discussed, the vast majority of her pieces have actually (in different ways) been 'site specific'. This reflects her early desire to do her shows '*anywhere*' and she has said that by preference she would always perform in public spaces in daily use, such as churches and school halls. This site-specificity extends not only to smaller-scale pieces like the *Table Occasions* but most of her larger-scale shows – so, for example, *Kitchen Show* premiered in her own kitchen, *How to Shop* premiered in a lecture hall and *Box Story* premiered in Bobby's own church, St Luke's in Holloway. Created with these spaces in mind, these shows were later adapted for touring.

*As indicated above, from *An Edible Family in a Mobile Home* onwards many of her performances have involved giving food to the audience. Sometimes this is handed in ways that foreground smell as well as taste, for instance in *How to Shop*, she fried garlic croutons on stage, filling the auditorium with their smell, before giving them to the audience.

AUTHORSHIP AND COLLABORATION

While the collaborative nature of most *theatre* practice has always problematised the ascription of authorship, for several centuries the work of (fine) art has usually been clearly understood as the product of a 'sole artist'. Even though Bobby has increasingly moved towards working with other practitioners – in contrast, for example, with the processes employed by Split Britches, which are intensively collaborative from the very start – Bobby says, 'I work on my own for a certain period of time, come up with the images and the ideas and *then* involve other people.' This was something she says she had to come to terms with early on in her working relationship with Polona Baloh Brown, or 'Pol', as Bobby calls her. When Pol suggested an 'alternative' ending to a piece Bobby was still developing, Bobby's immediate response was 'No' and she says, 'it was very difficult to negotiate that reaction but [Pol] was extremely generous. I said it's only really going to work if it's my images and my vision. I found it very difficult because it was like I was saying "I need your help, but don't do the fun bit." There have been stages where all that has got rather muddy and I have lost the lead in what I was doing – not only in terms of Pol's input, but other people's input and I would say that some of that work is not as clear as the later work.' Giving the example of Pol's role in the work with reference to *How to Live*, Bobby says, '[Pol] generally gets involved when everything was mapped out, everything was planned and then we had to make it into a kind of performance.' In terms of programme credits over the years, Baloh Brown has been often described either as director or co-director, but, after endless discussion she is now described as the performance director, but I don't know that that entirely covers the fact that she really is involved in the text and structuring.'

In a later exchange we had with Baloh Brown herself, she indicated that she is still not entirely comfortable with the term 'performance director'. Instead, she favours what she admits is a more 'cumbersome' designation – that of 'outside eye'. In this role, she says,

Kitchen Show (1991). LIFT, North London. Image from booklet: 'Roaming'.

> I perceive myself as a catalyst through which the work progresses and passes, and this catalyst helps channel it without destroying its original form, without challenging its basic shape, depth or colour ... An outside eye is also the bridge between the performer/author and the audience.

At the same time, however, for Baloh Brown, 'This means I must not have any preconceived ideas or expectations and take on board wholly what is given to me by the author/performer and work with it.'

If this role of 'performance director' or 'outside eye' is distinct from that of the 'traditional' director, equally it differs from that of a 'co-devisor'/performer who engages in the work from the start but also 'steps outside' to act as 'director/editor'. It is notoriously difficult to negotiate this latter role, although some, such as Lois Weaver, achieve it very successfully. It is worth noting that some other 'solo' performance practitioners (who also sometimes collaborate with other performers and/or artists) such as Kazuko Hohki occasionally work with freelance director Mark Whitelaw in a not dissimilar role to that played by Baloh Brown. The notion of working with this sort of 'performance director' or outside eye, brought into the process *after* the 'core' ideas and images have been developed, is therefore worth considering, especially by those primarily working as solo artists.

Interestingly, in her groundbreaking book on performance art, RoseLee Goldberg sometimes refers to the late 1960s to early 1970s generation of artists who rejected traditional fine arts methods and material to embrace installation, video and live art or performance, collectively as 'conceptual artists' (Goldberg, 2001: 152). In the public realm, this term is now mainly associated with figures like Damien Hirst and Tracey Emin and, while it may sometimes (potentially) be aesthetically and politically 'subversive', it lost much of its 'radical' edge when, championed by figures like Charles Saatchi in the 1980s and 1990s, it was firmly recuperated to the values of the commercial 'art market'. Nonetheless, certain aspects of Bobby's process and practice can still be allied to the notion and methodologies of 'conceptual art', although this is counterbalanced by her drive towards collaboration with other artists and more 'theatrical' staging in her larger-scale work. Equally, her incursions into film, radio and websites, as well as her decision to exhibit her drawings, indicate other directions 'formally'. Yet her body of work is nevertheless 'coherent' because what drives her formal experimentation is the search for 'integrity', as part of a passionate desire to communicate ideas in ways that open a debate about important social and political issues.

Upstaged by the Foodie Gaze

HELEN IBALL

'Well,' said Pooh, 'what I like best,' and then he had to stop and think. Because although Eating Honey was a very good thing to do, there was a moment just before you began to eat it which was better than when you were, but he didn't know what it was called.

(Milne, 1928: 168–9)

WINNIE-THE-POOH is a stop and think kind of bear, with the mind-set of a well-rounded hedonist. Here, his musings on pleasure begin with absolute conviction and end in a SALIVATORY blur. The process of his thoughts from consumption back to anticipation, with all the vividness of travelling in reverse, identifies an epicentre which Pooh (as lucidly befuddled as ever) christens the 'moment just before'. The distinction between this moment and the instant of absorption provides a model that, when applied to the manifestation of food and eating-acts in performance, raises key issues regarding the manipulation of audience response.

Human relationships with food extend far beyond moments of consumption. The appeal of just looking at food is enormous, and thus it is not surprising that, in live performance, it provokes audience response in a manner that is attributable to no other class of stage property, a point that is noted by Stanton B. Garner

From 'Melting Moments: Bodies Upstaged by the Foodie Gaze', *Performance Research: On Cooking*, 4 (1) Spring 1999.

Helen Iball teaches in the Workshop Theatre at the University of Leeds. Her recent publications are on Sarah Kane, Howard Barker, and on theatrical spectatorship post-9/11. Inspired by a workshop with Bobby Baker, Helen is undertaking a series of events and publications about academics, entitled 'Doctored Identities'.

Opposite page:
Table Occasion No. 4 (1998).
Purcell Room, London.

(1994: 99). Prior to moments of absorption, food draws attention to its own life, its own presence, and in so doing, highlights the 'liveness' of the theatre by forcing the acknowledgement of its permeability. Theatre is a leaky place whose artificial borders are crossed easily by the smells that waft into the audience. This sensory transgression of boundaries goes unacknowledged in key models of the conventionalised theatrical frame (Bennett, 1990; Elam, 1980; Schechner, 1988). The multi-sensory potential of organic properties enables a subtle, indeed invisible, invasion of the spectator, yet, on penetrating this target, its potential manifestation may well provoke a strong physical response, be this salivation or nausea.

> Objects of desire are not real but fictive, seen through a distorting lens. They furthermore enact a structure of desire that is a closed narrative system. Because the drive or pulsation of desire, in order to be sustained, must be unsatisfied, the objects desired (or the climax of the story) are ever distant or deferred. Thus the objects of a still life, although they appear accessible, are actually inaccessible, fictional, created; ideal as opposed to real.
>
> (Rowell, 1997: 10–11)

While this is not the space for a discussion of the ascription of the terminology 'nude' and 'naked' in the contexts of painting and performance, there is a parallel to be drawn here, in acknowledging the connection between the traditional nude in painting as a representation of the (female) body that succeeds in fixing that body's boundaries, thus containing its potential obscenity (see, for example, Lynda Nead's 1992 discussion of this point in *The Female Nude*) and the equally prevalent tradition of the 'still life' – the very title of which suggests capture through suspended animation and which, by convention, tends to include fruit, vegetables and game. Once staged, containment is difficult. The living, moving, naked body on stage provokes a response which draws attention to the propensity of the spectator to read the sign-system as significant and inclusive. The gaze can be directed/contained only so far – both in terms of the practitioner and the spectator, who attempts perhaps to 'see' in the context of the assumption of an 'expected response', but is drawn irresistibly into transgression and possibly even puerility. Similarly, staged food cannot masquerade as the 'ideal' object of the still life. Rather, like the naked body, it provokes a response that, in the first instance, is uncontrolled/uncontrollable because the food is both real and performed, echoing Barthes's notion of the ultra-incarnate actor (1954: 27–8). It is, to use Rowell's term, inaccessible only because the audience choose to respect the conventions of the theatre space, and, even then, the access point is shifted through potential seepage, as mentioned above.

This notion of seepage characterises the abject state of the body, as described in Julia Kristeva's *Powers of Horror* (1980), and it is the liminal capability of food as a key generator of abjection that has resulted in its frequent annexation within the work of performance artists seeking to make the (orificial) body *explicit*, to use a term attributable to Rebecca Schneider (1997). While this essay *will* mention Bobby Baker and Karen Finley, as subjects of the most 'foodie' performance analysis to date (Epstein, 1996; Baldwyn, 1996), its focus is upon the visibility and incarnation of *food itself*, rather than its function as a tool in foregrounding stage bodies that 'will not hesitate to come up close, close enough to be in danger of life' (Cixous, 1995: 134).

Food's own life-cycle, from freshness to decay, imbues it with a unique energy. The Poohvian struggle for words might, in this context, be related to the unspeakable potentialities of food. This is expressed vividly in Margaret Atwood's novel *The Edible Woman*, whose central character finds herself at the mercy of her own body, becoming obsessed with the imagined biology of an ever-increasing array of foods. She searches desperately for items she feels able to stomach, as rice pudding is transformed by her eyes into a collection of small 'cocoons with miniature living creatures inside' (1969: 203), while sponge cake 'felt spongy and cellular against her tongue, like the bursting of a thousand tiny lungs' (ibid.: 207). In *Food, the Body and the Self*, Deborah Lupton describes the manner in which food 'intrudes into the "clean" purity of rational thought because of its organic nature' (1996: 3).

In drama, dining scenes proliferate, bringing communities of characters together in convincing opportunities for social interchange (and their almost inevitable disruption). As a ritualised event, the meal-time is a significant resource for the theatremaker. However, feeding scenes are notable for their sparsity. A wariness of food's disruptive potential has meant that it has been 'disappeared' through containment, tokenism, even banishment. In Arnold Wesker's *The Kitchen*, a production note asserts that the preparation and cooking of the array of dishes are mimed, indeed 'it must be understood that at no point is food ever used' as 'to cook and serve the food is of course just not practical' (1960: 10).

Marcy Epstein's recent article 'Consuming Performances: Eating Acts and Feminist Embodiment' considers the ways in which a number of American women performance artists have reclaimed 'something forbidden to women onstage: something to eat' (1996: 20). Clearly women do have a different relationship with food in Western culture, and this is one which is imposed upon them, in direct relation to their ascription as most abject, most dangerous and thus most in need of containment. Indeed, as far as I am aware, all significant manifestations of food in

Displaying the Sunday Dinner (1998). Roast beef, roast potatoes, carrots, savoy cabbage, apple pie and baked custard.

performance art have been *created* by women. However, I am not aware of a theatre in which the women are forbidden something to eat, while the men indulge themselves. When this kind of gorging is permitted within stage representation, it is contained via careful contextualisation, its abject nature harnessed to communicate meaning. And, though perhaps to different extents, and certainly in respect of socio-historical gender to specific expectations, both sexes are implicated. This is evident in the examples given below.

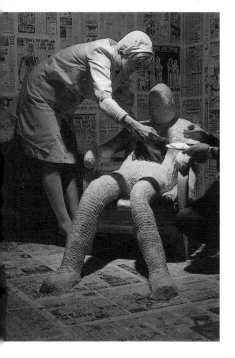

An Edible Family in a Mobile Home (1976). Stepney, London. 'Father': fruitcake, butter icing, food colour, chicken wire, fabric birds, armchair, newsprint.

Beyond tea-sipping, illusory nibbling and the chasing of cold peas around a plate to make the dining scene more 'realistic', food and its consumption on stage tend to designate a lapse in upright citizenship, an exposé of the deadly sin of gluttony. It is Stanley bringing home his 'red-stained package from the butchers' that Tennessee Williams chooses to give his audience its first impression of the character in *A Streetcar Named Desire* (1947: 4); and later in the play, at Blanche's birthday supper, Stanley ignores the social chit-chat of the party, interested only in the food. After he 'reaches way over the table to spear his fork in the remaining pork chop which he eats with his fingers' Stella chides: 'Mr. Kowalski is too busy making a pig of himself to think of anything else' before telling him to go and wash his 'disgustingly greasy' face and hands (Williams, 1947: 65).

The subversive potential of food is also packaged carefully and used under controlled conditions in *The Importance of Being Earnest* (1895). Oscar Wilde serves up afternoon tea in excess of social propriety as a device to physicalise the squabbles between Cecily and Gwendolyn, by making the gifts of food and drink unpalatable to the 'ladylike' sensibilities of the guest. Cecily brutalises the event she is hosting by sheer quantity, amassing sweetness in order to induce sickness:

> *Gwendolyn:* You have filled my tea with lumps of sugar, and though I asked most distinctly for bread and butter, you have given me cake. I am known for the gentleness of my disposition, and the extraordinary sweetness of my nature, but I warn you, Miss Cardew, you may go too far.
>
> (Wilde, 1895: 294)

Echoing Gwendolyn's identification of excessive behaviour, Cecily, determined and scheming in her actions, overfaces her rival. Via the minutiae of polite society she exceeds (ridiculously, of course) her role as host in order to act upon a code of self-honour which demands that 'to save my poor, innocent, trusting boy from the machinations of any other girl there are no lengths to which I would not go' (1895: 294). The food is given, but is inedible to Gwendolyn. An eating-act does not, and indeed, the point is, cannot, take place.

In these instances, the riskiness of food is being released

temporarily in a specific context, and the heightened behaviour of characters vies with the food for centre stage. Such situations rely upon a shared understanding of food etiquette and, as is clear from the examples cited above, are pinpointed as deliberate transgressions via the dialogue. In extreme cases, they may include the ultimate culinary taboo – use of the human body as a food source (the only exception to this taboo is breastfeeding for tiny babies). The impact of Bigas Luna's film *La Teta y la Luna (The Tit and the Moon,* 1994) is contingent upon the social horror of a boy of nine suckling at the breast; while Shakespeare's *Titus Andronicus* (1594), Sarah Kane's *Blasted* (1995) and Peter Greenaway's *The Cook, the Thief, His Wife and Her Lover* (1989) all portray the most extreme foodie *faux pas,* cannibalism. In an actualisation of Margaret Atwood's novel, in which the protagonist creates an 'edible woman' from sponge and icing to horrify her partner into recognition of his habitual objectification of her, Bobby Baker developed her fascination with cake baking and decorating to make her early installation work *An Edible Family in a Mobile Home* (1976). Baker describes to David Tushingham the way in which, over the course of the week of the installation (which was sited at Baker's then home, a prefab in Stepney) the cake family was 'completely destroyed' and 'actually smelt' (1994: 29). Tushingham's interview with Baker expresses vividly a key paradox that fuelled this piece and much of Baker's subsequent practice – namely, the instability of food as a sculptural material expressing the potentiality of such apparent gentility (cake at a tea party) to undergo a transformation characterised by decimation and decay.

Baker found most disturbing the total obliteration of the baby cake, as she identified the family she had created with her own, and with her place as the youngest of the family. In a number of her subsequent works are to be found less brutal, but disturbingly actual, body-based referencings of invitations to cannibalism, in a more subtle implicating of the audience as 'consumer'. For Baker is now the baked as well as the baker. She is the cake on the stand.

Figuring a performative blurring of a clear separation between 'fictional' and 'actual' worlds, Baker parodies etiquette. She stages the nurturing role of housewife and mother by treating the audience like visitors, welcoming them to the *Kitchen Show* (in which the original audience in 1991 were, literally, visitors to Baker's own home) with hot drinks and biscuits, emphasising stage food as ordinary and accessible. However, her performance space is one that also exposes the anxieties that 'politeness' demands be hidden. This is heightened by Baker's eccentricities in a manner that theatricalises the foodstuff in question to quirky, comic effect, while at the same time acting as a reminder of the 'gaze' to which prepared food is subjected: that is, the expectation with which the 'housewife' gazes at her family gazing at the food, wanting them to find it appetising. Which is the dichotomy of the gluttonous manner in which Cecily drinks in Gwendolyn's disgust.

MESS *en scène*: food is an ideal substance with which to *desecrate* the stage space, for childhood is characterised by being told not to knock it over or spill it on the floor or dribble it down ourselves, to such an extent that we recognise immediately and revel in the naughtiness of the act. This makes such incidents as the moment in Ayckbourn's *Absent Friends* (1974) when the jug of cream is poured over Colin's head, climactic and memorable. It imbues with particular impact the act of piling toast, which has been trodden into the floor, back on to the plate and offering it around as in Sam Shepard's, *True West*, (1980). It renders liberational the process of mapping out motherhood by throwing food over the floor and rolling in it as in Bobby Baker's *Drawing on a Mother's Experience*, (1988). Though, characteristically, Baker has put protective sheeting down first, to keep everything clean. Through such performance, food is released from its expected contexts. The usual 'food containers' – namely, the media's food programmes, magazines and advertising – indulge the foodie gaze, but on the pretext of a process of consumption. The food is contextualised as a proposal to emulate, cook, heat, eat.

As Stella chides in *Streetcar*, food stops Stanley thinking about anything else. As has been mentioned, performance artists such as Karen Finley and Bobby Baker have used food to 'up-the-staging' of the body; however, in the 'moment just before' contact with or absorption into the body, it might be suggested that the actor is upstaged by the food. Rather than an acute awareness of the performer's embodiment, the spectator's own corporeality is likely to be foregrounded, because the gaze has been claimed (seduced) by food, establishing it as a primary text at least momentarily, acknowledged both as potentially invasive and as distanced artificially through staging. Sam Shepard and Bobby Baker both seem to upstage the body of the performer quite deliberately, using foodstuffs as a key resource in the disruption of attention. In this scenario, the 'melting moment' is the temporary dissolution of the actor. This seems to be the reason that Wilde's moment between Cecily and Gwendolyn communicates so well, because it exploits a shared awareness of excess. The slab of cake represents a temporary disruption of the actor–prop hierarchy, which might be conceived as a continuum ranging from 'active' to 'inactive'. This makes an interesting point about food 'ownership'. The oversized piece given to Gwendolyn is, presumably, cut from a larger cake. Yet this cake, there to be subdivided and shared, is not perceived as excessive, and, as it conforms with expectations, remains inactive. The context of giving creates an expectation of an acceptable size of slice in 'polite society' and thus introduces the potential for excess, as overembodiment activates a jarring of response. The slice should be small enough to be overlooked, just as the forkfuls taken from it, to pass between the lips, should not stuff the mouth. By creating an oversized slice, the cake upstages Gwendolyn, who was, in any case, expecting bread and butter.

This paradox of excess under controlled conditions can be quite difficult to ensure, especially when the food act does not have a disruptive intention. For example, the lasting impact of Willy Russell's stage play *Shirley Valentine* (1988) is the meal cooked by Shirley during the play's first act. Shirley is upstaged by dinner. This is the Stanley Kowalski Factor: food melts all other thought. Thus, stage food can fight and bite back, demanding consideration not of the impact of ingestion, but of the Poohvian 'moment just before'. Never work with children or animals – or food.

Kitchen Show (1991): a space in which the preparation is the show – and this is a situation that, in itself, foregrounds the importance of food in 'the moment(s) before'. Bobby Baker's 'actions' focus upon acts of preparing food rather than consuming it. Indeed, eating is furtive, is guilty, and as such is described coyly in terms of 'grazing' and is manufactured to be as fragmentary and incidental as possible, so that it almost disappears. For example, the finger dipped in the peanut butter jar and the habit which she confides in us (and to which we can all relate) of eating only broken biscuits – and, if there are only whole ones, of breaking a bit off. Reclamation and recontextualisation seem central to Baker's intention. In food performance she has found a space that expresses the fundamentals of (her) life: 'Food is like my own language' (Baker in Tushingham, 1994: 30). It is her text, with which she is able to communicate on an intuitive level. We look at Baker looking at food. Baker plays for the acknowledgement of its significance. In order to achieve this and, concurrently, to cement the relationship she is seeking to establish with the audience, she draws frequently upon stock-images the audience will share; in *Kitchen Show* she discusses the merits of pre-prepared soup and enthuses over the beauty of the margarine 'nipple' that crowns a newly open tub of spread, she takes them to the supermarket in *How to Shop* (1993) and defamiliarises tinned fish by forcing the whole thing into her mouth, a preoccupation with food packaging that was reiterated in a recent piece, which involved smashing a jar of jam, then transferring some of the jam and glass mixture into her mouth in order to make a mark on paper (in Heathfield *et al.*, 1998). In these cases, it is almost as if she cannot wait to consume it, but, paradoxically, the packaging also sustains the 'moment before' consumption and the dubious safety of hygienic wrapping, a manifestation of an over-anxious society. Baker reclaims the misnamed kitchen sink drama and kneads it into refrigerator, chopping board, electric hob theatrical spectacular. Working even more from the 'inside', in terms of his (sub)version of domestic realism, Sam Shepard, in *True West* (1980) and, most particularly, *Curse of the Starving Class* (1978), turns out the cupboards, switches on the gas in the box-set kitchen, and moves the lamb-pen plus occupant/potential meal in from the yard.

Cheap margarine. Peanut butter. Toast. Soup. Ham. Eggs. Chocolate biscuits. The blandness of the food chosen by Baker and Shepard is its theatricality. They transform the banal into an ironic banquet, letting it boil over the top and spill across the stage. There is something of the Warhol Campbell's soup tin in their work, exceeding audience expectations by creating ultra-incarnate spaces in which the foods are both themselves and more than themselves, making the spectator take another look in a new way, *inflating* the sense of a stage object's semiotisation discussed by Elam (1980). There is pleasure in the mundane reconfigured playfully as outrageous, a quality that Marina Warner, in a recent article on Baker, links to surrealism, and one which relates closely to Bigas Luna's 'Sex and Food Trilogy' of films (*Jamón, Jamón*; *Golden Balls*; *The Tit and the Moon*). Luna believes that the purest form of surrealism in Spain is to be found in the food and, most specifically, in the garlic, to such an extent that 'society can be reliably divided into garlic eaters (surrealists) and those who abstain (sad realists)'. He adds that 'like all things surreal, garlic also has a life as a symbol – when we eat it, we eat a little moon ... a mixture of the real and the fantastic' (*Guardian*, 11 July 1996).

From high-impact blandness, it is but a small step to the massive impression a vanishing can make. With her installation *The Dinner Party* (1979) Judy Chicago conceived a reaction against the most familiar dining scene in the history of art, the Last Supper, which she aimed to rid of its male-only environment via a humorous reinterpretation 'from the point of view of those who have done the cooking' (Chicago, 1996: 7). In the completed piece, even when viewed simply from the photographic records, there is a deeply theatrical sense of waiting for the named guests to arrive and the event to begin, an atmosphere of an infinitely extended 'moment just before'. It is tempting to see Act I of Caryl Churchill's *Top Girls* (1982) as the staging of the arrival and meeting of a selection of Chicago's anticipated guests. It may be worth suggesting here that *Top Girls* perhaps does not allow the food itself to become foregrounded, except for Dull Gret as a 'gluttonous' character. Again, it is the location and consequent social situation that are significant for Churchill. In Churchill, the supper table becomes subsidiary to the characters seated around it. In Chicago, the table and its settings anticipate the women of a hidden history. There is a painting by Domenico Gnoli entitled *Without a Still Life* (1966) which depicts a table with a subtly embossed white cloth. Nothing else. An identification of a crucial distinction between the subject's disappearance from representation, and that disappearance from representation as

Judy Chicago, *The Dinner Party* (1979).

subject matter. Or, as Rebecca Schneider expresses in *The Explicit Body in Performance*, a 'striving to appear as invisible', a making of 'the body explicit as vanished' (1997: 117).

Food has been expelled so much from performance because it is a distraction. It is a distraction because it is so fundamental and so fascinating. The foodie gaze. The Stanley Kowalski Factor.

When food has been staged, and remembered, that memory has been vanished from critical writing because it is not the sort of preoccupation that is considered to be of acceptable depth. This paper is intended to function as a playful reclamation, stemming from an awareness of the fascination that staged food invokes. As such, it is defined partially by what it does not want to do. Most particularly, it does not want to succumb to the temptation to relate food used in performance immediately and automatically to issues of eating, consumerism, bodies and subjectivities. For me, as a spectator, it is the food that is most immediately foregrounded, it is fascinating and mesmerising as/of itself, in a moment and space before its annexation as a way of writing, smearing, or filling the performer's body. This determination bears strong relation to Pooh bear's acknowledgement that a label for the moment of gazing at food and the sensations that this provokes can be difficult to find. Food is in some ways 'unspeakable' because, as a feast for the eyes and nose and tastebuds, it is a highly individual experience – we cannot know quite whether others are having the same experience (a source of anxiety; do you believe them when they say it is good?). And it is as hard to avoid writing about 'eating' when writing about food as it is to sit on the sofa knowing that the red tartan tin in the bottom kitchen cupboard is still three-quarters full of plain chocolate digestives.

Writing about food in performance is undoubtedly challenging. There is a temptation simply to 'list' foods staged and/or to discuss symbolic function(s) rather than making any attempt in words to express pleasure and viscerality. But maybe I am also describing here the challenge of writing the 'disappeared' performance itself, trying to express it after the event. Deborah Lupton comments upon the fact that approaches to writing about food 'tend to be somewhat essentialist, assigning a single meaning to food-as-text without fully acknowledging the dynamic, highly contextual and often contradictory meanings around foodstuff ... the "lived experience" of eating' (1996: 12). Throughout my addressing of the foodie gaze I have been pressed by an urge to pluralise the already plural in order to emphasise the multifarious sites that the noun encompasses. I find myself wanting to write 'foods' to ensure constant reacknowledgement of variety, just as I aim to reference bodies rather than the body.

Food staged and screened has the capability of capturing the gaze – maybe only momentarily – but certainly, in that moment, totally, and propelling the spectator into a more bodily experience which, along with visual impact, etches itself on to the memory. This is the 'foodie gaze' and in the instances mentioned there is evidence of theatre and film playing upon it, just as Laura Mulvey (1975) describes the visual pleasure of the female body objectified in the male gaze being played upon by narrative cinema – itself a voyeuristic and infinitely sustained anticipation.

When food gouges out a place for itself in and as performance, eyes are compelled to gorge and nostrils to swell, until the mouth flows with desire and the mind runs away with the spoon. It goes without saying that those who *can* eat a fruit pastille without chewing it, or a doughnut without licking their lips, will probably not understand.

Opposite page:
Drawing from sketchbook
(1994). 'Release'.
Watercolour paper, pencil,
watercolour paint, aqua crayons.

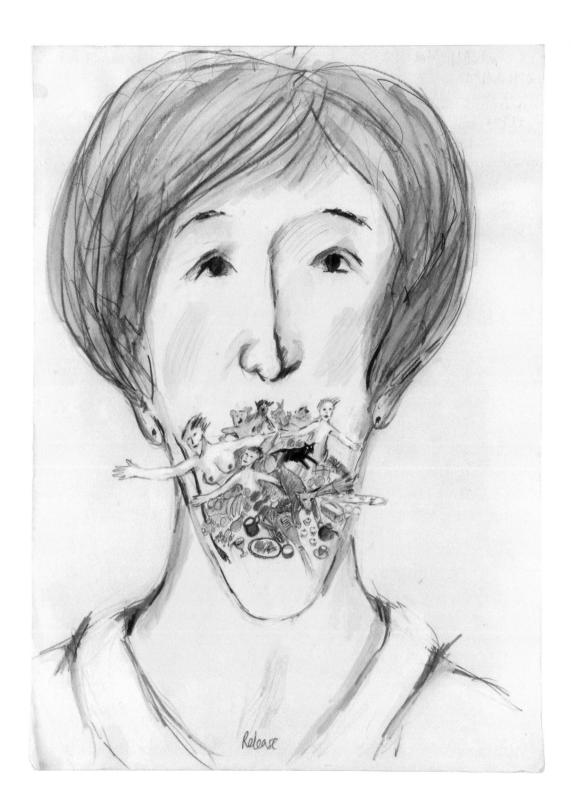

Release

Feminist Performance as Archive ELAINE ASTON

THE ONTOLOGY OF performance has, of late, been subjected to or made the subject of much critical scrutiny in the debate over the live and the mediatised. Peggy Phelan's discussion in *Unmarked* has become the seminal point of reference for performance argued as that which offers the possibility of representation without reproduction (1993: 146–66), while Philip Auslander (1999) is widely identified with the counter position: the mediatisation of performance and the possibility of the live as mass produced, reproduced.

I propose to align Phelan's interest in performance and gender representation with Schneider's discussion in *Performance Research* (2001) on the possibility of performance as archive. In her article Schneider challenges the conventional binary thinking of the archive (permanent) and performance (ephemeral) by arguing the possibility of performance remaining, but remaining differently. Feminist performance has an interest in neither being 'lost' to dominant cultural view (as has been the case in the past), nor recuperated or taken up by it in a way that neutralises its transgressive potential to disturb and to disrupt. How might the idea of performance remaining differently assist a notion of the feminist archive? How might feminist cultural activity become and remain visible without getting caught in the Western tradition of 'seeing' (of objectification)? Is it possible for performance to 'house' a culture resistant to and different from the dominant cultural order

From 'Feminist Performance as Archive: Bobby Baker's "Daily Life" and *Box Story*', *Performance Research*, 7 (4), 2002.

Elaine Aston is Professor of Contemporary Performance at Lancaster University where she teaches and researches feminist theatre, theory and performance, a field in which she is widely published. Her authored studies include *An Introduction to Feminism and Theatre* (1994); *Caryl Churchill* (1997/ 2001); *Feminist Theatre Practice* (1999) and *Feminist Views on the English Stage* (2003). She has co-edited four volumes of plays by women and, with Janelle Reinelt, co-edited *The Cambridge Companion to Modern British Women Playwrights* (2000). Her most recent publication, co-edited with Gerry Harris, is *Feminist Futures? Theatre, Performance, Theory* (2006).

Opposite: *Mastering the Art of Piping* (1977). Kettles Yard, Cambridge. 'Abstract Expressionist Piping'. Wood, canvas, icing sugar, food colour.

that would prefer to mark it absent rather than present. To pursue these questions, I locate my argument in the work of London-based performance artist Bobby Baker and her performances of *Daily Life*.

Schneider resources her discussion of the archive with, *inter alia*, citation of Derrida on the derivation of the word 'archive' and its patriarchal origins. Derrida argues that archive comes from the Greek '*arkheion:* initially a house, a domicile, an address, the residence of the superior magistrates, the *archons*, those who commanded' (1995: 2). The house of the Archon is where power resides, both figuratively (the Archons signifying political power) and literally (the place, house, where laws are made and kept, archived in the form of documents).

The whole 'business' of cultural (re)production is challenged through the hybridity of Baker as painter and performer. A painter usually desires to create an image that will last, ideally a 'masterpiece' for all time; an image to be bought and owned, by a private collector, or by a gallery, a public space, a visual archive to be visited by succeeding generations of viewers. Endurability, cultural value, consumption, ownership – all of these are con-tested through Baker's performance of art; her revisioning of the accepted permanence of art through the relative 'transitory' medium of performance.

Ephemerality is reinforced by the way in which Baker's mat-erials are foodstuffs not paints – are ones that will perish, will decompose. By painting not on canvas but on sheets that get washed and used again, nothing of the artwork is kept. Nothing can be bought and *housed elsewhere*. Her paintings – the Jackson Pollock-style food painting in *Drawing on a Mother's Experience*, the family sculpted in food in *An Edible Family in a Mobile Home*, or her creation-story food painting in *Box Story* are all gone by the end of the performance – erased by the artist, or consumed by the public.

Drawing on a Mother's Experience (1988) exemplifies this for us. We do not usually – unless, exceptionally, we have privileged access to preliminary sketches or drawings – see a painting in progress, as a process, a repeated process even, given that Baker 'draws' and then erases her 'experience' for each performance. A painting is generally offered only as a finished product, one that is usually contextualised, framed for us by an interpretative commentary, or a title naming the image, telling us what we 'see' as Derrida notes (1995: 2), by convention, it is the Archon who gets to interpret meaning.

However, the narrating presence of the artist enables us to 'see' the mother in the picture. Emulating the 'lost' tradition of women talking to each other while working, Baker narrates for us the maternal composition of her food picture as a painful, difficult, emotional and joyful process. There is no familiar, overseen, pure, Madonna-child imagery here. Rather it gives expression to the maternal abject, signed through the messy textures and colours of the foodstuffs that spill into the 'frame'.

The materiality of the object, the painting, is not preserved; will not be kept for cultural consumption as has generally been the case with 'images of women'. The artist-mother will not allow herself to be taken up again within the patriarchal feminine, and instead she authors her own disappearance. The 'whole' culinary image is taken, claimed back by the artist, marked on to the creating maternal body, exiting the space with the artist. What *is* preserved, what is kept, are the domestic, familial and autobiographical memories of 'daily life', those of the artist/storyteller and those of her audience/listeners.

As Warner observes, 'storytelling can act as a social binding agent – like the egg yolk which, mixed up with the different coloured powders, produces colours of a painting' (Warner, 1995a, 414). Performing, preserving the domestic through Baker's storytelling may serve as a means of binding her own experiences of daily life together with those of her listening audience. The uniqueness of Baker's domestic storytelling is its (potential) commonality.

If what remains is not the material art object but the (shared) experience, cannot we (as Schneider asks) understand and accept this as a different way of archiving: as one not dependent on an archival collection of the permanent, but one that embraces the possibility of the performing, storytelling body as archive – an embodiment of counter-cultural memory. If we accept this as a possibility, then it follows that we need to think of a different kind of archivist: one who 'collects', one who houses that which a dominant cultural order represses, desires to keep hidden. This may begin to explain the figuring of the hysteric in Baker's persona and performance register.

Feminist studies of female hysteria, particularly as it was (mis) understood in the nineteenth century, variously have argued that hysterical symptoms in women were produced by the experience of daily life as monotonous and stifling. Before the 'talking cures' pioneered by Breuer and Freud, treatment of the female hysteric, as, for example, pioneered by Charcot in his clinic at the Salpêtrière in Paris, involved putting the lives of the female patients into pictures rather than words (see Showalter, 1985: 145–64; Furse, 1997: 1–14). A patient would re-enact scenes from a traumatic past, but directed (possibly even authored) by the doctor. Female hysterics were medically archived. In particular, Charcot would take great pains to photograph scenes from hysterical seizures, would classify them, give them titles (according to his interpretation). Charcot referred to his clinic as 'our living museum of suffering' (quoted in Furse, 1997: 4); a museum that contained both flesh and bone (to use Schneider's terms); the live and the documented. Yet Charcot could not understand the 'museum' he curated, because he was only able to collect, exhibit, in the 'house' of the Father.

Baker mimics the idea of a 'living museum of suffering' by representing past experiences, traumas from the patient's – rather than the doctor's – point of view; performatively archiving the memories of the hysteric that medical *men* (like Charcot) could not 'see'. Narrating her own stories (some of which, she tells us, are too embarrassing to tell), Baker also connects with the collective social and cultural memory of the damaged 'feminine'; enters the cyclical, backward-looking (rather than linear, forward-moving) time of the hysteric; remains in the time (body) of a forgotten, repressed Other that is and is not her 'own'. Clément explains the body of the hysteric as one 'transformed into a theatre for forgotten scenes' one that 'relives the past' (1986: 5). Baker plays out 'forgotten scenes' of daily life, going back to school (childhood) in *Grown-Up School*, the kitchen or the supermarket (*How to Shop*). In *Take a Peek!*, which represents a women's clinic as kind of grotesque, fairground peepshow, Baker deliberately sets out to make an 'exhibition' of herself as female patient, hysteric. She puts herself on show, as an object of humiliation in the gaze of her audience, in order to alienate the 'naturalised' clinical and medical violence against the female body. The flesh functions as an archival sight/site, a repository of that violence.*

There is a risk, however, that Baker's hysteric as archivist will merely be read and dismissed as the hysterically funny ('mad') woman, not to be taken seriously. Commentaries on Baker's work frequently tend to elide the serious, angry side to her work, by focusing only on her comedy. Yet, to do so ignores the figuring of the hysteric as angry rebel – as Warner (1995) so insightfully describes her: 'the rebel at the heart of the joker'. As a counter cultural rebel, Baker mobilises (performs) hysteria in the interests of bringing down the Father's house.

If Baker is playing out 'forgotten scenes', bringing them out of silence, then how is she to make memorable in the future what has been forgotten? How is she to make these scenes endure, remain, beyond the moment of their staging? In addition to the tradition of orality (shared storytelling), as previously discussed, it is also important, in this respect, to note Baker's technique of 'marking' actions. Baker marks an action, a memory, abstracting it from continuous performance time for viewing so that it remains differently, is made more present both in the performance and in the after-performance memory. It is important to see these marks not just in isolation, but as they relate to each other. By the end of *Kitchen Show*, for example, Baker's body is marked by 12 actions/memories from the first mark of hospitality (the contorted hand of the hysteric bandaged into the action of stirring tea) through to the mark of roaming (blue J-cloths tucked into the back of her slippers), and shown all together in one final image (to make a 'Baker's dozen'). As Baker explains in the performance, it is important to see the image that these make when they are all

*That said, it is also the case that Baker creates photographic (and video) archives of her performances (which also merit archival discussion, but which I do not have the space for in this article). Food photographer Andrew Whittuck (Baker's husband) takes responsibility for the photography. It is interesting that in the case of *Take a Peek!* Baker recognised an affinity between Whittuck's photographs of her, and the images of hysteria that Charcot captured in his patients (see Warner 1995: p. 98 above).

shown together.

Marks are also central to Baker's composition. Marking actions is how Baker structures memory and gives an episodic shape to her work. Each mark, memory, has a story that is told, recollected, shared. That these marks are episodically arranged, narrated, is important – these are episodes from a life story, from lived experience, though never the whole story. As Baker marks her personal memories through objects, mostly food, which she frequently, in some way, takes on to her body, she makes a collage – but a collage with gaps and spaces. The white overalls that she usually wears for her performances, for example, get marked by

Drawing on a Mother's Experience (1997). Greenbelt Festival, Lincolnshire. Cotton sheeting, plastic sheeting, assorted food stuffs.

her memories (often splattered in food), but you can still see the white – a reminder that the stories we tell of who we are to give ourselves a past, an identity, are ruptured fictions. If the medical archivist thought he could catalogue the story of a whole traumatic past, he was very much mistaken.

PERFECT FOCUS

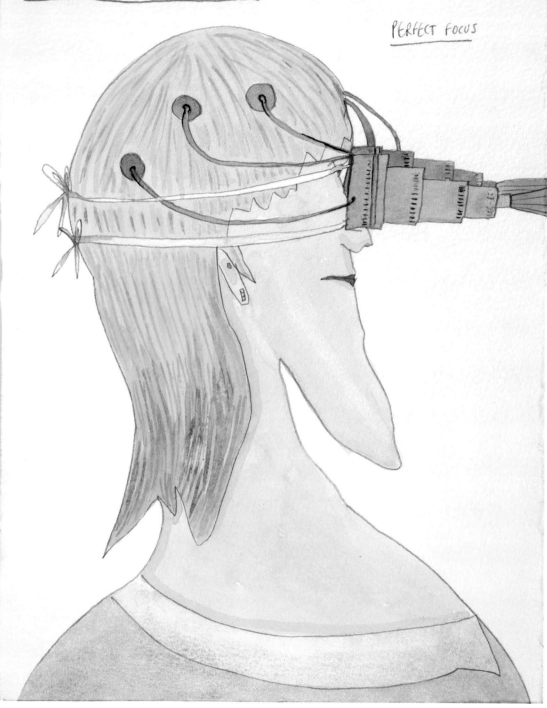

Saying the Unsayable

ADRIAN HEATHFIELD

A SECOND INTERVIEW

Adrian Heathfield It is eight years since we last did a formal interview.
Bobby Baker All of your cells are renewed within seven or eight years. So there's not a fragment of us remaining. Oh no, there'll be the bone.
A Well, in that eight years how do you think your relationship to your work has changed? Does your work occupy the same place in your life?
B There have been considerable changes and this is also related to my mental health, which has obviously changed considerably since then. The most significant development for me is that I have become more confident and clearer about trusting my judgement. Over a great deal of my working life I've had hunches, ideas, images or a whole set of very complex notions that I have sometimes been unconfident about. When I look back on early work, quite a few things were very precise because I followed the hunches, and then I think I went into a long phase where I had the hunches but I questioned them more because I was at the same time searching for more understanding or a more intellectual approach to what I was doing. I certainly feel much happier with my work life now. It's one of the main focuses of my life, rather than my mental health, which at that stage I think was still very much in the foreground. Now when I get ill in the gaps, that question is there, but the rest of the time I am making work. Also my life is much easier: our children are grown up. So I feel I'm in the happiest position I've ever been in with regards to my work and family and that has to be partly because of being at Queen Mary, University of

Opposite page:
Diary Drawing 489 (2004).
'Week 20 May 10 – Flat out work.
Perfect focus.'

135

London. I finally feel I've found a space where I can have conversations on an ongoing basis about ideas and get a variety of responses. Whereas before you know I've had this wonderful resource of working with Polona Baloh Brown, but that was very much focused on the making of the work. Now I find myself in a space that is like being in a hall of mirrors: I keep on getting dazzling glimpses of other things.

Though I'm not sure about that image of the hall of mirrors because it sounds rather grandiose, and as though you are looking at yourself. It isn't that. It is like being in a space where you have had some idea that you haven't been able to put into words or something that you have almost known and then you have a conversation and you are pointed in a direction, or towards reading the right book and it is like an extraordinary explosion of awareness. I do find that very comfortable. I feel the most optimistic or excited and lucky to be where I am that I've ever felt; whereas before it was always this relentless struggle or battle.

A Your work in some ways is closer to your life because you have been more able to draw on mental health as an explicit condition and resource?

B I have been thinking how odd the situation is that because I've been ill, I've had to do a great deal of thinking and talking. The most stimulating thing is engaging in this 'dialectical behaviour therapy'. I then went on to research this with Dr Richard Hallam, a clinical psychologist, that working process was more a social anthropological investigation. It wasn't like going into analysis or therapy and delving into my past, because I know more than I need to know about all of that. It was more a distant reflection on the whole phenomenon of therapy and mental illness, and that's where I have found a particular fascination in how it relates to being an artist. I've gradually been able to focus much more clearly in my work. I used to just hope for the best that I was getting things sharp, whereas now I feel like I turn the lens and move from thing to thing with a confidence and a lack of anxiety about getting it wrong. I just don't care. Because it is OK and it is funny, and I don't know whether it is going to be a successful piece of work, it is just part of a process. I am just the most totally bound up I have ever been in this process. I can't see it ending while I'm alive. Maybe it will; I don't care if it ends. But at this moment I'm in the thrall of this process, so it is a constant exploration and experimentation. I've got ideas to make all these new pieces of work. I might like them; I might not. You know it doesn't really matter. I'll make them and then they will inform the next stage.

A Well, you embarked on making a mammoth series of works that took you …

B Ten years. Yes, I'll never do that again …

A There's a strong constraining idea in such a series: the need for …

B Approval?

A … Well, for completion, and for such a long set of works to be representative and reflective of a life, so presumably, leaving that behind is quite freeing.

B It is absolutely liberating, and I'm glad I did it. The whole process of making these five shows was a learning experience. I feel the first *Kitchen*

Show and the last *Box Story* are the strongest pieces, although Pol and I rather like *Take a Peek!* at the moment. But going through the process of making those other shows – many elements of which I like and enjoy – was a way of gradually investigating and developing the ability to collaborate with people in a more reflexive way. It was a monumental idea, but that was the point. I still think it is quite funny, to do a quintet about domestic life: the absurdity of stating that you were going to spend ten years making five very ambitious shows about the minutiae of daily life. I still stand by that, but I'm really glad I've got it out of my system. I then got taken over with the bombastic project of *How To Live*, which had to be enormous for the same reason. Something huge on the Barbican main stage, to point out the absurdity and the significance of the subject at the same time. So it was a conceptual statement, but I'm rather horrified that I've now come up with an even bigger idea, which I'm trying not to think about or talk about too much because it is a tad overwhelming. I wanted to go back to just doing small, simple pieces but it doesn't seem as though that's going to be the case.

A You've always oscillated between scales of production and proper and improper sites.

B Yes and I can't see myself doing a huge amount more in the theatre after *How to Live*, for a while, if ever …

A If your earlier work centred on questioning the institutions of the family and the domestic sphere, *Box Story* brings you closer to the institution of the church, and then *How to Live* obviously to the machinery of psychiatry and therapeutic culture. These are all institutions that have played pretty big roles in your life. The attitude towards each institution is different in each piece, but in the last piece *How to Live*, you are heavily in the mode, if not of parody, then of pastiche. You inhabit the form of the therapeutic talk whilst commenting on that form at the same time.

B It is also quite constraining to be within that form. It is slightly puzzling when some people don't realise that I'm trying to throw a grenade into it, to explode it. But people take it in so many ways. With *How To Live* the radio version and indeed the live version, people quite often seem to take it as a self-help guide. I mean quite literally, it seems to make people feel better. I find that astonishing, satisfying, but very surprising considering my initial intentions.

A I'm sure the quality of parody works differently in the different forms it takes. The DVD, say, which is already a form that a self-help guide might be distributed in, will be read very differently from the theatre show, where there's already a real disjunction of form in place between a theatre show and a rather warped psychology lecture …

B Yeah, I remember going back to *How to Shop*, that sort of model. I have a bit of a love–hate relationship with it. I find the pastiche element rather irritating and yet I couldn't have done anything else in terms of relating to the whole subject. So the next major piece I'm working on is a bit of a pastiche. Ah, damn – I've done it again.

A In what way?

B I want to do a version of *Big Brother* or *House of Tiny Tearaways*: like a reality TV event, but complex in terms of what I'm doing in there. It's about family history and mental health: revisiting *An Edible Family in a Mobile Home*, reworking that in a very different way, with my knowledge and experience of having a family of choice as opposed to a family of origin, and how the two connect. Oh, god that's really irritating! And yet I really can't resist. I want to be Dr Tanya Byron, the psychologist, but also a farmer and artist 'fat controller'. At one level, I want to be the expert. But I think it's a much more complex piece in its form, its location and how people will relate to it.

A Yes, the expert is an important recurring figure in your work, but it is always a fallible expert.

B The absurd expert. Questioning the whole notion of there being a 'true' authority and expertise. I am chipping away at those authority figures: the posturing that goes on in life. I can't say that I'm not part of that, but I really object to it on a quite regular basis. Those people who invest themselves in these bodies of knowledge and the status that goes with that, and then strut around the world telling people how to live and what to do. I'm constantly fascinated by it: it isn't that I don't think they have valid things to say, or useful advice or skills or strategies or processes. I suppose it is a recurring infuriation with a lack of awareness that we're all just part of some giant hamster wheel! You know? I suppose I want to step outside and say 'Look, this is all a bit of a joke really.' That's one aspect of what I've done. Even with *Drawing on a Mother's Experience*, there was quite an angry side-swipe at my education in the art world, at art history, and its canonical figures. But I could never say that I am knocking something totally because I'm in an ambivalent position of really loving it at the same time. I love Jackson Pollock's paintings, for instance. So it is a tension that I never quite resolve.

A This is the tension of pastiche, which has an affinity with the form that it mimics; it never quite destroys its values. Say, for instance, at the beginning of *How to Live*, your use of 'profound' philosophical quotations, in one way, you could see those as being utterly ridiculous things, and yet at the same time they do have some good philosophical value!

B I am trying to constantly keep that tension.

A You haven't really returned to the earlier pieces like *Kitchen Show* to restage them in any way, have you, though I am sure you are asked to?

B Occasionally, yes.

A Do you take up the offer?

B No, I wouldn't do that piece again.

A You have a window of a few years after a piece is made when you can re-stage it?

B Yes, I was thinking of doing *Drawing on a Mother's Experience* again recently and then it didn't happen and I was really relieved. I thought it was absurd to do it at my age now, with the distance I have from it. My experience is so different now. But then I got myself caught up the other day in thinking *Cook Dems* and *Table Occasions No. 19* were quite a good package. I've done them a few times, and I thought 'Ooh, I'd quite like to do that again', but too much repetition is tedious. Yet, we are talking about that, for the launch of this book, potentially doing a mini retrospective but what would I do? What could I do? I was thinking about *Packed Lunch* because I really liked that and *My Cooking Competes* that I did in 78/79, but I think it would be quite odd.

A Perhaps this says that there is something inherent in the work that ties it to your body and presence in a particular time. Perhaps there would be something dishonest about restaging a piece 15 or 20 years later, unless you genuinely encountered and worked with the difference between doing it now and doing it then.

B Yes, changing the piece, which I assume would be the only way of doing it – to do it from my current age. It is an odd notion, and yet, look at what Pina Bausch did with that piece where she worked and then reworked the same show with much older people.

A Oh yes, *Kontakthof.*

B Yes. I didn't see it when she first did it, I had just read about it and I think it is one of the most inspiring things I've seen. The knowledge that this was a piece that was done with younger bodies and then redone with some of those performers when they were older, and a whole range of other older people. It was remarkable.

A … The way in which the age and experience of the performers fills the piece with a different content is extraordinary.

B Also, to watch it with the knowledge that it had happened in this different way with those particular sorts of bodies at a certain stage in their lives. I found that just wonderful.

A But of course the work that you were doing, say with *Kitchen Show*, is of a different order, in that you were directly speaking from the place that you were in at that time. It doesn't aspire to timelessness. It interests me why certain performance works lend themselves to repetition, re-enactment, and re-circulation. What aesthetics enable or disable this.

B With *Kitchen Show* it was my intention to make versions of it that I could bung in envelopes and send off all over the place. My assumption was that it would be the book that had an afterlife, but that sold out relatively quickly. What astonishes me is that the video version that I made with Carole Lamond, which was such an experiment (I had never done anything like that), has had an extraordinary life. It is the economics of it: video is relatively easy and cheap to reproduce and to disperse. So in a sense that became the show, not the original live version, which I find really fascinating and funny.

A You have increasingly been using and playing with more popular media. What drives that interest?

B It was a very conscious decision. If you've got a set of ideas or a set of images or a set of experiences or knowledges that you want to bounce off people, you need to put them out and about and see what people think, what happens as a consequence, where it will lead. I gradually felt more frustrated with the simple doing of something for itself. Especially with pieces that I've worked on for long periods I just can't stop thinking about how to document them – it isn't just documentation, it is how to make the work into some other form that could communicate it in a slightly different way. But while I'm doing that, I also realise that it is problematic. There is a tension in the motivation for doing that, so again there is a commentary on the whole idea of documentation and archiving. With *How To Live*, we made a DVD and we have developed a website, but this was all about the posturing of having a truth that would save the world.

A As an artistic strategy it also means that an artwork can have a life in many different forms, and because of that, it can access different audiences as well.

B That's always the hope, because I must say I'm always terribly attracted to the idea of art getting to as many people as possible in whatever way they want to take it. You know that serial questionnaire in the *Guardian*, it is like the form of *Desert Island Discs*: they ask the same questions every week, and one of the questions is 'What is the trait in others that you most deplore?' I decided this morning that it was elitism. I went through meanness, martyrdom, misogyny and hypocrisy. Today I picked elitism. I can't stand bodies of knowledge that are exclusive to a set of people, which is why I think I object to psychoanalysis to the extent that I do. It is about secret knowledge and the power that knowledge gives some people over other people.

A Some bodies of knowledge are keen to defend their borders and professions are often very keen to police entry. You've worked with 'experts' before, haven't you? How has that worked in terms of their perception of the relation, because you are often clearly appropriating and playing with their knowledges?

B Well, yes. It feels slightly manipulative. The collaboration I had with Richard Hallam was very equitable, though. It was an ongoing discussion. It was really enjoyable. He'd give me information; I'd give him information. I was learning a lot from him. Though it got to a point where I took his knowledge and I ran away with it and it was at that point that I changed the way I work: making decisions much more clearly about which bit of knowledge fits in, using an editing process. I feel that other people's ideas can become part of the work. Other people's images, even. For instance, Deborah May's amazing animation of the pea in *How to Live*. That would never have been anything that could come from my mind, and I feel it is a very important part of the show. It is being at ease with collaboration, while at the same time keeping control of the whole project.

A Perhaps this confidence also arises from the way you are dealing with 'what is your own', as well. In *Box Story* you are delivering material that is traumatic in terms of your own past. In a sense one can never finally control this, but there is an expanded capacity to make it present, to speak to and through it with ease.

B Yes, that is a power, because some people don't talk about these things. When it happens in an autobiography, or when I experience it in people's day-to-day stories in whatever form, I never cease to be delighted or enjoy it. So to make that more formal is quite empowering, because you've said the unsayable, which I'm now in the process of doing by talking about madness. This has been a bit of an exploration, because when I first started to talk about it I somehow colluded with people's embarrassment.

I would be telling somebody about an experience I'd had, which I thought was very funny or weird and there was just this appalled embarrassment, or desire to change the subject, and that experience has made me more determined to do more. Maybe in a more effective, generous way, so that people can see what I'm saying. I insist on and defend the use of humour as part of this process.

A It is a much riskier project with illness and with madness (whatever that might mean) …

B More vulnerability …

A … Yes, because there is an assumption with grief that it is always

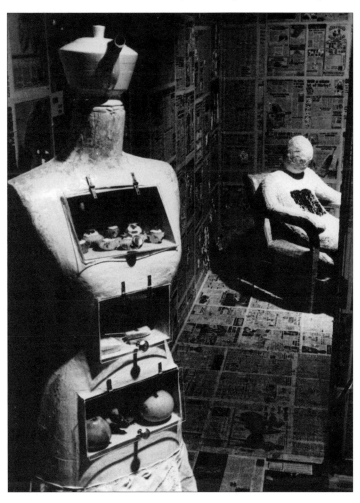

An Edible Family in a Mobile Home (1976). 'Mother': stool with wheels, dressmaker's dummy, tablecloth, cardboard, Perspex, Fablon, gloss paint, teapot, rubber spout, iced buns, sandwiches, fruit. 'Father': fruitcake, butter icing, food colour, chicken wire, fabric birds, armchair, newsprint.

shared, but there's a tremendously strong cultural investment around not having mental disorder shared, to sustain the mythology of rational being and ordered exchange. So presumably in doing this work you are meeting other kinds of resistance, other kinds of hostility and silence.

B Silence and embarrassment is the way it manifests itself, but I was very excited by discovering Foucault's position on reason and unreason: that was a turning point. Something I was going to add to my list of what I most deplore: this constant necessity for people to categorise things I do as eccentric, or odd, or quirky. I find that so tedious and very naïve. It is no odder to do what I do than to go to a church and say you are drinking somebody's blood! I mean, is that not infinitely the oddest thing in the world? And yet that's what happens. Psychosis is really metaphor – a metaphor for extreme suffering.

A Well, 'eccentric' is an identity that allows others not to engage with whatever the 'eccentric' person is doing or saying. It is a kind of sanctioned exception that doesn't trouble the order of things.

B Yes, it comes from fear …

A Even though it manifests itself in many different forms in your work, this rupture of the irrational, of disorder and a certain kind of abjection has been a strong refrain throughout …

B Yeah, I'm not sure I really understand what the whole notion of abjection really is and how I relate to it, because I understand the abject as the pathetic and the defiled, the exposed, raw innards of something. I've probably strayed very close to it, but it is always with a level of control and knowingness that for me is not abject. Do you see what I mean?

A I do. In its simplest form, the abject is just something that refuses to be a proper object, to have clear borders, to be contained: something that has fallen into an in-between space. Thinking about the phenomenon of abjection across your work, in the early pieces, *Drawing on a Mother's Experience* and *Kitchen Show*, abject physical states are enacted, whereas in the later works, *Box Story* and *How to Live* your abject states are powerfully narrated, but the on-stage falls of your body are cleaner and more classically comedic …

B What I've found is a refrain – I'm worn out with it – is that I always fall back on numbers. They are a system, a very simple mathematical system, of ordering disorder. It is spurious, really: it is absurd to impose a number on such a complex line of thinking and association. Which is why I got so thrilled to bits with prime numbers when I discovered them. They are just beyond anything we can understand, so they are the ultimate sense of mystery!

A Have you always had these separated periods of creativity and illness?

B When I talked to you last time, they were very much muddled together. Now they are much more separated.

A Does that separation arise from the fact that you are much more able to use the material that emerges in periods of illness within your creative work?

B I think I'm much more able to contain it, or make use of it. What I've noticed over the last three or four years is that, when I'm very troubled or in a very bad space, the best way of dealing with that, is to focus on my work. So it might seem like the ideas and images come out of being completely barking but they don't actually – they come out of a refusal to succumb to that. I'm much more aware now that I might be feeling anguished and, rather than just be agonised or look for someone to help me with that, I'll just think, 'Oh, I've got this particular problem to think about' (to do with my work) that's infinitely more endurable. It is such a necessity to escape the misery that it is incredibly productive.

A People tend to say this is avoidance, running away into your work, but it isn't quite that, is it? It's a working through of troubles without taking the direct route, but being beside them, allowing them to move, by addressing other things.

B I quite agree. Not being flattened by despair. So that's why now, although I do still get ill, and say 'OK, now I will look at this because I have to', an awful lot of the time it is just infinitely better not thinking about it, because it is going to take time to resolve this. Maybe it'll take another 35 years! Since I was five and became friends with Mrs Aspinall who was blind and benevolent, I've had an ambition to be 90 and wise. I used to go and visit her and sit in a little chair and stare up at her in awe. She must have found me engaging, as she left me the chair in her will. I lost it in some squat years later, but the memory of her acceptance and peace is a beacon. I dare say there'll be a lot more to say on the way to finding that!

A What interests me about conversations like this, is that you never know what they're going to produce. The relational aspect of these encounters means that you become a different person or articulate yourself as a different person in different relations and that movement always fascinates me.

B Yes, what intrigues me is that it is an opportunity, which perhaps I don't have all the time, to examine why I do things. I find it impacts on what I then do, but it is all part of the ongoing process. When I started making work I was just astonished that nobody asked me why I'd made certain decisions. I just assumed they would, and what worried me was I didn't know at that point why I was making decisions. I suppose people do ask me more now, but quite often they don't and you're sort of waiting for somebody to say, 'Well, why did you put that on your head or why did you wear shoes that colour?'

A Do you find recorded and written interviews such as these useful for your creative practice?

B That was what was rather special about our first interview: it was the first time I had considered the wording in such detail. It was really helpful because it took the whole process a stage further in terms of engaging with another form. I write applications rather a lot, so in those I am constantly assessing/evaluating/stating my aims or my motivations, whereas this is a much more reflective way of doing that. I know I will be very careful about this.

A Transcribing is itself an act of interpretation, usually done by one person, and then there is the editing of that transcript, another level of collaborative interpretation. I love the relay of this process, the negotiation and contest of meaning that takes place around what was said, or what ought to have been said. For something that seems like a form of spontaneous speech, there's an awful lot of rewriting.

B Yes, it's a form of spin, but it is actually about meaning and it is about communicating intentions or ideas. That is what Michèle and I are doing when we are constructing this account of my work.

Comment

ROY FOSTER

THE FIRST WORKS I saw of Bobby's, over 30 years ago, were delicate, wistful paintings – portraits of things that belonged to people, their old toys, or their clothes. Then in 1976 I saw *An Edible Family in a Mobile Home* in Stepney. As we trooped around, cannibalising the chocolate-cake mannequins, I realised that she was still using the detritus of everyday life, but in a more elemental and slightly menacing way. She has gone on doing that ever since. But in the process she has herself come into the limelight, as her own subject – white-coated, peremptory, obsessive and confiding all at once, veering between Joyce Grenfell and Bette Midler. And through a series of riveting performances comes the manipulation of food – as staff of life, as currency of comfort, as aggressive weapon. Tragedy comes in unbearably moving moments, such as the sausages on the beach in *Box Story* or the surreal dance at the end of *Drawing on a Mother's Experience*, wrapped like an Egyptian mummy in the Jackson Pollock-spattered sheet that records her eating journey through depression. But there is also the euphoric naked plunge into the glass of wine in *How To Shop*, or the endearing little pea-patient who is taught *How to Live*.

Daily life is conjured by Bobby in its traumas, its horrors, its bizarre conjunctions and its moments of transcendence. In some ways, she has moved from the domestic to the public, from opening her own kitchen to an audience, to conquering the Barbican stage, without ever losing the vulnerability and the unnerving quality which have always drawn people to her work. Nor has she compromised in her critique of patriarchies, consumerism and marketing: of art as of food (or the two combined, in *The Art Supermarket*, an entrancing ICA show where she re-created iconic paintings in icing sugar which were so beautiful that I deliberately missed the point by wanting to buy one and preserve it for ever). The cut-glass diction and ineffably middle-class manner of her stage persona actually expresses an unwavering attack on elitism; as she has said, born into the world of the Chislehurst golf club, she was determined to avoid the golf club of art. Asked to define the desired effect of her work, she has used the word 'renewal'. In its bravery, self-mockery, sadness and resilience, Bobby's oeuvre reminds me of Beckett's Winnie in *Happy Days*. Though its heroic protagonist is sustained by a picnic basket or a grocery-carton instead of a handbag, she is similarly saluting the world and clarifying her life by creating the means of survival amidst a landscape of daily terrors.

Mastering the Art of Piping (1977). Kettles Yard, Cambridge. 'Cubist Piping'. Wood, canvas, icing sugar, food colour.

145

Part Three
The Shows

IN THIS PART of the book we thought it would be useful to group the selection of material available around specific shows. We start with *Drawing on a Mother's Experience*, first performed in 1988. A performance in 1990 was transcribed by Katy Deepwell and published in *n.paradoxa*, and we reprint that here, alongside an extract from a much-quoted interview with David Tushingham. Next there is an example of the kind of ephemeral, but historically interesting, review that Baker's work receives – a piece by Lynn MacRitchie on the very early *My Cooking Competes*. We then move onto the *Daily Life* series of shows, which occupy the 1990s. *Kitchen Show* has generated an enormous amount of interest, and has been performed in many locations around the world. We print here a transcript of an entertaining rendition of 'Action No. 3' (the pear throwing) on Australian day-time television. Baker decided to produce a booklet, with her own text to accompany the performance, and this text is included here, along with an abridged version of the essay by Griselda Pollock that was commissioned for the booklet. Lesley Ferris discusses the performance as she saw it in the original site, Baker's own kitchen in Holloway, North London; this is followed by a discussion, by Helen Iball, of the politics of touring this show.

The next two shows in the *Daily Life* series, *How to Shop* and *Take a Peek!* were performances involving more collaborators and different media (such as integrated film sequences). They triggered some lively discussions, particularly among performance studies academics interested in theories such as Julia Kristeva's approach to 'abjection'. Illustrating these debates, we print extracts from longer essays by Geraldine Harris, and by Elaine Aston, in the company of cheerful audience responses from Lisa Jardine and Nigel Slater. *Grown-Up School* is one of the more difficult of Baker's shows to represent in a book – as Aisling Foster points out, you just had to be there. Lauris-Morgan Griffiths previewed it in the *Independent*, and we include some pictures with that piece. With *Box Story*, Baker returned to a format that makes a transcription possible, and the one we include has been made from a recording of the Barbican (Pit theatre) performance in 2004. This is accompanied by my discussion of the redemptive mood in Baker's work (published in the booklet of the show), and Deirdre

Heddon's exploration of confession, in Foucauldian terms, in this work. Finally, in bringing the *Daily Life* series to an end, we thought it would be interesting to ask some younger performance artists for comments on Baker's work, and include these from Franko B, Maria LaRibot and Tim Etchells.

The last section of part three of the book concerns work that Bobby Baker has made since deciding to make public her experiences on the issue of mental health care and the politics surrounding it. Sarah Gorman, in this brief extract from a longer paper, describes the blank incomprehension of some first year students in the face of any work (such as Baker's film *Spitting Mad*) that challenges their rationalist assumptions. One of the shows described in Baker's 'Chronicle' is *Pull Yourself Together*, in which in conjunction with the Mental Health Foundation she drove around central London, bolted to a flat-bed truck and with a megaphone in hand, urging people to 'get a grip'. Baker herself described the event, in a published diary she kept at the time, as 'a fabulous experience with great responses' (Baker, 2001b: 38). *How to Live*, first performed in 2004, was the result of a collaboration, funded under the Wellcome Trust's 'Sciart' programme, between Bobby Baker and the psychologist Richard Hallam. Bobby Baker had been treated with a form of cognitive behaviour therapy for some while, and Hallam was an academic expert on it. Together they devised a substantial programme of research that informed the new show. The emphasis on politics was strengthened in one post-show discussion of human rights and mental health, with Bobby Baker in conversation with Jon Snow. *How to Live*'s spoof of the grandiosity of therapy, of the therapy-empire phenomenon, should be taken as one side of the coin of her experience, *Diary Drawings* being the other. Here, as Griselda Pollock explores, we see the raw experience of human psychic suffering. These images, chosen specifically for their value in terms of educating the public in relation to mental health issues, form an important aspect of Baker's visual chronicle. *Redeeming Features of Daily Life* offers, we hope, a broad context for reading those images.

MICHÈLE BARRETT

Drawing on a Mother's Experience

This transcript was made by Katy Deepwell from a video recording of the live performance at Wren Street Studios, London, in 1990. It was originally published in *n. paradoxa* Vol 5 (2000).

(BAKER ENTERS AN empty space carrying two large John Lewis shopping bags, walks around in a circle to face camera.)
Hello! My name's Bobby Baker.

I've come here today to my husband's studio – he's a food photographer – to make a drawing for you about my experiences as a mother. I'm very experienced as a mother but I'm not very experienced about being on TV.

I'm going to do this drawing for you out of food. I'm a very experienced mother and one thing I've learnt is that you should always think ahead and avoid unnecessary mess, whenever possible.
(Baker starts laying out plastic sheet on the floor.)
And I particularly don't want to make too much mess on the floor because I'm going to have to clear it up afterwards. It's quite tricky but I do like to try and do things as neatly and as perfectly as possible. Almost there! Now, I don't want any bubbles. I want to get it just, just so. *(Smoothes out plastic sheet on the floor.)*

I'm going to do my drawing for you on a sheet, a white double sheet. *(Baker starts laying out white sheet on top of the plastic.)* The wonderful thing about

doing drawings on sheets is that when you've finished it you can wash them and then either use the sheet again for a bed, you know, or for another drawing. It is quite difficult to get all the stains out. It takes quite a lot of boiling and soaking but it's worth it. I've actually drawn four times on this sheet and you'd never know, would you, as there isn't a mark on it. I always buy these sheets, as I'm an experienced mother, in the sales at my favourite department store and thereby I save just a little money.

I'm going to unpack all the things for my drawing – and I really have to concentrate on this. So, I don't make any mistake.
(Gets out ingredients and kitchen equipment and lays them out in a neat row behind the sheet.)

This is my mother's mixer. I've got a plug here and I'll just test it. Yes, it's working! She gave it to me quite a while ago and sometimes she says she'd like it back but I feel it's mine now.

I've brought with me this damp cloth in a polythene bag so I can mop my hands as I go along. I'll put the bag here. I should know this really exactly now but I get a bit flustered. I'll just think it through and check if I have everything now. There! Now, I'm ready to start. Whew! Now I'm quite hot and bothered!

I'm going to start at the very beginning with the birth of my first child nearly ten years ago. Don't worry. I'm not going to embarrass you with any nasty details. What happened was, you see and this does happen quite often I gather, is that we decided to move to a bigger place when I was pregnant and we ended up moving on the day the baby was born which wasn't a very good thing. I went into labour and we'd asked these friends over to help us pack up and it was a week before the baby was due. I'd prepared this lovely lunch ready for all of us. We had cold roast beef, cold potato salad with fresh chives from the garden – I grow my own – a green salad and then we had strawberries and cream but as it turned out I couldn't eat any of it because I was upstairs. But I think they enjoyed themselves very much. In fact, we then finished the packing up because things had slowed down a bit and we left the old house. I went into hospital in the middle of the night and had the baby which was a wonderful little girl, just what we wanted, and then we moved into the new house the next day. It was marvellous! *(Takes slices of beef from a tupperware tub and gently presses them into the corner of the sheet.)* I'm going to start with some sensitive marks, delicate impressions with some cold roast beef. Now, you needn't worry about waste! I don't like to waste money. I'll probably use this again for another drawing or feed it to the cats. I'll probably freeze it. It's a very subtle, lovely start here to mark the birth of our first child. I'm going to clear up as I go along! I'll put those away. I'm already using the cloth.

OK, so there we were in our new house with our wonderful daughter – in a sort of degree of shock but very very excited. Now I'd always thought that the one thing that would be really difficult about having a baby was whether I would be able to love it, but that came really quite naturally actually, but the thing that consumed me was this worry about feeding. It became quite an obsession! This is quite normal. I was quite lucky I was able to breastfeed. I won't go on about it. I have too much milk actually. I used to – what they call – express it and send it to the special care baby unit. It was a great feeling of satisfaction and pride. I used to freeze it.

(Picks up one of two babies' bottles, takes off lid.) This is only ordinary milk with water. I think I'll

drop it in these possets and dribbles, which I think are so subtle and sensitive and remind me of those early days. I can feel it splashing on my legs. It's quite chilly.

There, I really like that start. I'm going to put these tops on as I put them back in the bag, otherwise the tops get lost and you have to get a whole new set. It's a bit of a rip-off, they don't give you spares.

So, here we are – with feeding established and our drawing coming on. The next major problem was – and nobody told me about this – was I used to get very hungry. Nobody planned who was going to feed me and my husband was busy rushing off to work

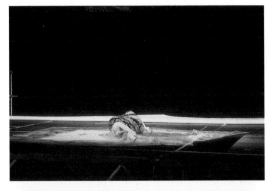

Previous page: *Drawing on a Mother's Experience*
(1988). Publicity photograph.
These pages: *Drawing on a Mother's Experience* (1997).
Greenbelt Festival, Lincolnshire. Cotton sheeting, plastic
sheeting, assorted equipment and food stuffs.

and dealing with the rest of things. I used to get incredibly hungry. My mother lives quite a way away. She was absolutely marvellous and she used to come and give me these frozen fish pies. Very nourishing! I've made them here but I haven't been absolutely true. She always used these orange breadcrumbs. I just

couldn't. I used wholemeal ones instead. I'm just going to pop that in! *(Drops contents of two freezer cartons onto drawing.)* These nice foil cartons! I buy them new, but my sister – a very clever idea – she saves them from the Chinese takeaway and uses them again. And another one over here!
(Drops second.) Quite solid and nourishing! I'll just wipe my hands.

Although these meals were nourishing, I didn't find them to be really nourishing enough. I felt very hungry a lot of the time. I had been told that stout is a wonderful thing to drink for a nursing mother – full of vitamins and minerals. I never liked it before but I discovered that I actually loved it. I was told a pint a day was the thing. *(Holds up bottle of stout.)* These of course aren't quite pints. I found nearer four a day was the right thing for me.

I'm going to put these in in a really subtle way. I hope you can see this. *(Rolls bottle, contents spill out.)* I missed! I'll just roll it in here – this is quite skilled and tricky. Oh dear! I'll have to try again. *(Tries again – bottles hit each other and clink together.)*

That's what I wanted. That clink is what I wanted because it reminds me of taking the empties back in the pram. I used to load up the pram around the baby and to fill the special tray at the bottom to take the bottles back to the off-licence. I remember meeting the health visitor once and it was months before I realised why she was looking at me slightly concerned. I'll step back – so you can see properly. I love those marks!

I gained in confidence after the first few weeks. Confident enough to visit my mother, to drive to her which was slightly nerve-wracking and then she'd give me lovely meals and she'd really feed me. My mother has always been keen on puddings. She likes milky puddings. When I was little she used to make me eat them up, which is not done today. She used to make junket and rice-pudding. She's moved with the times. Now she likes ice cream and what have you. And she's discovered this wonderful – I don't know whether she realises it – sheep's milk yoghurt.
(Spoons yoghurt into a bowl.)

And she puts blackcurrants with it. She would of course boil her own blackcurrants. I've used tinned but they are in apple juice. It's absolutely beautiful the way the red moves into the white. Exquisite! When I go to my mother's I always eat everything up and then, when I've helped clear up, I always eat a little bit more in the kitchen. I don't know why, well actually, I do, I have a fairly good idea. I'm going to introduce this into my image like this!

(Throws contents of bowl across sheet.)

I don't know why but I always get this great urge to pop the blackcurrants with my feet. It's, well, very satisfying. So, as you can see, this does extend the chroma. There we are! It's a lovely red. Pink. Sorry! I know from experience, I should take my shoes off, otherwise I might fall over. So I'll do that.

This is coming on fairly well!

I got very very worried at this point about not earning any money and we were finding things a little bit tight. New house! And I got very manic really with all sorts of these money-saving schemes. And one of these things I found very satisfying was making chutney and preserves. *(Holds up a jar of chutney.)* Can you see that piece of greaseproof paper! The one thing about making chutney is the smell. It's very horrible really. You have to sterilise the jars. You're recycling. In those days you were saving money and you put the jars into the oven. Today I have a dishwasher. You put hot chutney in hot jars and wiped them down nicely and you'd have rows of these beautiful shining objects that you've made. And it's so satisfying! I always like to introduce these, although I'm not a dancer, in dancerly way. *(Spins around with jars in hand, throws chutney onto the sheet as she turns.)* I don't want to spill any on the camera equipment. It makes me giddy! I don't know quite how to deal with that. Maybe in years to come, I'll become a brilliant dancer.

I like that brilliant red. You can still smell it. My son when he saw me making this drawing he said, 'It really stinks, it really stinks, Mum.' I'm going ahead of myself, bringing him in.

The next bit of the drawing I get a bit embarrassed about! I don't know why but I had been rushing around too much and hadn't really recovered from having a baby and became very ill. I got women's trouble. I don't know if you know but if you're in a terrible amount of pain and everyone around you thinks it's your nerves and people think you're mad. I went into hospital a couple of times but it didn't help at all except for people assuming it was my nerves. I spent about five months in bed and it's really terrible with a small child and your husband is trying to cope with everything, but it was the only thing to do.

(Lies down in the centre of the drawing.)

The wonderful thing about lying in bed is that it gives you time to think and ponder over your past life. My mother used to come and visit me and bring me these boudoir biscuits – I called them sponge fingers – but they're boudoir biscuits. I'll just show you what it's like to lie in bed surrounded by biscuit crumbs – it's really horrible.

Anyway I did get better. I got better than I'd ever been in the long run. I felt absolutely wonderful. So much better. And I got pregnant again. And this time I wasn't going to go into hospital, as I'd had such a bad time. So I had this baby at home – which was quite frightening but it was so romantic. I got the house really spotless. I remember my sister when she was pregnant scrubbing floors and I thought she was loopy.

I was in the bath and I'd started labour. I noticed a spot on the floor and I said, 'Andrew, look, there's a spot on the floor.' And he just rushed and got the vacuum cleaner. He wouldn't do that now, but he knew how I felt.

It was very romantic – with classical music – we spent the night in the living room and we'd planned to have the baby in the bedroom. But carrying a baby – it's very heavy. I'll demonstrate. And I didn't reach the bed. I had the baby on the floor just by the bed – and it was on the one rug that I hadn't cleaned. And I was quite worried about that. And we had a baby boy which was marvellous and just what we wanted. A beautiful boy. As soon as I was alright, I told them to put the rug in the bath and give it a wash. I'd been told that camomile tea is a very good thing to have around, but I prefer good strong tea with just a little sugar in it. *(Opens flask of tea, drinks and throws contents of cup on to sheet.)* It's extraordinary. It doesn't make much impression on the image. It's the same as the stout!

Then, there we were with our boy and our girl – supposedly a perfect family. I feel so ashamed but I got, well, post-natal depression. I couldn't believe it was happening to me. I was lucky though. I joined a post-natal depression group and got better quite quickly. There's something so therapeutic about being in a group with people in the same position. My theory, that no professional has queried, is that depression is connected to anger and I was certainly very angry by this stage. That's why I love this bit. I think it's my best bit! I want to make these really strong marks with the black treacle. *(Starts pouring treacle from two tins.)*

Isn't that stunning! It's so powerful! I had a tutor. You know, I trained as a painter. He used to say just when you've finished a painting, add some black to it. Now, perhaps, I see the point. It used to be very irritating – but it's not only black. It's a very dark brown. You can see this very fine line. I could go on for hours. But as it's TV I have to keep the pace going. I'll just do one more line. A little bit later you'll see these lines feather into the stout. It's quite stunning. Anyway, I don't want to go on too much.

I got better – I was fine – and as I came to my senses – I realised we were in considerable trouble what with me being ill or having babies. I became a working mother. I went out to earn money. I was very skilled and experienced at minding the house, looking after the children. I find it very odd, but at that stage we were very ambitious and we used to do a lot of entertaining on a rather grand scale. It seems quite extraordinary. I wouldn't dream of doing it now. So I'm going to show you one of my recipes. I'm going to do this carefully now. *(Starts breaking and separating eggs into two bowls.)* So, you know, when you separate the yolk from the white, you should do this one by one. I've broken one there and I could have ruined everything. If you get any yolk into your white you can ruin the whole recipe. And I've got so much on my mind. I'm hoping that the children are in bed and whether Andrew got them in the bath. So, I shout up the stairs. 'Andrew, have you got those children in the bath?!'

The guests might be coming soon. Unfortunately, I should really do this over hot water properly. A bit of strong spirits to pop in there and a lot of sugar. I don't need to measure it as I'm very skilled. You beat this over hot water for a long time and you get this exquisite pale yellow thick cream. You won't get it today. If you imagine this as thick, luscious, smooth. It's a very beautiful yellow cream. But I haven't got time.

I need my sugar over here. *(Runs round to other side of sheet with egg whites and sugar, squats down next to electric whisk.)*

I'm going to do my whites. I wonder if you can see this, if I do it over here. Of course it would be far too long to get a really true white. *(Starts electric whisk.)*

I find this very soothing, mesmerising even. About halfway through you put in the sugar. This is where you are going to get a peak. Exquisite, so pure!

I'll bore you if I go on too much about it.

I'll just clear it up. We'll get a really good image. *(Drops whites on to drawing.)*

I got some white on the floor, I'm afraid, and now I'll sling this here. *(Adds yolks, mixes them together on drawing.)* If you did this with a pale yellow it wouldn't move so well. Of course, these eggs are organic. Can you see the feathering?

(Points to patterns on the sheet.)

There is one element I always seem to find very hard to talk about in public. It's the most important element in my life. So, I won't. Strong white flour from my supermarket. This is so beautiful! *(Begins sifting the flour on to drawing through a sieve.)* It isn't actually white, it's sort of creamy. I know from experience I must have two packets. It's so beautiful! I hope you can see all this. You see how experienced I am. Doing half with one pack. *(Covers the whole drawing with sifted white flour obliterating the image.)*

I hope you're not bored, but it's truly worth pulling this off. It's truly wonderful. It's finished, but there's something else I'd like to do … to sort of symbolise how one takes one's past into one's future. However, I'm not going to take these fish pies into my future. *(Removes them from drawing.)* I'm going to roll myself up. I hope you can't see my knickers. I did this drawing in Cardiff and I was described as a human Swiss roll. *(Rolls herself up in drawing.)*

At this stage, I wonder whether I am going to get out! I panic that I'm stuck but I'll keep calm and just slowly ease myself out and up. *(Stands up wrapped in sheet.)*

There is one more thing I'd like to do. To celebrate the whole thing … A dance. I've chosen some music I really like. It's Nina Simone. It's not very significant. *(Music begins.)*

My baby don't care for shows
My baby just cares for me
And this care is not a style …

(Baker dances slowly whilst gathering in the corner of the plastic sheet and with great difficulty, collecting it all together and pushes it into the bags.)
Thank you! *(Exits, carrying both bags.)*

Drawing on a Mother's Experience DAVID TUSHINGHAM

An edited extract from
Tushingham's interview 'Bobby Baker:
"Food is my own language"', in
Live 1: Food for the soul.

David Tushingham is a dramaturg,
writer and translator. He has worked
for a series of leading European
theatre festivals including the Wiener
Festwochen, Theater der Welt and
Theaterformen. He is currently
dramaturg for the RuhrTriennale.

David Tushingham *Drawing on a Mother's Experience* was one of the very few experiences in theatre where I've been made to laugh hysterically and cry at the same time. I was very struck by your courage and naked honesty in that piece. It was very, very powerful.

Bobby Baker It came out of such a passionate set of feelings, of experiences, that the conviction that I had to try and communicate this with people was very strong. I still find that, performing it. I feel just as angry, just as desperate to explain that process because the things that happened to me and the significance and importance of what happens in daily life isn't looked at and acknowledged.

It took me a long time to work out the form of that piece and what information would go into it. Obviously it comes very much from my interest in painting. And also it was essential that the painting was made of food, because food is like my own language. Food has this wonderful endless way in which it can be used: the fact that it can be eaten or thrown on the floor – or I can eat it – or other people can eat it. It has such possibilities. So that was the obvious thing to draw with and I just loved the idea of doing something like a painting in public, rather than to do it in a studio, but to actually act it out or paint it in front of people. And then to use foodstuffs that reflected a whole range of things that happened, were happening in my life and still happen.

I'm still quite surprised by the strength of the image. It's framed, it's put within this sheet on the plastic sheet on the floor, so it's not going to

Opposite page:
Drawing on a Mother's Experience
(2000). Jacksons Lane Arts
Centre, London. Cotton sheeting,
plastic sheeting, assorted equipment
and foodstuffs.

make too much mess. And then the last thing I do is I roll myself up in it to show how you take your past experience into your future life. And I'm absolutely covered in it, from head to toe. But what's so extraordinary: because I've covered the whole sheet at the end with a layer of flour, that obliterates the image but it comes through anyway on the other side, this spectacular, dripping stain of treacle or blackcurrants or what have you. And then I do this little dance to celebrate the whole experience.

D I found that very disturbing, that final image; for me it seemed to be an image of grief, sackcloth and ashes … It seemed a kind of abasement too, the way you dirtied yourself, smeared yourself.

B Well, it was the final taboo thing of throwing food on the floor – but playing with that idea. To actually roll in it and get all besmirched and stained is obviously very shocking. What's interesting about it – and I find it very disturbing – is that people, all the way through, find things funny, hysterically funny. It's on the edge of what's safe and what's not safe and the humour – it's almost the only way to be able to cope with what's happening – is my reaction to difficulty, but it's also how society, the audience, react to this.

D You mentioned that you were aware of having evolved food as an artistic vocabulary for yourself. Were you conscious of that when you went through the experience of motherhood – and do you think that that made having a baby and breastfeeding and all this sort of thing a different experience for you?

B When I had small children I found the first few years so shocking, so extraordinary, I couldn't believe what was happening to me, what was actually going on. It left me unable for a while to know how to articulate that or proceed.

One decision I made really early on was that what was important was to actually examine things from the inside out. That to use my own experience was the only valid way to proceed. Everything kind of crystallised. But it took a long time – because it was very difficult to know how to use what I'd observed.

It seems to me every detail, every aspect of our life is so packed with meaning and profound significance. It came together with the idea I had very early on of wanting to make work that related to those moments in time where just for a split second you experience an extraordinarily complex set of realities, associations. I know the first time it happened was at St Martins where I was standing in the middle of a studio. I tried painting that moment, which didn't work. It's like when you're a child and write your address with the universe at the end and try and go further.

And that's what happened when I had children: it led me to look at things on a much deeper level. What I actually did from moment to moment was send out a ripple and I felt so angry that that wasn't acknowledged – not just for me, but that our society wasn't observing, valuing and examining that. So what I've done ever since is a developing process, the *Daily Life* series is a way of investigating ranges of issues.

D One of the interesting things you said about wanting to do performances in the first place was wanting to see the audience and wanting to see their reaction. What sort of things do you look for in an audience?

B It's an extension of the way I relate to people on a daily basis. And it's very risky, I suppose. There was a great risk in opening my kitchen to the public: to be in such an intimate environment where you can't avoid seeing what's actually happening. I've become so bound up with the people during the performances that I actually think I know them. I quite often see people at a later date and think I've met them and then it comes out they've been in the audience. It worries me, this confessional aspect, the voyeuristic, the exhibitionist side of it: whether it's really connecting with people and how they respond to what's happening.

D I find a powerful sense of compassion there. You present yourself as an example of humanity and your work is clearly from your own experience – but we too are examples of humanity and can have lives which are entirely comparable in their ordinariness and their remarkableness in that apparent ordinariness and I think because of that the audience feels extraordinary sympathy for you.

B It's great when that works. I do feel sometimes that there's a sort of sacrificial element to what I'm doing which is so excruciating.

D I think it's very generous. I didn't want you to feel that there was anything selfish about your confessions.

B There does seem to be this great need or excitement that people experience about being allowed, given permission to look at what is going on within their lives. On one level they love to look at the mundane, superficial details of, say, shopping – their day-to-day experience. I must admit that I'm more interested in where God and sex come in.

My Cooking Competes LYNN MACRITCHIE

An extract from a 1980 review, reprinted in full in Parker and Pollock (eds), *Framing Feminism: Art and The Women's Movement 1970–1985*. Lynn MacRitchie's review was originally published in *Primary Sources* (Christmas, 1980).

Lynn MacRitchie is an artist and writer based in London.

Opposite: 'Coffee Break'. Colour print. One of a series of classic food photographs, which were hung in a row behind the table on which the actual meals were set out, village fête style. *My Cooking Competes* is described in Bobby Baker's 'Chronicle', pp. 46-47.

FOOD PREPARATION AND serving is a universal female task. Men may work with food as professionals — highly paid chefs, for example, whose creations are admired — but ordinarily, domestically, cooking is done by women. Skill in baking and cooking is usually passed down from mother to daughter. An unusual aspect of what is normally a private task is the tradition of the show of baking, jam and preserve making at venues such as the Women's Institute, church fête or agricultural show. Bobby Baker drew on this reference in her piece *My Cooking Competes*.

Perhaps what made this piece so appealing, even touching, was the sense it conveyed of shared experience. The audience knew that this presenter had actually performed all these tasks, that they had taken up her time, just as they wear away the time of countless women, day after day. Those women who in all their frustration will still take a blue ribbon to decorate that despised iced bun, because, after all, it's an 'anniversary tea'. Cooking is indeed one of the ways, however damaged, in which we experience love. Bobby finished the performance festooned in the rosettes from her creations. She managed to look at the same time both bashful and wise.

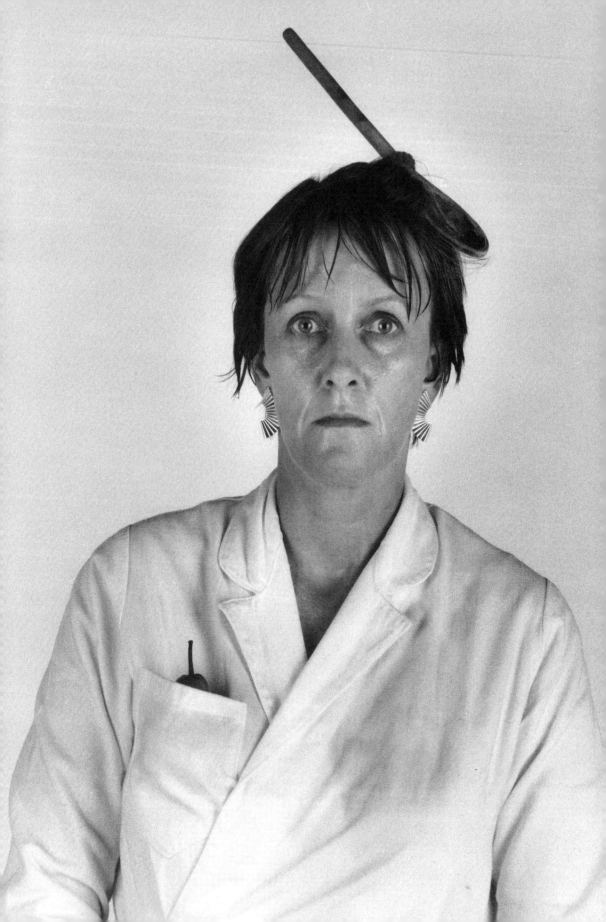

DAILY LIFE 1
The Housewife's Philospher

In 1993, Baker appeared on Australian daytime television programme *The Midday Show with Ray Martin*, where she was dubbed 'The Housewife's Philosopher'. This transcript is of her demonstration of 'Action No. 3' from *Kitchen Show*.

Ray Martin Now you're out here for the Adelaide arts festival?

Bobby Baker That's right. Yes.

R To open a kitchen?

B Yep. I'm opening a kitchen for three weeks. I have actually opened my own kitchen in London, and I've been to a couple of other places, and I'm going to Canada later in the year to open a kitchen there. You know, to really draw attention to what goes on in kitchens. I'm going to be showing a range of things that I do in my kitchen.

R Do you put on your passport kitchen opener?

B No, I put artist, actually. But it sort of ties up.

R What could we expect – the sort of thing we see, that you do when you open a kitchen at the Adelaide arts festival, for example?

B Well, there are a dozen actions, but one that's quite easy to understand maybe is the one – I've got this – shall I show you?

R Please.

She stands and turns to address the audience.

B Well, I've got this skill of dealing with anger, you know when you're intensely angry and frustrated, and I find it's best to actually let that out, to get it out of

your system, otherwise it becomes sort of destructive. And the way that I do it – I've done some very stupid things in the past, and I want to show people what not to do.

R Right.

B Once I threw an electric typewriter on the floor and that was a real mistake, because it's quite expensive. I had to pay for it to be repaired. And I've also thrown a glass, which could be very dangerous, into the corner of a room, carefully. So what I recommend is to get a really ripe piece of fruit – especially, I like pears, you know when they're sort of slightly too old – *(She takes one from a bowl on the table in front of her.)* – and just sort of hurl that with great force. Preferably, I prefer a kind of washed-down paintwork so you can actually clear it up quickly afterwards, but I was a bit worried about your set because it's this wonderful paintwork, and so I've got a tablecloth to put up, because I'm going to show you my technique – hang on a minute… *(She unravels a tablecloth; audience laughter.)* I've got a paper tablecloth. Um, if you don't mind, can I just –

R No no, please, go for it, yeah.

Audience laughter. Bobby moves some potted plants

out of the way to clear a space against the wall of the studio.

B I think it's best, you see, in these moments, to actually think ahead and avoid – *(She moves an ornamental vase out of the way.)*
Audience laughter.

R And you'd normally do this in the kitchen, would you?

B Yeah, well I don't need to in my kitchen because I've got a gloss paint door.

R You can wipe it off?

B Yes.

R Okay.

B But I'd hate to damage this. If I put that up there… *(She secures the tablecloth to the wall.)* There, right, okay. And then –

R So you're in the kitchen, you're pretty angry?

B Yep, I'm really furious. *(Audience laughter.)* And I know – I mean I am slowing it down, so that you can understand how I do it. I would normally be much quicker. But I use a sort of cricket bowling technique – *(Audience laughter.)* – because I used to want to be good at cricket when I was young. So, I don't do the sort of sissy underarm. *(Audience laughter.)* I do a proper overarm.
She eyes up her target.

R So you're angry, you're upset about something, you're in the kitchen?

B Yeah. Take a real sort of close aim. Do be careful, because once for instance I hit the light fitting. Which was – *(Audience laughter.)* – and then just slowly… *(She mimes the action slowly; audience laughter.)* I'm going to really do it now.

R So you're angry, right?

B I'm really angry. *(She takes a run up and throws.)* Arggh!
The pear hits the cloth on the wall and explodes.
The audience laughs and applauds.

R And do you feel better?

B I feel great. You notice I shouted at that last moment.

R Yes.

B That really kind of lets it all out.

R Yes.

B And then I can rush over there and clear it – I'm sorry about the carpet, but it will wipe out. *(Audience laughter; she turns to them.)* Just don't leave it to dry, because it goes very hard, when it's dried on.

Page 160: *Kitchen Show* (1991). 'Mark No. 4: To splash water from the running tap all over my face and chest – so that I'm drenched'. Image from booklet.

Opposite: *Kitchen Show* (1991). 'Action No. 3: Throwing a ripe pear against a cupboard door'.

DAILY LIFE 1

Kitchen Show: One Dozen Kitchen Actions Made Public

Reprinted from the *Kitchen Show* booklet, available to attendees of the performance.

Opposite page: *Kitchen Show* (1991). LIFT, North London. 'Action No. 13: Showing all the marks whilst standing on a cake stand placed on a coffee table'.

No. 1 When I welcome people into my kitchen, I always offer them a hot drink straight away – 'Coffee? Tea?' I don't like them to sit there with nothing. It makes me feel anxious.

People often say – 'Oh, I'll have one, but only if you're making one' – or – 'I'll have whatever you're having!' How exasperating! Of course I'll have a cup of tea with them and I only like tea. What if they'd really like coffee?

I prefer a clear precise response, for example: – 'Coffee – a touch of milk, one and a half sugars, please.'

Then I can try my hardest to get it right, adding intuition and flair to attempt perfection. I always do the milking and sugaring myself. With family or friends I try to remember what they have as it's embarrassing to forget. I stir the sugar in very quickly so as not to waste time. It's hard to get the drinks just so.

Action No. 1 Stirring milk or sugar into a hot drink.
Mark No. 1 To bandage my fingers into the right shape with elastoplast.

No. 2 I think about all sorts of things while I cook. My mind wanders through recent events and conversations. Sometimes I'm stunned by the beauty of what I'm cooking, the changing colours and shapes, the picture in the pan.

The way my friend cooks has influenced me a lot. She's Slovenian and

I'm impressed by her kitchen techniques – well, almost intimidated really! She seems so thorough and competent and she always prepares such delicious, nourishing and complete meals. Slovenians are probably more generous than us.

I was very struck by the way in which she always rests the spoon she's cooking with on top of the pan lid while the pan is simmering for a long time. I thought that this was a curious Middle European habit but I was puzzled to notice that her mother did not do the same thing, so, eventually, I asked her what it meant. She explained that a woman had once said to her, when she'd left the spoon standing in the pot – 'Oh, you don't want to cook the spoon, do you?' Ever since then she's put the spoon on top of the pan.

I try and do it whenever I remember to for friendship's sake but secretly I wonder what's so wrong with cooking the spoon!

Action No. 2 Resting a wooden spoon on top of a saucepan.
Mark No. 2 To fix a wooden spoon into the hair on top of my head with a blue hair toggle.

No. 3 When I get angry in my kitchen, I feel the need to do something violent in order to release the tension. I find that throwing something is better than hitting someone.

Once I tried throwing a wine bottle on the floor – but it made an awful dent. Another time I threw an old glass tumbler carefully into the corner of the room but it took ages to clear up and could have been dangerous. When I hurled an electric typewriter on the floor it was very expensive to repair.

I think that the best throwing action is to take a ripe pear and hurl it against a cupboard door. It's a good idea to have a practice, just to make sure that you're going to get it right. I have a run-in of about 10 feet and I use an action similar to the one I tried to learn when I was young – that of bowling a cricket ball overarm. Underarm would be 'sissy' of course.

I hurl the pear at the opposite wall so that it explodes *blam/splat* and I SHOUT at the top of my voice just at the moment of hurling.

I choose a cupboard door to throw against because it's painted with vinyl silk and the pear washes off more easily than from a vinyl matt wall. When I clear up the mess, I check inside the cupboard for little bits of pear. I don't like to see them when they get all brown and dried on.

Action No. 3 Throwing a ripe pear against a cupboard door.
Mark No. 3 To put a pear in the top pocket of my overall – all ready for the next occasion.

No. 4 One of the most soothing things that I do in my kitchen is to rinse and prepare vegetables under fresh cool running water from the tap. I know you shouldn't waste water but this is one of my luxuries. In fact, nowadays, I put the plug in the sink, so that I can use the water for something else whenever possible. I don't feel so guilty that way. I like the carrots best of all because of the colour and because they are so simple and satisfying to peel.

I know that one should remove as little of the skin as possible because the *goodness*, the *vitamins*, are just under the skin apparently. However, I can never leave a carrot unpeeled – it just wouldn't look right to me.

I have a very skilled technique for peeling them. I hold the carrot in the palm of my hand and I peel from the centre of the carrot towards myself and then turn it round and peel the other half – so quickly, neatly and lovingly under the running water. I watch the splashes and drops of water flying out as they catch the light. It's best when the sun is shining. I turn my hands so that the water pours over my wrists and palms – cleansing and cooling.

The whole experience is overwhelming – the noise of the water gushing out, the sparkles of light from the drops of water, the colour of the carrots, the sensation on my hands. I am shot through with joy.

Action No. 4 Rinsing and peeling carrots under water running from the tap.
Mark No. 4 To splash water from the running tap all over my face and chest – so that I'm drenched.

No. 5 I feel so lucky to have a lovely garden leading straight out from my kitchen but I only manage to get out there occasionally to hang out the washing, tidy up or to look after the plants. It's a treat just to gaze out of the window when the weather's fine, especially in the springtime.

My husband always cuts the grass. It looks so smooth, green and cropped – so lush.

We have three black cats. I admire the way they wander around – nonchalantly striking poses in the kitchen or garden. One of the most thrilling sights is to see a cat bounding across the lawn. It's usually George, the youngest, the most confident one, who does this. He's so graceful. He moves so swiftly and elegantly from one side of the garden to the other. The jet black of his coat against the green grass is breathtaking.

I always feel the urge to copy him. It thrills me to think of being so wild and free. I bend down on all fours and lope across the grass. I really envy him because I'm so clumsy compared to him.

Action No. 5 Pretending to be a cat bounding across the lawn.
Mark No. 5 To fix a shiny black plastic bin bag from my shoulders, with two pegs, like a cape.

No. 6 I buy one particular brand of margarine because it looks so beautiful when you first open the tub.

I get so excited as I ease off the lid – will it be perfect or not? The margarine is obviously piped into the tub with a huge nozzle. The undulations in the surface are smooth and voluptuous. But the best bit is the little pointed nipple in the centre. It's such a wonderful shape, so exquisite. I gaze at it lovingly just for a moment and try to fix that moment of beauty in my memory. The milky yellow colour is so soothing to look at.

I've said it before and I'll say it again – it's moments like this that make it all worthwhile.

Action No. 6 Opening a new tub of margarine to see its unsullied perfection.
Mark No. 6 To smooth some of the margarine carefully onto my cheeks using the tip of my finger.

No. 7

I like to have little tastes, all the time, of as many different things as possible, it keeps me stimulated I think. I call them 'taste sensations'. I think, 'Oh, I must have a taste sensation of that cake mixture' – or 'that biscuit' – or 'that bit of butter'.

Sometimes I think that it's like grazing – moving from one little bit of nourishment to another. Perhaps it's not the stimulation I need but to be constantly fed – to keep a continuous supply of sustenance in order to maintain my blood sugar level.

I never eat a whole biscuit, say, or a whole slice of cake. I just have little broken pieces, little edges and dippings. I was surprised when discussing this action with my friend that she said that I sometimes put the tiny piece of food into my mouth and suck it from between my fingers slowly. I was shocked and embarrassed that she'd observed my actions so minutely.

Sometimes I make stupid, and possibly unhygienic, mistakes. The other day I picked up what I thought was a crumb of cake only to discover that I was chewing a small piece of masking tape!

I chose the mark for this action because of something that happened when I was little. We went to visit a friend of my mother's who had just had a baby. My mother went upstairs to see her friend and the baby in the bedroom. I went up too but they were embarrassed and annoyed at my interruption because she was breastfeeding. I saw the woman's nipple. It looked bright red like a cherry. I thought she'd put lipstick on it.

Action No. 7 Picking up small pieces of food between my thumb and forefinger and popping them into my mouth.
Mark No. 7 To put bright red lipstick on my puckered lips.

No. 8
I try very hard to say the Lord's Prayer every day but I'm hopelessly disorganised about it. I know that I should have a regular structure to my day but I never manage to achieve it.

Consequently I say the Lord's Prayer whenever it pops into my mind – at any time of day or night. When I happen to be in the car, I obviously can't shut my eyes and I just try and move my lips very indistinctly so as not to embarrass anyone. I always feel a bit embarrassed about it, you see. Or at least I'm not embarrassed but I think other people will be if they know what I'm doing. I'd rather not explain it at all but it's such an important action that I *have* to include it.

When I say the Lord's Prayer in the kitchen, I usually just rest my head in my hands with my elbows on the work surface – sort of bending over. But *really,* of course, one should kneel down to pray. I show this action, in my kitchen, by kneeling on the patio with my face pressed against the window – so that people can clearly see my lips moving.

Action No. 8 Saying the Lord's Prayer while kneeling on the patio.
Mark No. 8 To put on gardening knee pads to protect my knees.

No. 9 I do love to listen to music while I work. Sometimes I have the radio on but it can interrupt my train of thought too much and so I choose music to suit my mood.

My choice is a bit limited really. I don't know a lot about serious music and I'm always forgetting what things are called. I've always found opera very hard to cope with. I went to the opera once when I was at college and I had to *crawl* out on my hands and knees because it made me laugh so much.

I had a breakthrough when I heard that wonderful tune that Pavarotti did for the World Cup. I bought his LP and now I listen to that all the time. It always makes me want to dance. I get carried away and sprinkle spinach leaves or other foodstuffs around me as I dance.

Action No. 9 Dancing when inspired by operatic music.
Mark No. 9 To pin a large spinach leaf to the lapel of my overall with a safety pin.

No. 10 There are certain areas of the kitchen which have become repositories for certain types of possessions. I am very skilled at organising large quantities of objects belonging to our family as I'm in charge of them all. I move them from one place to another in a ceaseless attempt to maintain order – shifting, sifting, keeping track.

I find that the best way to do this is to designate storage areas as goals or targets for each category of possession. Then I know where to aim them and where to find them in the end.

To save time I often throw things in the direction of their goal. People sometimes interpret this as an aggressive action but it's not, it's practical.

These storage areas can become very cluttered so they have to be tidied. Sometimes I start this task but haven't the time to complete it. I take the drawer out but have to put it away again before I've finished. It's so frustrating but I have to remember that every action is ultimately contributing to order.

Action No. 10 Pulling a drawer right out so as to tidy the contents.
Mark No. 10 To hang some cutlery round my neck with a piece of string.

No. 11 From time to time, in my kitchen, I am overcome with weariness. I feel that I can scarcely move another step.

If I'm lucky then I can have a rest. I often have one after lunch – which is when I used to have a rest as a child. Sometimes I manage to get time for a nap when my children come home from school. I like to curl up on the sofa with a pillow forced into shape under my head. I put on the radio or TV. They always send me straight off to sleep. If I'm on my own I might feel cold and so I use my big black overcoat as a cover. If my children are with me then they sit and watch TV and keep me warm.

The telephone very often wakes me up. It's always a shock.

Action No. 11 Lying down with my head resting on a pillow so as to take a short nap.
Mark No. 11 To stuff a pillow in place, under my overall.

No. 12 This action is the most significant as it ties all the others together. I roam about my kitchen, sometimes in a state of euphoria, completing only parts of a whole range of tasks — never necessarily seeing one task through from start to finish but having a 'stab' at it and then roaming on to the next.

There is a great deal of skill and versatility attached to this action. It is like keeping a set of juggler's balls in the air. I might, for example, sweep some spilled flour and spinach into the corner of the room to be picked up later with a dustpan and brush — answer the telephone and, while I'm talking, sort out some notices on the board — throw the bits of paper towards the bin under the sink — put away some cassettes — get a warm, damp J-cloth, blue, like the sky — wipe some bits of pear off a cupboard door — pick up the bits of paper on the floor and put them in the bin — rinse the J-cloth — put on the kettle, etc. etc. etc.

This ceaseless swirling kitchen action is like gliding through the sky.

Action No. 12 Roaming around the kitchen from task to task.
Mark No. 12 To tuck two new blue J-cloths in between the sides of my heels and my slippers so that they fly out behind.

No. 13 This is my 13th action — to make my Baker's dozen.
I put the cake stand on a coffee table so that I can be seen better. That's a high enough pedestal for me as I suffer from vertigo and I might find standing on the kitchen table too frightening.

The cake stand is a very strong professional one that I bought years ago. I wouldn't advise posing on an ordinary one as it might break.

I stand with one foot on the cake stand and revolve round slowly so that all the marks can be noted and remembered. It's the image they all make together that matters most.

Action No. 13 Showing all the marks whilst standing on a cake stand placed on a coffee table.
Mark No. 13 To show this image to the public.

Opposite: Drawing in sketch book (1990). Paper, ink.

6.12.87

[Oh.... trotting, trotting, trotting, trotting,
round about we go....

tithuping about the room
tit, trot, trot, trot, tit trot...]

DAILY LIFE 1
𝒦itchen 𝒮how LESLEY FERRIS

From 'Cooking Up the Self: Bobby Baker and Blondell Cummings "Do" the Kitchen', in Sidonie Smith and Julia Watson (eds) *Interfaces: Women/Autobiography/Image/Performance*.

Lesley Ferris's publications include *Acting Women: Images of Women in Theatre* (Macmillan) and *Crossing the Stage: Controversies on Cross-Dressing* (Routledge). She is a professor of theatre at Ohio State University.

Opposite page: *Kitchen Show* (1991), LIFT, North London. 'Action No. 10: Pulling a drawer right out so as to tidy the contents'.

WHEN, IN THE summer of 1991, I purchased a ticket for a performance of Baker's *Kitchen Show*, I was given a small map with directions to Baker's house. She lives in North London, in an unassuming terraced house, on a tree-lined street about a ten-minute walk from the nearest underground station. My two daughters, aged 7 and 12, and I were among the first people to arrive, but slowly a very small line formed. This was a quintessential liminal theatre moment for me: hovering on the threshold of Baker's residence with a theatre ticket in my hand. When we were admitted to the house, the ticket was taken from me at the kitchen door by a woman with a LIFT badge. The programme proffered, the sense of change was heightened, perhaps even more by the presence of my two young daughters. Baker has a large kitchen that looks on to a back garden in a traditional London terraced house. The kitchen table had been removed, and in its place were three rows of chairs seating 25 people. The chairs faced the stove and the sink area.

When Baker entered her kitchen, she was dressed in her signature white smock, appearing as part-doctor, part-chef. She greeted her guests shyly, warmly, and introduced herself: 'I'm Bobby Baker. Once a long time ago someone expected to see a man, so I want you to know that this is me.' I later learned that she uses this introduction for her various performance works. The

performance begins, then, with her identification of herself as a woman with a gender-ambiguous name and a costume that says 'I'm ready to get to work.'

Baker subtitles her performance 'One Dozen Kitchen Actions Made Public'. Her dozen is, of course, a Baker's dozen, or thirteen, and each of what she calls her 'actions' is accompanied by an autobiographical monologue. She begins by pulling out a trolley loaded with cups and saucers from a cupboard and proceeds to put the kettle on the stove. She speaks as she prepares tea and coffee for her audience.

> When I welcome people into my kitchen, I always offer them a hot drink straight away – 'Coffee? Tea?' I don't like them to sit there with nothing. It makes me feel anxious.
>
> (Baker, 1991: p. 165)

With remarkable ease and efficiency, Baker delivers her speech, along with a cup of coffee or tea, to each member of her audience. A characteristic of her language, repeated over and over again throughout her performance, is the sense that she is speaking aloud an inner, private monologue. We are privy to her personal thoughts, and this privilege is double-edged: while on one level she plays a straightforward homemaker concerned with her day-to-day travail in the kitchen, on another level she ironically performs a certain kind of dutiful womanhood. Her delivery is disarming; we are caught up in the moment: teacup in hand, sipping and listening, we are guests in her home. It is only later, when I look at her programme, that I see that she distils this activity into a single action that she identifies as '*Action No. 1* Stirring milk or sugar into a hot drink'.

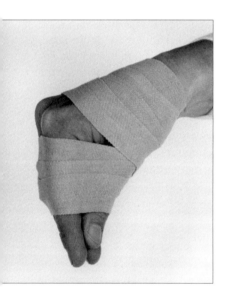

Kitchen Show (1991). 'Mark No. 1: to bandage my fingers into the right shape with elastoplast'. Image from booklet.

There is a ritualised quality to each of Baker's thirteen actions. Each monologue – which articulates the action while she is doing it – is followed by what she calls a 'mark'. For Baker, the mark is literally marking her body in some way so that she physically retains a 'memory' of the action throughout her performance. For example, *Action No. 1* is followed by '*Mark No. 1* To bandage my fingers into the right shape with Elastoplast'. She describes the bandaging of her hand in the shape required for stirring a cup of tea. The notion of some ideal hand shape for stirring tea gives Baker the opportunity to layer her performance with the inescapable issue of class so present in British culture. Her hand and fingers remain taped in this way during the entire performance and foreshadow that her body will become 'bound' by the tea ritual.

The effect of this ritualised marking is that by the end of her performance Baker is covered with a variety of kitchen utensils and objects, in addition to being bandaged, smeared with margarine and partially soaked with water. She carries the burden of both her performance and her kitchen with her. The kitchen space becomes a site for sharing, telling, demonstrating and enacting her fantasies of chaos and violence. The kitchen is the space where we serve our guests, but it is also a daily battlefield of onerous tasks and repetitive activity.

In Baker's playing space, the kitchen becomes a haven for just such detail in its provision of factual evidence: routines of daily life are examined, minutiae of domestic work are performed and social life is enacted. But interwoven into all this are hints of comic madness, a suggestion that chaos lurks just below the surface. In *Action No. 3*, for example, Baker describes her occasional need to vent her anger and then proceeds to demonstrate this by smashing a ripe pear against a cupboard door.

Action No. 7 is a surreal juxtaposition opposing eating and cosmetics. Baker, snacking on small pieces of food that she calls 'taste sensations', describes how important it is to keep up her blood sugar level. She stages how her constant feeding and need for oral gratification in the kitchen have led to some embarrassing mistakes. For example, Baker 'picked up what [she] thought was a crumb of cake only to discover that [she] was chewing on a small piece of masking tape!' She then, seemingly incongruously, marks herself by putting on bright red lipstick and explains her action by linking it to a childhood experience.

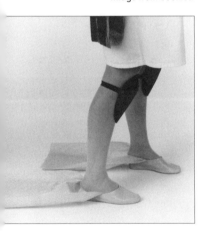

Kitchen Show (1991). 'Mark No. 12: To tuck two new blue J-cloths in between the sides of my heels and my slippers so that they fly out behind'. Image from booklet.

> We went to visit a friend of my mother's who had just had a baby. My mother went upstairs to see her friend and the baby in the bedroom. I went up too but they were embarrassed and annoyed at my interruption because she was breastfeeding. I saw the woman's nipple. It looked bright red like a cherry. I thought she'd put lipstick on it.
>
> (Baker, 1991: p. 168)

Connecting her constant snacking, or 'grazing', as she calls it, to a childhood memory of her embarrassment at discovering a woman breastfeeding is a startling imaginative leap. The kitchen and the remembered woman are linked as sites of potential nourishment, a private association made by her narrative. Baker plays on the duality here – she is both the feeder and the one who feeds. To mark this connection she gashes her mouth – the body part that receives the food – with red.

For Baker the kitchen is a site of constant work, but also of memory and engaging fantasy. In *Action No. 9* she dances to operatic music while sprinkling spinach leaves around the kitchen. In *Action No. 12*, which she calls 'the most significant as it ties all the others together', she moves about the kitchen trying to finish a whole range of uncompleted tasks. She says, 'There is a great deal of skill and versatility attached to this action. It is like keeping a set of juggler's balls in the air.' For the women in the small, intimate audience such as myself, this notion of 'juggling balls' is a recognisable part of the domestic terrain. The never-ending routine of housework is a commonplace experience, with its rush to pick up, straighten up, clean up. To mark this action, Baker attaches two blue J-cloths (disposable kitchen cloths) to the heels of her slippers, providing us with a hilarious image of winged heels, à la Mercury, the Greek god of speed and flight.

Using her own kitchen, Baker transforms the traditional stage space from one of public, open exteriors to an intimate interior space that is literally lived and worked in. Her autobiographical monologues reposition – one could say semiotise – the audience, transforming them from conventional spectators to invited guests. We witness Baker's rituals of kitchen life just as her friends and neighbours may have occasion to do. But in this duality of audience as guest/spectator, conventional woman's work becomes a performance, an artistic event. Indeed Baker's performance is a means to 'transgress the boundaries within which woman is held separate from, the antithesis of culture, society, meaning' (Pollock, 1991: n.p.).

Because we are in Baker's own kitchen, witnessing her talking and working with her own dishes, utensils and appliances, because such work is marked visually (for the spectators) and physically (for Baker), the specificities of this woman, this body, this kitchen, this work are highlighted. Baker's body is both the guiding artistic intelligence and the body artistically marked in performance. As Ellen Donkin has suggested, she is both the creator of meaning and the carrier of meaning (Donkin, 1998: 65). Or, as Baker demonstrates in *Action No. 7*, applying bright red lipstick to her lips, she is both the feeder and the one who feeds. This deliberate conflation of the woman performer and the artwork transgresses cultural boundaries that demand the separation of private and public spheres. Baker turns the misogynistic notion of women actresses *merely playing themselves* on its head. Baker makes playing herself a deliberate creative act, one central to her work. Locating this performance in a kitchen, a site culturally identified with women and women's work (and a site and activity most often hidden from public viewing), adds another layer to this conflation.

In Baker's final action, laced with irony and humour, Baker displays herself as a kind of fantastically decorated cake, turned awkwardly and uncomfortably around on her pedestal. When I saw her performance, Baker, in what appeared to be an impromptu gesture, invited her daughter to come into the kitchen and play the piano for her final pose. She commented that her daughter happened to be available for this touch, so her final image on a cake stand featured her shy daughter's hesitant, charming chords. For me her daughter's appearance in the kitchen/stage paralleled my own in the audience with my daughters as guests/spectators.

This moment emphasised the autobiographical nature of Baker's work for both performer and viewer.

Baker's final pose – her marked body displayed on a cake pedestal to the tinkling strains of her daughter's piano – is a tongue-in-cheek reconfiguration of the Pygmalion myth. Bobby Baker debunks this age-old myth of man transforming woman by presenting herself as an artwork. Instead of the idealised beauty of male fantasy, she is increasingly defaced, soiled and stained by the traces of her kitchen work. Women on pedestals have been served up to us as artworks created by men. They have neither autonomy nor self-definition. But here, standing precariously on a cake stand overtly used for consumption, Baker connects her body to her domestic life and to her artwork. She underscores the importance of this connection in her final line, 'It's the image they make all together that matters most' (Baker, 1991: p. 170). This final image – both serious and tongue-in-cheek – stresses Baker's active participation in interpreting her 'self' for us. As Paul Smith argues, 'a person is not simply the *actor* who follows ideological scripts, but is also an *agent* who reads them in order to insert him/herself into them – or not' (Smith, 1988: xxxiv–xxxv). Baker's self-insertion into these scenes of the kitchen both remakes it as a site of agency and stages her send-up of conventionalised domesticity.

DAILY LIFE 1

𝒦itchen 𝒮how GRISELDA POLLOCK

An extract from Pollock's essay in the *Kitchen Show* booklet.

Griselda Pollock is Professor of Social and Critical Histories of Art and Director of Centre for Cultural Analysis, Theory and History at the University of Leeds.

Opposite page: *Kitchen Show* (1991). LIFT, North London. 'Mark No. 7: to put bright red lipstick on my puckered lips.'

ART IS THE transformation of material – social, psychic, physical – into a form which so alters what we are familiar with, that we come to know it differently. Art uses affect cognitively. Women's work, however, is not often the material of art because it doesn't affect us and it seems to defy being known at all. It falls below the threshold of recognition and it is not really accounted as work. It is what mothers do because they are mothers. They cook and clean, prepare food and wash clothes, shop and run households as a natural extension of the ability to gestate and deliver babies. Decide to have a child and the whole package of domesticity lands on an unsuspecting adult's head to take over and redefine what you are. Who is there when all this happens – who is the subject (psychoanalytically speaking) of women's domestic labour? A person, a woman, a worker? The worker – there's a word loaded with historical and political force, empowered all the more by the debilitating nature of the work workers are forced to perform in factories, mines and offices. But the mother – that has no political charge, no identity even. 'Mother' is a not a person so much as a place, a supportive texture for other people's lives and personalities like wall-paper or a comfortable arm chair, a thereness which is the opposite of our idea of the individual, neither agent nor sensibility. And woman, well, there's an enigma. What do they keep going on about?

Bobby Baker's work is about the subjectivity of the woman who works as a mother. Bobby Baker's work is about an artist

23.10

My life is gaining an epic quality at last.

A still-life of great beauty – light streaming through a window with drops of water on it. – curtains drawn – a line of light.

THEN – a moment of great joy a turning point –

THIS GOOD KIND OLD BODY OF MINE

– why not make the most of it?

Drawing in sketch book (1990).
'My life is gaining an epic quality at last. A still-life of great beauty – light streaming through a window with drops of water on it –
Curtains drawn – a line of light.
Then – a moment of great joy
A turning point –
this good kind old body of mine – why not make the most of it?'
Paper, ink.

*Bricolage is a term from anthropology which defines a making process which involves the combination of many found elements, the accumulation of hybrid materials and items to create a cultural form.

who works with the materials of an experience which is lived as and seen to be the antithesis of being an artist. There is no doubt Bobby Baker is very good at her job as an artist. There's no doubt Bobby Baker is good at her job of being a mother. There's no doubt that it cost Bobby Baker a lot to disappear into a job at which she was so good it made her all the more invisible.

To make art at all is to change the terms of being a worker who is a mother making art about working in a kitchen.

How can this topic of all topics be made to touch us, for it is blighted by a culturally endorsed tedium. The Mothers know it already, all too well, though it is both shocking and comforting by turns to recognise a familiar pattern of rage, anxiety, ecstasy and pain experienced in an emblematic form of *Kitchen Show*. The Daughters don't want to know, because they must believe it will be different for them. The point of being a Daughter is exactly not to become like the Mother. The Son doesn't want to know because it might make him feel confused. He is already looking for a Mother substitute. The Father doesn't understand because when he became a Father his Humanity, his place as a social subject, didn't evaporate in a cloud of talcum powder and napisan. Anyway when he cooks he clocks up the brownie points. This work is not narrowly addressed to those who know – or can bear to know. We are not all Mothers, but we are all the children of Mothers. It happens to the Mothers and we live off it. It is one of the central experiences and social institutions of our cultures – in all the complex facets – of our society and it should enter representation, so that it can be confronted imaginatively.

Kitchen Show is a highly formalised piece of work. There are to be a dozen actions, variations of stirring, throwing, peeling, eating, praying, dancing, tidying, resting, roaming. What is an action? Like pieces on a chessboard which have prescribed movements through which it realises its function, these actions are ritualised movements through which are realised, made actual and made into experience, the functions a woman fulfils in the kitchen, that core domain of the domestic economy, the familial community, that private space of reverie and emotional bricolage.*

In the kitchen people's needs are supplied. There are actions like offering a cup of tea or coffee which are both simple tasks and dense social rituals. Lest the little moves which encapsulate the attentive concern that all needs should be anticipated and met be overlooked, Bobby Baker focuses attention on the gesture of stirring by fixing her hand into that pose with lengths of adhesive bandage. Suddenly the hand that stirs the coffee in this sunny and plant-filled kitchen becomes a kind of bondage, an injury on a body marked and incapacitated like the bound foot of old China in its submission to the invisible bonds of hospitable service patriarchal cultures call femininity. The placing of a spoon on a saucepan lid is a reminder of a friendship, a network of mutual obsessions and shared tips and hints in the perpetual improvement and elaboration of cooking rituals that begin to have charm as tokens that pass between women, invested with memory and association. It is proper that this should be celebrated – the spoon becomes an adornment for the hair. But there it transgresses two spheres – women's service and the rituals of cooking and women's service and the rituals of beauty.

Hair in food or food in hair are taboo, dangers, signs of things being out of place. This gesture of spoon in hair reminds us that there is a person who bridges these places and an artist who by marking her own body with this emblem grounds the shock and the transgression in the actual and the visible, not allowing the metaphor to derealise the social bond, the communication between women that the 'mark' commemorates.

What is an action? Actors acting use the body in space to dramatise words and to make meaning acquire a vivid image through our identification with a sentient, expressive being. The Kitchen is a theatre for many emotions. But *Kitchen Show* makes us see the actions without an overdressing of drama. They are performed, not acted. The action of bowling a pear at a kitchen cupboard as an emblem of anger is shocking in its calculated nakedness as an action. Angry women are a cultural anathema. Mothers are never meant to be angry. It is always one of the shocks of becoming a mother and a housewife how anger is unleashed in hitherto peaceable and self-controlled people. The anger has deep roots in the violence brewed both in any ordinary family and in the mother's own childhood. The pear is a fruit of soft and sweet flesh. Women are often pear-shaped. As it crashes against the hard wooden surface (vinyl silk so that it will wash off easily), it is bruised and explodes – producing a shocking image of violence coupled to vulnerability. The careful housewife takes precautions that her guests are not splattered with her anger. A table cloth protects them from the fall-out. The artist places another fruit in her breast pocket, for another time, a disruption of that metaphor of women's fruitfulness with a potential missile.

Managing emotions is part of good acting, and the next three actions alter the mood dramatically. The kitchen is a space for surprising moments of sensual pleasure and ecstasy because it allows for the unexpected delights of playing with colours and textures. Note the joys of revealing that intensely saturated orange hue of a carrot beneath its drab and often hairy skin. Note the delights of running water 'shot through with joy' as the interior and the workplace connect via that humdrum instrument of modern technology, the faucet/tap. Remember James Joyce's lengthy chapter on the modernity of water works in *Ulysses* as Bloom fills the kettle for a cup of tea. Pause for a moment to note the almost forgotten sensualities of food as the artist opens a tub of margarine with its pristine, glossy surface and rippled swell

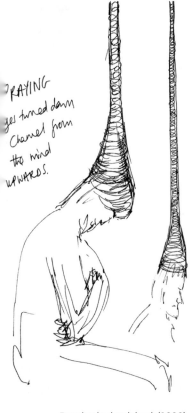

Drawing in sketch book (1990).
'5 April praying. Eyes turned down.
A Channel from the mind upwards'.
Paper, ink.

into that tiny sign-off nipple. These joys are undoubtedly sensual, but the careful control which art exercises by asking us only to look at colour and texture but not touch is breached as the artist swamps herself with water and moisturises her face with marge.

Food is a complex field for women, who must both spend their lives feeding others and yet exercise perpetual control over their own consumption. Haunted by the cultural taboos on body size, the mother experiences childbirth and feeding as a potential disaster. How many women never regain their girlish form after that amazing hormonal transformation which allows one body to sustain two and then produce that life-giving liquid? Eating has been identified as a feminist issue – where pleasure and pain perpetually interfere with each other across that formative threshold of the inside and the outside, the mouth. *Action No. 7* produces a mark – lipstick applied to make the mouth a cherry. The narrative which leads to this overlays that adult act of female sexual adornment with a childhood memory, the startled child's inadvertent discovery of a breastfeeding mother and her exposed

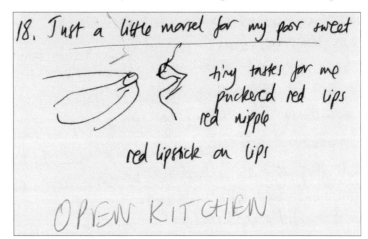

Drawing in sketch book
(1990). Paper, ink.

nipple, red like a cherry on top. Lips, especially reddened lips, are usually taken as a sexual sign – an advertisement of other lips, a fetish against that female wound. But that is in an economy of masculine sexuality. Oral imagery is here wound through memory and image into a more specifically feminine pattern. It is also suggestive of the permeability and mobility of the female subject, at once a mother feeding a child, yet projectively able to experience the lost ecstasies of the child's utter abandon to the pleasures of its lips around the cherry of life. Freud wrote of a little girl's shock at seeing her mother's body and knowing it was lacking. Bobby Baker invents another startled girl-child encountering what is much more interesting and strange about the adult female – the breast, a fullness, a redness, a capacity to sustain life out of the body itself that precisely poses the singularity of woman not as closer to nature, but as a more complex site of human subjectivity as it lives its psychic and symbolic realities in and through a body.

If such a range of human emotion can be lived in the kitchen, just what is it that denies this space both social status and poetry? Women's domestic lives are not empty any more than workers' who are otherwise required daily to perform repetitive tasks which service other economies. *Kitchen Show* presents us with a person, a range of memories, reveries, meanings and resistances to the domestic as something which threatens women's hold on a singular identity and yet is also the site of its elaboration. Each subjectivity is a product of constructions of class, race, gender, sexuality and each speaks necessarily from its own, localised experience. But each attempt to expose the tension within which a particular class, race and gender subjectivity is pinned to a culturally prescribed identity and its performance has something to say beyond the conditions of its own existence – if it does not claim its experience as exemplary or normative. Each attempt to speak of and represent that combination of subjection and resistance makes a difference because it brings hitherto-disregarded areas of social experience into view. Bobby Baker's art form, performance, makes us the audience, the necessary witness to the cultural marking of an individual body. The persona in the piece functions as the visible crossover point between the action of culture upon this woman and the cultural action of this artist.

The effect of marking is to make us remark upon the process of living inside a culture which makes the artist and the woman antithetical terms. Where else could this become so remarkable than in Bobby Baker's workshop – a kitchen?

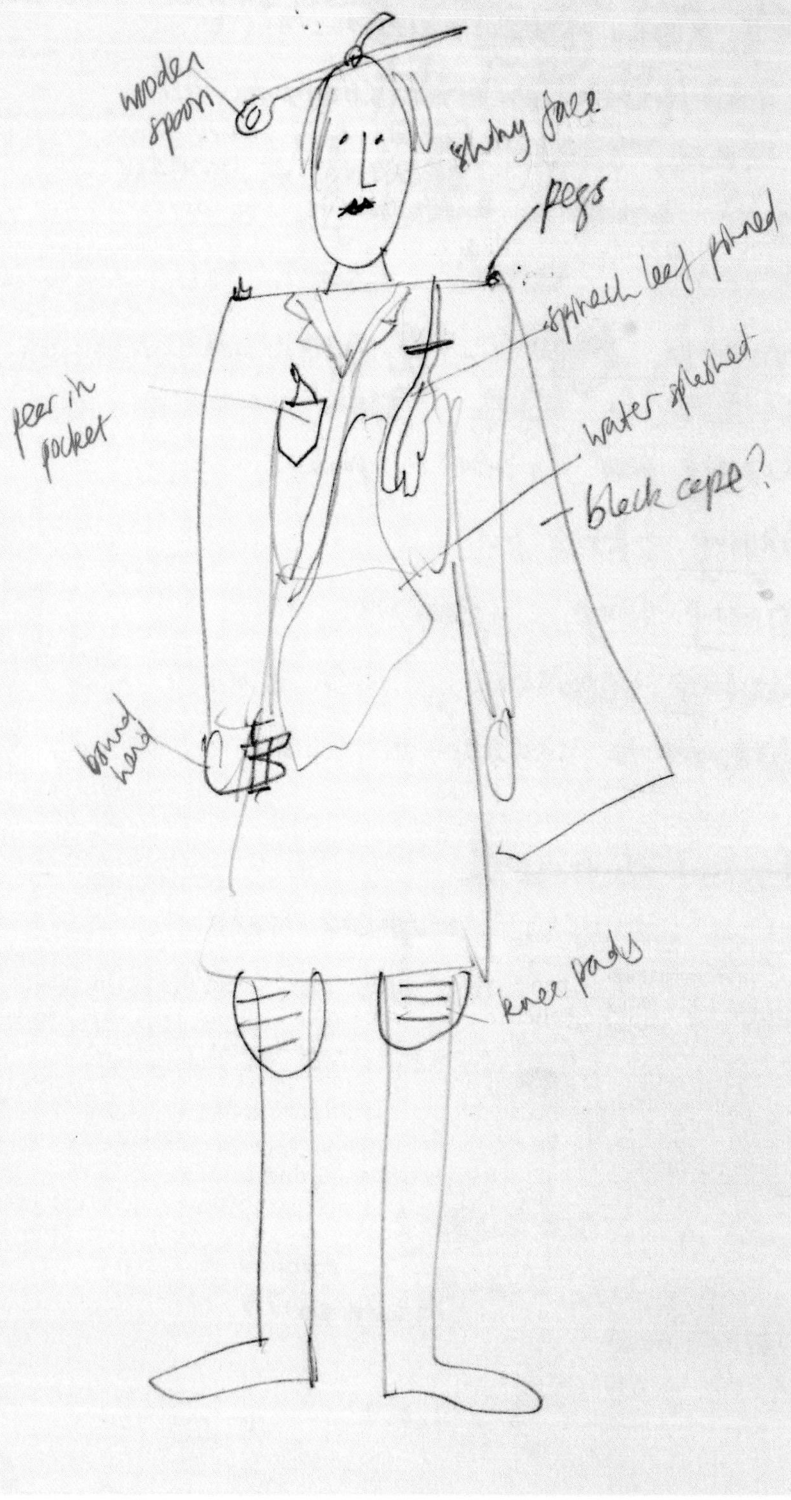

wooden
spoon

shiny face

pegs

spinach leaf pinned

pear in
pocket

water splashed

black cape?

bound
hand

knee pads

DAILY LIFE 1

𝒦𝒾𝓉𝒸𝒽𝑒𝓃 𝒮𝒽𝑜𝓌   HELEN IBALL

From 'Taking Ownership of "Her indoors": Performativity as a Theatrical Dis-location of the British "Housewife", in Laura Lengel and John T. Warren (eds) *Casting Gender: Women and Performance in Intercultural Contexts*.

Helen Iball teaches in the Workshop Theatre at the University of Leeds. Her recent publications are on Sarah Kane, Howard Barker, and on theatrical spectatorship post-9/11. Inspired by a workshop with Bobby Baker, Helen is undertaking a series of events and publications about academics, entitled 'Doctored Identities'.

Opposite: Drawing in sketch book (1990). Paper, pencil, felt tip.

ON OCCASIONS SPANNING more than a decade in Adelaide, Brighton, Bristol, Canberra, Cardiff, Ljubljana, London, Nottingham, Salisbury, São Paulo, Sydney, Utrecht and Wellington (NZ) audiences have watched a white, middle-aged, middle-class English woman – born in the south of England to a Protestant family and now living in North London – demonstrate a series of a dozen actions that take place in her own home. 'They responded to it as a kind of extraordinary cultural event. But, what seems to happen in these shows is that there is something about them which touches people' (personal communication, 26 November 1999). The hub of the action is Baker's kitchen, and she makes every effort to evoke its particularities within the space she has been allocated for her performance: be this a small marquee (Cardiff), or a show home on a new housing development (Canberra), or a chic celebrity kitchen (Sydney).

As a globetrotting artist, Baker takes 'her indoors' with her to a diversity of other places, remaining tied to the metaphorical kitchen sink with an elastic binding of anecdotes, photographs, mugs and spatulas. She sources these as a form of gently ironic seduction that operates on the level of her willingness to expose her experience in all its domestic detail. In each place Baker performs, her strategy is to create a temporary and powerfully unstable transformation through the energies of a fundamentally theatrical discourse: conscious of its own conventions and potentialities, celebrating the active presence of its audience, and accessing the heightened potential of blurring the borders between performance, theatricality and autobiography.

Baker points out that her co-director, Polona Baloh Brown (Pol), is Slovene and that this 'adds a great deal in that she has a more objective view of British culture (laughter)' and so 'we can expand on that' in making the work and translating it for its various audiences. One of the issues Baker and Brown have discussed at length is:

> The Protestant ethic behind British culture, the sort of control and meanness, almost, of the lack of delight or expressiveness in enjoying things. Yes, the tightness of it all. That's the one thing we've observed a great deal. She particularly harps on about the eccentricity, which bugs me [laughter]. I like to think I'm deeply normal.

Baker adds, however, that people's perceptions are different in different countries.

> I mean, in Australia and New Zealand and Canada it is a sort of ex-colonial perception of the British and a delight at my subversive attack on that. But in Germany, for instance, they are just astonished and delighted by the sense of humour and they relate to it as being particularly British and eccentric and they put it into the context of Monty Python – relating it to what they see on television, making it just one more strand of that – which interests me. That happens quite a lot in Europe. But in Madrid they were less bothered about what it is to be British; they have less context and less contact with us. They related very strongly to what the work was about and how it related to their own daily lives.

The international reception of Baker's housewife persona is undoubtedly affected by her own recognition of the peculiarity and, indeed, insularity of her work. She works diligently with Pol on the process of translation in its various, and more literal, aspects:

> I speak a bit of French and so when I perform in France, I add quite a lot of French to the show. But in Spain – I don't speak Spanish so we had a translation and synopsis of the show, during the show; because the shows are very structured, it was possible to break it down into sections, so that the audience just had a short synopsis of each section that they could read. But the shows are very physical and expressive, they communicate on different levels. It worked extraordinarily well, in fact.

Asked whether the fact that there was this kind of translation taking place made a difference to the performance and her feelings about it, Baker replied:

> One of the differences was that I was extremely anxious about how it would work before the show. I think, intuitively, I was far more physical in the way that I performed and used much simpler language and told the stories in a different way. That's one thing we work consciously at in the way that the shows are put together. I generally tour with Pol. She and I, because we have a great deal of experience at touring now together, do quite a lot of research when we arrive at a place and talk to whoever's organising the show – and when we're rehearsing we concentrate on how we think it might communicate best and then like it particularly if the show's happening more than once, so that we can develop it according to what happened.

Bobby Baker acknowledges herself as an import. The citational strategies and vital modifications to *Kitchen Show* ensure its unique presence in new contexts; each performance never seeks to repeat precisely the 'original'. So, based upon Baker's own reflections, it might be suggested that, in diverse cultural frames, the fondness and the pain come up close because she is unafraid of reperpetuating myths of Britishness and a particularly localised expression of women's experience. Lucy Baldwyn describes Baker as 'employing a peculiarly British gamut of emotions – reticence, irony and embarrassment' through which 'she concocts theatrical images that resonate with unspoken desires and frustrations' (Baldwyn, 1996: 37). Baker 'speaks from and avoids speaking for' (Heddon, 1998: 53), in that she is not attempting to impose a false sense of global sisterhood, but enabling an active spectator (also see Blumberg, 1998: 201). It is in this manner that Baker's work avoids the pitfalls of appearing patronising or artificially unified. An example: she establishes her tone through the subtly parodic appreciation of Weight Watchers' Mediterranean Tomato Soup; which she implies is rendered rather exotic (Mediterrean) by the inclusion of flecks of red pepper. In this context, she praises the greater culinary competence of her Slovene friend – 'I think they're more generous and skilled than us', she told her Cardiff audience in a tone gently mocking of middle-class, postcolonial reverence.

If *Kitchen Show* accesses a 'global' experience, this capacity stems from the recognitions generated in each member of each audience. Everyone needs to eat. Tradition usually has it that the preparation of family meals is part of the woman's role and, thus, that the kitchen is primarily her domain. And so it is that substitutes come into play to ensure a satisfying correlation at the very moment that cultural particularities are identified and stereotypes of the British housewife paraded. Baker takes a low-sided, large, round container from the refrigerator, showing it to the audience and preparing them for one of the special moments in her domestic life: when the time has come to open a new tub of 'Vitalite light' margarine.

When asked whether she received particular responses to such objects from the audience, Baker remarked that:

> People relate to these shows by constantly and to an extraordinary degree relating them to their own experiences, to equivalents in their culture. So, when I performed in Cairo, in relation to the 'Vitalite' people were talking about a paste called phool, so it doesn't matter that mine might be margarine – theirs is chickpeas. It happens with all the shows. People get, almost, very boring [laughter], telling the whole of their experience and how extraordinary it is to recognise that this aspect of their lives goes unacknowledged.

This fascination with comparative cultural instances addresses Elaine Aston's recent observation that 'the uniqueness of Baker's domestic storytelling is its (potential) commonality' (Aston, 2002: 81), to a more diverse canvas by considering the work on tour. It is thus that Aston's useful footnote is complicated – she cites Mike Pearson's tripartite categorisation of the 'watchers' of performance into: 'fans/aficionados (colored by expectation, memory, history), first-timers (incredulous, extreme), and "foreigners" (those perceiving a different order of connotative meaning' (Pearson, 1994: 134). Aston observes that the commonality of Baker's storytelling will inevitably be affected by which kind of watcher is watching. The Father, for example, may find himself a 'foreigner' in Baker's audience (Aston, 2002: 85). Certainly, even when showing video extracts to students – when one becomes aware of the rather overbearingly enthusiastic responses of the Magdalena audience, which were recorded in the process of making the available video – discrepancies between watchers of Baker become evident. However, first-timers and 'foreigners' do, as Baker suggested several times during the interview, become drawn into the performance as it progresses. They are lulled in because 'Baker refers only to that which is non-threatening, safe, in order to mobilize that which is extraordinary, challenging and dangerous' (Aston, 2002: 80).

The potential of merging the theatrical and performative, as a strategy for the 'overcoming' of architectural and cultural boundaries must, of course, be balanced with an acknowledgement of the demographic of Baker's audience, both nationally and internationally. She recognises that because *Kitchen Show*'s contexts have often been international festivals 'the audience will be at the wealthy end of that culture and we will have nothing to do with what goes on beyond the smart streets'. Baker reflects that this situation both 'does and does not bother' her, 'because the work

Drawing in sketch book (1990). 'My cup runneth over'. Paper, ink.

that I suppose interests me the most is the work where I reach people in their daily lives ... and it doesn't matter that I'm middle aged and middle class'. In an interview with Alison Oddey, Baker described the energetic tension of 'the fact that I appear to be a very normal middle-aged, home-counties-type woman' within which persona she finds 'the power is for people to feel lulled into security in that appearance and then to break out of that' (Oddey, 1999: 272). Thus the form and context of the work are as vital tools as its content. Baker identifies that perhaps the most fundamental aspect of her international appearances is the hope offered by the very fact of her presence as an artist, and that

> If it only works on this level then I feel very positive. That it is very empowering to see a woman doing work on her own. Women making work is relatively unusual, particularly for women of my generation. That in itself is a very strong part of what the work communicates to people. I find it very much with young women that I teach or run workshops with or I talk to after shows – that they see me as a role model.

The work clearly takes on radically different meaning in certain cultural contexts. A rare instance of disjuncture, recounted by Baker in interview, was her appearance at the Canberra International Comedy Festival, where a faction in the audience, expecting to see 'stand-up comedy', became disruptive and began to throw Baker's own pears at her. There have also been moments when her privilege has been thrown into sharp relief:

> Cairo was the most difficult to deal with because of the way women are viewed. I was most anxious about that. I suppose I have performed mainly in Western cultures: the US and South America, Canada, New Zealand, Europe. Also, what's slightly predictable, as in Sao Paulo, are International Festivals [...] I think three times there has been a potential tour in India with the British Council, but [...] always, there has been the concern about the way I use food. It is appalling to go into a country where there is starvation and throw food on the floor and tread on it, a really shocking and disrespectful thing to do.

Baker is strongly aware that it is the spectator who engages in identification, recognition and parallel, aided by shifts made to the performance. She uses comic irony to create an in-between space, thus 'making-do' with the available resources and venues. She is making each place do – taking 'everything but the kitchen sink' on her travels, with a dogged strategy of foregrounding that keeps her looking at that world with her hands in the sink that she has left behind in Holloway.

COMPASSION

Corkscrew slowly moving in to a bottle of ROSÉ wine

→

merging of my body with the image of the corkscrew

↗ possible close up 1 - transition stage

toe pointed into bottle - slowly swivelling row to get in ungainly

in an attempt - very

Disappearing into wine bottle? - glass

Swimming sequence in rosé wine - Esther Williams (water tank)

DAILY LIFE 2
How to Shop GERALDINE HARRIS

An edited extract from Harris's much longer piece 'The Active Consumer' in her *Staging Femininities*.

Geraldine (Gerry) Harris is Professor of Theatre Studies at Lancaster University, UK. Previous publications include *Staging Femininities* (1999), *Beyond Representation: The Politics and Aesthetics of Television Drama* (2006). With Elaine Aston she co-edited *Feminist Futures: Theatre, Performance, Theory* (2006) and co-wrote *Performance Practice and Process: Contemporary [Women] Practitioners*, (Palgrave Macmillan, 2007).

Opposite: *How to Shop* (1993). 'Compassion'. Part of a sequence of five story board drawings done in 1992. Paper, pencil, watercolour, crayons.

THE 'PATIENCE' SEQUENCE of *How to Shop* remarks the sort of 'incoherence' that, according to Julia Kristeva's *Powers of Horror*, is produced by the foregrounding of the 'abject', a concept and a work of particular relevance to *How to Shop* because of the show's religious content. According to Kristeva, 'Abjection accompanies all religious structurings and reappears, to be worked out in a new guise, at the time of their collapse' (Kristeva, 1980: 17).

In this essay, Kristeva throws into relief the ways in which the modernist, 'scientific' discourse of psychoanalytical theory draws upon and remains imbricated within the historical discourses of institutionalised religion, particularly the Judaeo-Christian tradition. Kristeva traces out the evolution of Old Testament purity laws as a process of creating rules and boundaries for an ideal 'clean and proper subject', fit to speak to his god. She argues that these laws, which were related both to hygiene and to the sacred, developed into a classification system of differences and oppositions separating out subject from object, masculine from feminine, heterosexual from homosexual, the spiritual from the corporeal, the clean from the unclean, inside from outside. According to Kristeva, this system then served to define the limits and borders of orderly, proper subjects, defined in obedience to cultural taboos, which must be maintained to achieve socialisation and provide a sense of the self as a discrete and unified whole. The abject marks these limits and borders which, when transgressed or even simply remarked, can provoke the recognition that this wholeness is only a construct, producing a sense of instability and incoherence or of being 'out of control'. Above all, the abject relates to a fear of the fragility, permeability and 'uncontrollability' of the

How to Shop (1993). Part of a sequence of five story board drawings done in 1992. 'Courage – oil poured on my head – dripping on to shoulders/floor, etc.'

COURAGE -
oil poured on my head
-dripping on to shoulders/floor etc

body, and so the subject's 'wholeness' is threatened by the sight of blood, the appearance of other bodily fluids and the ingestion and expulsion of food, all of which serve as reminders of, and prefigure, the ultimate loss of self – death. Paradoxically, these same objects simultaneously serve as a reminder of birth and of the primary, physical and psychical process of separation from the maternal body, necessary to the achievement of this discrete subjectivity in the first place. As a result, within this process of classification, the feminine comes to be associated with the corporeal abject, and the abject with the feminine, so that for Kristeva food induces abjection when it recalls the 'archaic relationship between the human body and the other, its mother' (Kristeva, 1980: 75–6). However, as Kristeva puts it, abjection 'is caused by what disturbs identity, system, order. What does not respect borders, positions, rules. The in between, the ambiguous, the composite' (1980: 4). It would therefore be wrong to associate the abject *only* with the maternal feminine. In *Powers of Horror*, Kristeva then turns to the New Testament, where she explores the sublimation and recuperation of the threat of the corporeal/abject/maternal/ feminine through its incorporation into the figure of Christ, a god made flesh, whose body is subsequently purified through physical suffering and death and then resurrected so that he is assumed 'whole' into heaven. By this means the abject/corporeal/feminine is inoculated and transcended through this figure, who thereafter represents an impossible, ideal model for achieving 'true', rather than 'symbolic', wholeness (Kristeva, 1980: 120).

Clearly, 'Patience', like much of the rest of the show, can be read as playing on social and sexual taboos in a fashion that borders on the abject in various ways – hence the contradictory, excessive, if not incoherent, nature of Baker's identifications. The tendency towards 'abjection' throughout the piece was often concentrated around the use of food products which were also quite specifically connected to religious iconography. Yet the attitude Baker demonstrated towards this iconography in the show was in itself ambivalent, ambiguous and contradictory. At times, this imagery seemed transgressive, foregrounding the historical, discursive abjection of the feminine within the Judaeo-Christian tradition. At others, Baker appeared to accept her position as the feminine abject and at others again to identify with Christ as an ideal of unity and wholeness, unifying the split between masculine and feminine, the pure spirit and the sinful flesh. This may indicate a reworking of this religious structure at the time of its collapse, and, interestingly, it was the sections where Baker appeared to express genuine religious belief, rather than those that were more obviously transgressive, which seemed to evoke uncertainty, if not instability, within the audience. For example, just before launching into her exemplary shopping trip, Baker repeated the little prayer 'Lord send me', which she told us she always said before engaging in such activities. In contrast to the comic tone previously established, this prayer was delivered quietly and seriously, a switch of mood that caused a hiatus, after which Baker shrugged self-deprecatingly, muttered something inaudible and once again changed registers.

Yet 'Obedience', for which, following the prompting of her 'inner voice', the voice of the Lord, Baker placed an unopened tin of anchovies sideways in her mouth, was received with much hilarity despite its masochistic and Christian framing. This action was shown first taking place in a supermarket on film and then on stage where, still with the tin in her mouth, Baker performed a clumsy dance to the music of 'When the Boat Comes In', therefore obediently and/or ironically dancing for her 'daddy'. The implicit, biblical reference to 'fish' was consolidated through linking this act to a story about friends swimming with a shoal of fish in Greece, but Baker also said she may actually have got this image from the film *Shirley Valentine*. This act was most definitely a mortification of the flesh, and yet Baker's personal anecdote dwelt on the pleasures of the senses. Moreover, *Shirley Valentine* is a story of a 'disobedient' woman who leaves her husband and rejects domesticity to 'find' herself through worldly physical experience, in a sort of reversal and repetition of *The Pilgrim's Progress*. Finally, enacting this gesture in the supermarket in itself was socially a transgressive and disorderly act that failed to respect not only the boundaries of inside and outside the body but also the 'rules' of the appropriate public behaviour. Similarly, for 'Joy', Baker mimicked Eve's original sin of eating the apple which brought death into the world, thereby quoting the Old Testament construction of the feminine as standing for, and enslaved by, the corrupt and corrupting temptations of the flesh. Yet her citation of this religious archetype was performed as a playful celebration of the body, if not a positive reclaiming of disorderly female desire. Yet again, this whole section was framed by reference to the experience of drowsing in an apple orchard on a late summer afternoon surrounded by the scent of windfalls, a highly sensuous image but one which in turn is not so far removed from notions of death and decay. These, then, like all the sequences in the show, were sort of double or triple exposures in which contradictory or opposite images, narratives and identifications were layered on top of each other, in a manner that was contiguous and overlapping, rather than dialectical. This produced clashes, convergences and dissonances that were somehow both obedient *and* disorderly, celebratory *and* troubling, simultaneously affirmations of life and *memento mori*.

This contradictory, dissonant layering was much in evidence with reference to the last two items on Baker's shopping list. Red wine, for Baker, stands for 'Compassion', and she said she needed a great deal of this to get through the day. She held up

How to Shop (1993). LIFT, London. 'Courage' sequence from live show.

a corkscrew to the audience, flapping its arms and saying, 'My friends say this is me.' Under the influence of the show's religious framing, this corkscrew seemed not only to signify 'out of control' femininity but also a crucifix. A film sequence used trick photography to show Baker being transformed into this corkscrew to open a bottle of wine in which she then swam apparently nude. This again, then, is a series of double images bringing together the masculine and feminine, the martyrdom of Christ with the 'hysterical' woman, the partaking of the cleansing blood in the ritual of the Eucharist with more mundane, literal consolations. This reference to the Eucharist was consolidated in the final action for 'Love'. Using 'Mother's Pride' bread and taking pains to let the audience enjoy the smell of frying garlic, Baker made garlic croutons which were placed in baskets, passed out and shared with the spectators. Of the ritual of the Eucharist, Kristeva says that, 'By surreptitiously mingling the theme of "devouring" with that of "satiating", that narrative is a way of taming cannibalism. It invites a removal of guilt from the archaic relation to the first pre-object (abject) of need: the mother' (Kristeva, 1980: 118). This sequence was described by several reviewers as 'touching', but it is also potentially a reminder of the way in which Mothers are often 'devoured', both literally and metaphorically, and therefore, although presented as an act of love and willing self-sacrifice, it did not necessarily allow for the removal of guilt. In fact, *How to Shop* was shot through with moments when Baker foregrounded the self-effacement demanded by her role as mother and housewife as a sort of martyrdom. This is a mortification of both the flesh and the spirit, which is not entirely willing and happy – hence her need for courage and compassion and her ambiguous relationship to obedience. She was shown breathlessly rushing around the supermarket in order to fit in all her daily tasks, she said she never got to watch a film all the way through because she would always either fall asleep or be popping in and out of the room, and before picking up her halo at the end of the show she muttered darkly that, of course, 'You've got to pay.' In both the 'Love' sequence and in the final act of assumption, the image of the nurturing, everyday housewife and mother, weighed down and 'devoured' by mundane, domestic duty, overlaps simultaneously with Christian from *The Pilgrim's Progress*, transcending his body to reach the celestial city, the body of the abject, 'archaic (M)other', the image of Christ as an ideal of both loving self-sacrifice and 'wholeness', and also perhaps with that of the Virgin Mary who, like Christ, was bodily assumed into heaven (as is Bobby in the final image of the show). This final figure, venerated as a mother but only in so far as she achieved maternity without any recourse to sexual intercourse, again represents both an incorporation and erasure of the feminine at the same time. This layering and juxtaposition of contradictory imagery opens up a space of defamiliarisation to

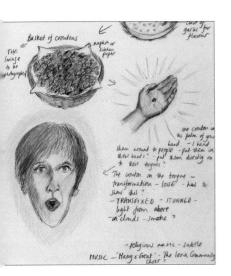

Part of a sequence of five story board drawings done in 1992. 'Clove of garlic for flavour. Basket of croutons. The image to be photographed. Napkin or kitchen paper. One crouton in the palm of your hand – I hand them around to people – put them in their hands? – put them directly on to their tongues? The crouton on the tongue – transformative – love – how to show this? – transfixed – stunned – light from above – in clouds – smoke? – religious music – subtle music – "Many and Great" The Iona Community Choir?'

underline the ambivalent, if not incoherent, fashion in which the maternal feminine has been historically, discursively constructed and is concretely experienced by Baker in the practice of her everyday life.

However, since *How to Shop* is, above all, a performance, it would be a mistake to take some of Baker's 'masks' in this show as transparently reflecting the truth about her 'real-life' subjectivity, while assuming others only to be part of the act, not least because the subjectivity performed is unstable and unreliable. To do so is to assume the meaning of the show in advance on the basis of Baker's apparent sex, gender and sexuality and paradoxically to close down the space of agency out of which, in Linda Kintz's (1992) terms, Baker is successfully manipulating these images. Since it is the proliferation of 'masks', identities and identifications Baker performs that produces this defamiliarisation, it is important to take all her 'roles' in this piece equally seriously or equally as jokes. This includes her identity as artist and her role as lecturer. Paying more careful attention to the staging of the show within the lecture theatre as a social space and to Baker's role as lecturer allows for another reading of the piece to emerge which confirms much of my analysis so far but also places more emphasis on Baker's 'agency' as a socially and historically located subject.

As the lecturer, Baker stated that she was offering a 'deconstruction of the shopping experience' and that one particular source of 'inspiration' had been the book *Lifestyle Shopping: The Subject of Consumption* (Shields, 1992), from which she read a quotation from Lauren Langman's essay 'Neon Cages: Shopping for Subjectivity' (1992). Examining this quote, its original context suggests that Baker has indeed studied this work which offers a deconstruction of the shopping experience, and that to a large extent *How to Shop* is a repetition, a reversal and a resignification of this work – in short, a deconstruction of this deconstruction. This reading is of course entirely based on information collected *after* seeing the show, but Baker did strongly urge the audience to take notes and gave enough information for us to follow up her citation of Langman's essay. She also stressed that she chose the lecture format because she felt that in previous pieces, like *Kitchen Show*, the audience became too relaxed and failed to pay attention to the '*very important points*' she was trying to make. In short, she invited us to accept the validity of her knowledge and her right to speak as an equal authority in a field where, as she remarked, the strength of academic interest indicates that 'an understanding of the shopping experience is central to any analysis of our modern society'. At the time the audience laughed, and it was left open for them to finally decide whether or not this authority was only a joke and whether or not to become active agents in the construction of meaning *after*, as well as during or before, the event.

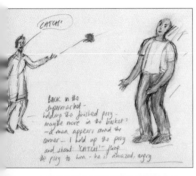

Top: Story board drawing for *How to Shop* (1992). 'Back in the supermarket – holding the finished posy – maybe more in the basket? – a man appears around the corner – I hold up the posy and shout "CATCH!" – fling the posy to him – he is amazed angry'. 'Humility sequence'.

Above: *How to Shop* (1993). LIFT, London. 'Humility' sequence.

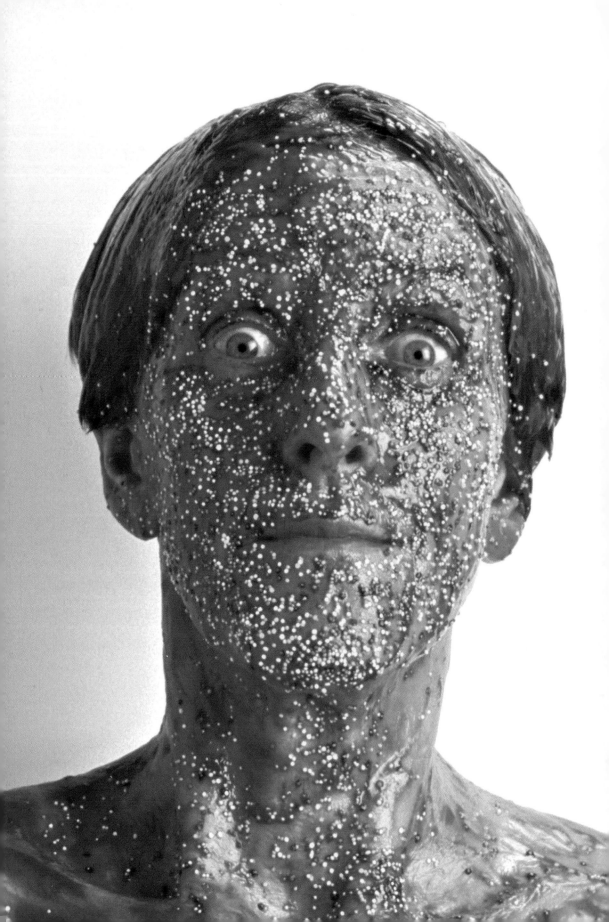

DAILY LIFE 3
Take a Peek! LISA JARDINE | NIGEL SLATER

LISA JARDINE
Centenary Professor of
Renaissance Studies, Queen Mary,
University of London.

I BECAME A passionate Bobby Baker fan in 1995. That is when I fell hopelessly in love with her stage persona, because she so perfectly captured my own ambivalent relationship to my body, and the equivocating and uncertainty of my relationship with food and health.

I can remember the precise moment when it happened – the moment at which I knew that Bobby had changed my life for ever, and that neither food nor feminism would ever be quite the same again.

It was at the South Bank, watching her perform *Take a Peek!* In the final scene, beatifically, to the strains of Annie Lennox singing 'Keep Young and Beautiful', Bobby stripped and immersed herself in a bath of skinless chocolate custard, emerging to be sprinkled from head to gleaming chocolatey toe with rainbow-coloured hundreds and thousands. She was bold, she was brave, she was beautiful.

And with what acuteness, then and always, has she unpeeled the wrappings from packaged modern femininity, and given us, quite literally, food for thought.

Thank you, Bobby!

NIGEL SLATER
This review was originally published in
the *Observer*, 9 July 1995.

IT WAS ALL SO embarrassing. Having to ask the assistant in the book shop where I was, and how to get to the collection point for Bobby Baker's *Take a Peek!* (I was about ten feet away), then having to follow the artist herself, dressed in several white gowns and pink fluffy slippers (her, not me) along the busy terraces of the Royal Festival Hall. By the time I reached the the first of the white booths in which I was to sit or stand, my palms were sweating and I was beginning to wish I hadn't come.

Bobby Baker led us along the Hall's hidden terraces, past the much maligned and absurdly named People's Palace restaurant, then left us, in appropriate hospital waiting room style to look at the walls, the floor, each other. As we sat on hard wooden benches, far too close for comfort, I wished I had made time for a bath before I came. I had been cooking fish all afternoon and knew I smelled of salmon. I was grateful to the woman next to me who smelled ever so slightly of Pernod.

'You'll love it, it's full of food' was still ringing in my ears as Baker's brutal assistants, Tamzin Griffin and Sîan Stevenson, made her perform for us: Bobby Baker as the fat lady patient (how we laughed), Bobby Baker as fairground turn (how we loved throwing those nuts at her), and Bobby Baker stuffing herself with preserved plums, the juice dribbling down her snow-white hospital gown. *Take a Peek!* follows *How to Shop*, Baker's triumphantly successful show, part of LIFT 93, in which our dotty, delightful host lectured her audience on, amongst other things, 'trolley technique'. She serenaded toffee apples and covered herself in cooking oil. She cooked for them too, producing garlic croûtons for all, continuing the vein of food that runs through much of her work.

Every time the patient's gown fell open to reveal a flash of her sensible spotless white knickers, I warmed to her. By the time her nurses had tied her in knots, confused and contorted her, I desperately wanted to take her home, away from the humiliation and the laughing, peeking audience.

There was more then a whiff of Dame Edna Everage about Bobby Baker's show. Some of this was due to the creeping feeling that any second I might find myself as much a spectacle as Baker herself – a fear realised when the the white screens slid back, opening stage, artists and – Oh God – the audience, to the voyeurs on their way to Waterloo, all of whom of course stopped to watch both nurses wielding their knives on the confused patient and the audience sitting in our waiting room.

The uneasy spectacle of patient as performer, as fun-fair freak show, reached its glorious climax when Bobby Baker shed her white gown and knickers and plunged naked into a bath of chocolate custard. How I longed to help her assistants throw the rainbow sugar-strands at her afterwards, turning our spectacle into a human cup cake. The scene was sensuous, unnerving and delicious. Bobby Baker is a joy. I had been entertained, tantalised, unnerved and comforted. I would go without food for a week just to get a ticket for her next show.

I left on a high, though deeply relieved to have been on the outside looking in. Then I took the wrong way out, through the double doors that led to the trash cans and service area. I broke out in a sweat as everyone watched the guy who couldn't find his way out of the Royal Festival Hall.

Page 196: *Take a Peek!* (1995). 'Lucky Dip'. Photograph for souvenir poster. Opposite page: *Take a Peek!* (1995). LIFT, Royal Festival Hall, London. 'Lucky Dip' sequence.

DAILY LIFE 3

ELAINE ASTON *Take a Peek!*

An edited extract from Aston's much longer piece 'Making a Spectacle Out of Herself: Bobby Baker's *Take a Peek!*', *European Journal of Women's Studies* 2004 11: 277–94.

Opposite page: *Take a Peek!* (1995). Publicity photograph.

IN *TAKE A PEEK!* Bobby Baker makes a spectacle out of herself, turns herself into a 'spectacular' demonstration of 'failed' femininity in a way that constitutes a site/sight of critical feminist 'work'. Her performance demonstrates that a social and cultural shift in the economy of the feminine and the maternal requires alteration not only to the symbolic, male-defined objectification of women, but also to women's own collusion in the 'compulsory' feminine: the policing 'matronizing' voice that keeps women fearful of making a spectacle of themselves.

In *Take a Peek!* Baker is relatively and curiously silent. She functions mostly as a dumb show at the mercy of her two speech- and action-empowered assistants. Manipulated and silenced, her presence works emblematically: she 'pictures' feminine suffering and pain through a series of mostly wordless tableaux. Aside from the fortune-telling sequence in which, although she is invited to talk it is not long before she is told to shut up, it is only in the final episode as Baker recites her recipe for happiness that she comes into speech. Tracing a line of argument through Tania Modleski's observation on the function of feminist writing as necessarily concerned with the '"mute bodies" of women', as opposed to 'the "speaking bodies" of men', Peggy Phelan argues that 'for performance the opposition is between "the body in pleasure" and, to invoke the title of Elaine Scarry's book, "the body in pain"' (Phelan, 1993: 150). As a performance, *Take a Peek!* may be argued as locating the 'mute' woman's body as a 'body in pain' that comes

eventually to 'voice' and to pleasure.

There is a further observation to make in respect of Baker's silence, however. While, on the one hand, in line with Modleski and Phelan's thinking it can be argued as 'speaking' to the position of women who historically, socially and culturally have been denied a 'voice', on the other hand, the silence is also evocative of suffering in a Christian and, by implication, symbolic, sense. Both possibilities are made present and are a reflection on Baker's unusual combination of feminist and of spiritual beliefs.

In *Take a Peek!* Christian imagery is present from the outset: it is part of the show's setting up and sending up of the feminine, the maternal, presented as the burden Baker has to bear. Baker's demeanour was penitential, her head bowed, checking to ensure that her audience were following, but seeking to avoid their gaze as much as possible. Walking, processing with Baker, here, and in the tableaux to follow, where spectators stopped at and then were moved on through images of suffering, was Baker's own version of the stations of the cross. Her burden, her cross, was the overly large (she was wearing several, not just one, white gowns) and ungainly (she had on pink, fluffy slippers that, with her multi-gowned body, made it harder to walk) female body. As a 'fallen' woman, a woman 'failing' to live up to the feminine 'ideal', Baker commits her body to spectacular suffering.

In her analysis of *Powers of Horror*, Mary Russo argues that 'the privileged site of transgression for Kristeva, the horror zone par excellence, is the archaic, maternal version of the female grotesque' (Russo, 1994: 10). The 'maternal version of the female grotesque' figures in Baker's House of Horror as she unleashes the monstrous-feminine on her spectators. Ghostly laughter and blood-curdling screams, as from a horror movie or fairground ghost train, fill the air as spectators walk to their next point of viewing, one that reveals Baker in a glass-fronted window display, flooded in pink light and in reclining porn pose position, with red fruit juice dripping from her mouth. She snarls at her audience and 'vomits up' her 'insides' (juice). The imaging of menstrual blood (juice) suggests a 'maternal authority': an archaic return to a playing with bodily fluids, waste, that the 'symbolic law' (of the father) does not permit (Kristeva, 1980: 72–3). The abject body on display is one that menstruates, births, miscarries and aborts. Importantly, however, Baker's display is one of mock-horror. The maternal 'beast' behind the glass screen provokes laughter rather than (self-) loathing, or rather plays with, makes fun out of the ways in which the feminine is made monstrous.

Baker's various masquerades of femininity might, for example, be argued as performance equivalents to Judith Butler's explorations of 'gender trouble', her exposition of 'compulsory citationality', for example, that demonstrates the production of femininity as 'the forcible citation of a norm' (Butler, 1993: 232).

What is different about *Take a Peek!* as a performance, however, is the way that spectators are invited to become active producers of gender 'norms'; to assist in the process of gender 'normalisation', and so come to be persuaded of the need for change.

Baker is clear in her own view about making public the 'failings' of her abject body. As Warner explains, 'she "wants to share feelings of no worth, of being humiliated", and does not feel that by enacting them, she compounds them, but rather gives herself back power in the act of wilful imitation' (Warner, 1995: see p.103 above). Does this argument obtain for her spectators? Are they also empowered through her 'wilful imitation', or masquerade of the feminine? Here, I would argue the issue of affect and the necessity for Baker's acting out to produce an acting upon. The desired emotional response of spectators to the invitation that the show offers for them to participate, actively participate, in the construction of the feminine, must be to *feel the violence of the feminine and need for a different arrangement of social subjectivity*. A spectator of *Take a Peek!* is encouraged to *feel* Baker's humiliation through observation and participation in the construction of the feminine: to 'stone' the woman and to see themselves stoning

Take a Peek! (1995). LIFT, Royal Festival Hall, London. 'Show Girls'.

the woman being stoned; to feel the violence that comes from participation in and observation of the feminine.

Arguably this spectatorial experience equates with the way in which Teresa De Lauretis theorises women's position in relation to dominant representational systems: the ways in which women are forced to recognise themselves 'in' or to identify with the sign 'Woman', at the same time as knowing that they 'are not *that*' (De Lauretis, 1987: 10). Observation–participation positions the spectator as dangerous collaborator in an economy of the feminine that is not just Baker's burden, but a part of their (our) own – is a part of women's experience/s, albeit variously and differently figured according to how any one individual is situated in relation to the representational economy of 'Woman'.

Moreover, as women's relation to 'Woman' is multi- (rather than uni-) lateral, it also calls women's relations not just between themselves and the economy of the feminine into question, but between themselves, the economy and *each other*. The presence of the two female assistants in the show suggests a need to look beyond a male-identified objectification of women to the collusion of women in their continued production of the feminine. In their role as barkers the two assistants join in the commodification of woman as spectacle; are supportive of the idea of a 'paying' audience for the female body. Their discourse is masculinist (breasts are 'melons'; the mouth/vagina is a 'hole'). Their actions are cruel and uncaring. They operate hierarchically, denying the disempowered 'patient' a voice, treating her as though she is absent, not present at all (forcefully imaged in the post-operative episode of recovery as Baker's body is arranged and manipulated between them, while they talk over her and only to each other). In brief, an economy of Woman makes women 'blind' and violent towards each other.

In the final analysis, it is the spectator who is brought to a border, the spectator whose 'viewing' is disturbed, made abject, through the sight of Baker's living sculpture: the chocolate-coated body of the artist, 'grotesquing' the idea of the classical body – corporeal perfection set in the smooth white stone of antiquity. Witnessing the martyrdom and rejuvenation of Baker's body, the transition from self-loathing, humiliation and shame, to self-celebration, acceptance and pride, the spectator is situated at the border between the spectacular suffering of the feminine and the spectacle of the 'grotesque' body taking pleasure in its own (maternal) waste. As a 'polluting' presence, the feminist agency of Baker as artist lies in the power to create bodies of dis-ease: to 'infect' her spectators with the desire for an affirmation, rather than an expulsion, of the 'disorderly', 'irregular' female body. Baker's invitation to laugh at the grotesquing of her own body may serve to empower those who look to look differently at the ideas and 'ideals' that shape the feminine in contemporary cultural and social systems, and to expose the symbolic feminine for what it truly is – a freak show.

DAILY LIFE 3
Grown-Up School
LAURIS MORGAN-GRIFFITHS

Reprinted from the *Independent*, 21 June 1999.

Opposite page: *Grown-Up School* (1997). Camden, London. Publicity photograph. Strawberries, cocktail sticks.

Bobby Baker actively seeks odd places for her performances, out of the ordinary spaces where artists don't normally go. She has opened her own house to audiences; performed in Chelsea's Physic Garden; in community halls for Women's Institutes – in the grey nether lands where art is seen as cultural extravagance.

Her latest performance, *Grown-Up School*, is being performed at a fully functioning London primary school, where 37 languages make up the rich colourful mix of an inner-city school. Inhibiting? Definitely. But Baker has no fear that they won't get the message. When she toured *Cook Dems*, *Drawing on a Mother's Experience*, *Kitchen Show* and *How to Shop*, previous audiences got the message loud and clear.

To consign Baker to the ditsy parameters of performance art is to miss the point. The simplicity of her work is not to be confused with it being simplistic. It's powerful, with hard realities being sweetened by humour. As Baker herself observes: 'It allows people, particularly women, to examine their own experiences.' Thus she has explored the creative and meditative aspects of housework, and relived early motherhood when she splattered foodstuffs Jackson Pollock-style on to a sheet. Using treacle for the whirling pits of post-natal depression, with flour settling like the healing power of love over 'the "canvas"', she wrapped the smothered sheet around her, imprinting all those experiences on to herself – and walked off stage.

The response is laughter and sometimes tears with quiet recognition and identification. The battiness sugars the political aspect as she rummages in the vast underbelly of life; by concentrating on the specific she blows the particular into the universal experience. 'I decided very early on, when I was in my early twenties, that I wanted to base my work on my experiences. It was the only way I would have any integrity in what I was saying. Then I just had to hope for the best that it was accessible.'

Grown-Up School is Bobby Baker's fourth in the *Daily Life* quintet commissioned by LIFT – the London International Festival of Theatre. It investigates areas of daily life that are normally taken for granted and 'how larger, more important aspects of life are reflected in the minute and mundane details of our everyday existence'.

In the midst of the chatter and clatter of the school day, 27 members of the audience will gather in the playground, be taken on a tour of the school, see the pupils' view of *Grown-Up School* and then revisit childhood sitting on tiny chairs facing each other at square blocks of desks. Dressed in white overalls, pink, knee-high, lace-up boots, Baker will give the lesson with the help of three school pupil monitors.

It has been the most harrowing and risky project that Baker has undertaken. Examining her childhood and youth from the perspective of middle-aged motherhood has been painful. However, having embarked on the course she is not someone to balk at it. Baker does not hide behind an alter ego when performing. 'It is me – but different versions of me.' Rooted in her 1950s experience, it is as much about how she related to her parents and how she was treated, as about her own childhood. 'It is terribly important how we relate to children because that is where it all starts. It strikes me as bizarre that we take for granted how we treat people. If we dealt with people with more care and attention so many things would not go wrong.'

On to this stage come 'the berries', strawberry stick people. The berries, like ventriloquists' dummies, give Baker the latitude to act vicariously through the squashy, vulnerable beings. The performance is an adventure about what happens to the berries. Within that is a layered, complex examination of life and how children are treated and how we view our childhood which in turn feeds into thoughts about society, life in general, good and evil. It is also funny.

Grown-Up School is a two-pronged project. The school has bent over backwards to accommodate this production. Baker is emphatic that the play is her and her ideas, not the children's. But everyone is very aware of what is happening and what the subject matter is. Baker, her director Polona Baloh Brown and Mark Storer, have run workshops with the children to explore the same topic. The results (some themes reflect Baker's *Grown-Up School*) are documented in a book revealing their thoughts on uniforms, buildings, self-esteem, problems and punishment. '*Grown-Up School* is for children to teach adults what it is to be a child.' A common comment is 'parents need to learn to understand their children more', or 'learn to understand each other'. Out of the mouths of babes and sucklings ...

DAILY LIFE 5
Box Story

This transcript was made by Duncan Barrett from the video recording of a live performance at the Barbican Pit in 2004, now part of the Daily Life Ltd DVD set.

Opposite: *Box Story* (2004). BITE, The Pit, Barbican, London. Assorted foodstuffs, assorted boxes.

AN EMPTY, BLACK *studio space. Two white plinths at either side. A large back-projected screen upstage right on which a choir is visible, sitting in silence.*

A large box emerges gradually into the light from stage left. It is about six feet, by two feet, by two feet in size. Bobby Baker is pushing it along the floor. She wears a brilliant blue overall, and blue high-heeled shoes. She lifts the box with effort – it seems very heavy – and steps awkwardly with it to centre stage.

Audience laughter.

I'm alright.

Audience laughter.

She drops the box upstage centre.

Hello.

(Audience member: Hello.)

I'm going to start, as I always make a very firm point of doing, on every single occasion when I appear in public, by introducing myself.

She draws an awkward breath/nervous laugh.

I do this out of necessity, but also I have to admit with a sort of *obsessive* need to repeat myself. Because, from time to time, mistakes have been made – and people have expected to see a man. *(She laughs; audience laughter.)* And I'd like to make

it absolutely clear, yet again, that I am *(taps her head)* Bobby Baker, and I am... *(gestures to her breasts)* a woman! *(Audience laughter.)* Good! I'm glad we've got that straight.

I shall also add, because it seems to be a topic of such interest these days, with regard to myself and others like me, it's quite often mentioned to my face, it's been written about me, but some of you might not have noticed, so I will explain that I am middle-aged.

She smiles reassuringly at the audience, as though to check they've understood.

Audience laughter.

Okay? I'm fifty-three years and a quarter.

I'm absolutely thrilled to be here in the Pit theatre as a part of BITE. However, before we go any further, I should like to draw your attention to the most important and significant part of the evening. That is – my shoes! *(Audience laughter.)* Don't you think? *(Audience laughter.)* They're absolutely wonderful. They're the most expensive shoes I've ever bought. They cost a hundred and forty nine pounds, fifty pee in New Bond Street – if you should want some. They've got little jewels on them and they sort of sparkle up my ankles – you don't seem very impressed! *(Audience laughter.)* I just think, they sort of reflect everywhere and, I feel – *(Audience laughter.)* Don't you? *(She walks around, showing them off.)* There's something very wonderful about the way I walk, I just feel if I walk round and round and round all evening we'd all be happy.

Audience laughter.

However, I sort of know, intuitively, what's brought you here. The big, big question of the evening: what – is in – the box? Yes? *Are* you interested?

(Audience: Yes.)

Oh phew! *(She laughs.)* Because if you're not you'd better just go now. *Audience laughter.*

Quite seriously though, the issue for me is – should I really open it? *Dare* I open it?

A pause.

But we all know I've got to, so I'd better get on with it.

She walks over to the box.

Erm… I'm not sure…

She taps it.

Oh yes – I've got a pair of scissors. Let's get in there if I can. Tight.

She starts to cut the brown tape which seals the box shut at the near end.

Little shivers of anticipation. Uh-huh… It's quite difficult.

She cuts through the rest of the tape and the box flaps open. She gasps.

Audience laughter.

She opens the end of the box up fully.

And… Oh! *(She laughs.)* I don't know if you can see, but there's hardly anything in there at all. What a disappointment! Never mind, we'll get it out.

She lifts the box from its closed end and tips the contents on the floor. They are a collection of smaller boxes:

A Corn Flakes cereal box;
A box of Bryant & May matches;
A Colman's Mustard Powder box;
A box of Domaine de Larroque white wine;
A box of Rowntrees raspberry jelly cubes;
A box of Ariel Essential washing powder;
A Just Juice orange juice carton;
A box of Tate & Lyle icing sugar;
A Black Magic selection box;
A box of Ginger Thins biscuits.

Is that everything?

She makes sure all the boxes are on the floor, out of the larger box.

Get this out of the way.

She moves the large box so that it lies lengthways across the stage, behind the other boxes.

Just a few boxes. Basically, just a bit of measly – shopping.

She kicks the smaller boxes around, examining them.

It's quite hard to know what you can make of that. Hmm. I know.

She picks up the Corn Flakes packet.

Corn Flakes.

When I was young, which as I've already pointed out was an extraordinarily long time ago – *(Audience laughter.)* My memory is quite hazy, I don't know if you find that, you sort of remember things, well you know things you've been told, but there's huge chunks of time you don't remember, but certain things for some reason stand out, even from very early on, really clearly. I remember that my mother used to take my brother and I shopping every day, in a big old-fashioned double-ended pram – he's two years older than me. She carried on putting us in the pram until we were quite big, I suppose it was convenient to do the shopping because it had a metal tray at the base for the shopping, and she'd trundle us up the road to the high street, do the shopping, stuff it in around us, and then trundle us back again – and we'd kind of jiggle and giggle and play with the shopping, it was great. *(She laughs.)*

Well one day we'd got up to the high street, she went into the grocers and she came out with a packet of Corn Flakes – not dissimilar to this, it has to be said – but before she put it in the pram she showed us on the back these big black letters, which we couldn't read – it said 'Funny Faces', and underneath there was a pair of glasses with dotted lines round to show that you could cut them out, and make yourself look funny. *(She laughs.)* Well, it just captured my imagination, and I started to make funny faces – and do you know, they loved it, they laughed, they laughed, even my mother was amused, and my brother was hysterical, and before long we had a little group of shoppers around us, laughing at *me*! I felt – oh, I felt so important! We went back home, and my mum rushed into the house to get the camera and then she posed us – I've still got the photo – of me holding up the box

and going – *(Makes an odd face)* – like that. *(Audience laughter.)* And then I suppose she must have taken the camera back into the house to be safe, because I distinctly remember being on our own, and I suppose the excitement of all the attention *(laughs)* went to my head – oh! – because I'd got this brilliant idea, and I took the Corn Flake packet, and I opened it – *(An embarrassed gasp; she opens the box of Corn Flakes)* – and my brother, gosh, he was so shocked at my naughtiness – I found it quite difficult with my stubby little fingers, but eventually – it was greaseproof paper in those days, this is foil – eventually I got in there, ate a few corn flakes… *(She does so, enthusiastically.)* But then I got the best idea ever. I took the whole box – *(She inverts it, the Corn Flakes fall out; Audience laughter.)* – and I tipped it onto the front garden path.
Choir sings:
Oh Bobby. Oh Bobby, Bobby.
Bobby laughs.
Silly me.
She stands the Corn Flake box up on the stage right end of the larger box.
I don't know why, but I just get an irresistible urge – to walk on it.
She walks on the Corn Flakes.
Audience laughter.
I really recommend it.
Audience laughter.
Especially in these shoes.
Audience laughter.
But I know, you're probably all finding it quite difficult to concentrate on the story, with the beauty of me in these shoes on.
Audience laughter.
Well I have to admit that they don't come naturally to me and they're actually killing me. *(Audience laughter.)* So, I'm going to take them off, put them up on these boxes, so you can continue to admire them.
She removes the shoes and places them on the two white plinths.
Oh, what a relief! This is me.
Now, this might not be, strictly speaking, historically or geographically correct – but here we have the start of our map. Here – *(the mound of Corn Flakes on the floor)* – we have *land*.
She goes and picks up the matchbox.
Bryant and May matches. I had a passion for matches when I was young, like most children I think.

I used to pinch them from next to the cooker. I'd hide them in my shorts pocket and then I'd go out to this little hiding place I had in the side passage, and I'd take out the box *(nervous laugh)* and I'd take out one match at a time, and light it – *(She does so)* – and then I'd flick it out – *(Does so)* – and then I'd – *(She does)* – put it on my tongue. You ought to try it, you get a little zzztt. *(She laughs.)* Very satisfying. *(Audience laughter.)* And then I'd eat the end of the match. *(She does so.)* It's disgusting, but I thought they were delicious. *(Audience laughter.)* I used to work my way through a whole box at one go. It must be, must have been some sort of nineteen fifties deficiency in my diet.
Audience laughter.
Anyway, my brother and his gang, the big boys, they had a passion for matches too, but they used them – they used to pinch them, buy them, that sort of thing – they'd tie them into little bundles and make them into bombs. My brother actually put one in the boiler, and blew it up.
Audience laughter.
Well one day – I was a sort of honorary member of the gang – one day we decided to make the Biggest Bomb Ever. It was really exciting, we all went off to different places to get matches and eventually we got together, and we had enough to make a bundle *that* big. *(She gestures with her hands, about the size of a basketball).* We tied it up with string, somebody made a rudimentary fuse, and then we looked around for somewhere to set it off – and I remembered there was a stone in the middle of the lawn that my mum used for the washing line stick, it was a sort of strange triangular stone with a kind of groove in it. She used to kick the stick into place every time she hung the washing up. Well, we got rid of the stick, and we put the bomb on it, and we all went to the edge of the lawn, and then the bravest boy went and lit the fuse. And it went zzzz and then out. *(She laughs.)*
This went on for hours – sort of terror, and then nothing. But finally some clever person made a new fuse and there was a zzzzzzzzzz and booom! Incredible explosion, I mean literally flames right up into the sky, oooh! Sort of scary and exciting. Well when the flames had died down we went to have a look – and we saw, to our horror, that the stone on which the matches were resting was black and charred and cracked into three pieces. We knew we were in big, big trouble. My

mum was really scary.

Choir:

Bobby! Bobby!

Oh Bobby, Bobby, what were you thinking of?

Bobby! Bobby, Bobby, Bobby! What were you thinking of?

Oh Bobby, Bobby!

As the choir sing, Bobby cowers at stage left, hiding her face from them and shaking her head. Then she moves back to the centre.

Here we have one tiny seed falling onto the land. *(She drops a match onto the pile of Corn Flakes.)* And I think we'll have a whole shower of seeds – *(She throws the rest of the packet down)* – waiting to grow.

She places the empty matchbox on the larger box at the back, next to the Corn Flakes box. Then she picks the next box up off the floor and reads the label.

Colman's – of Norwich!

She places the Colman's Mustard box next to her shoe on the stage-right plinth.

When I was young, I was very lucky, well we were lucky as a family because we always used to go on holiday to the same village in Norfolk, called Brancaster – I don't know if anybody's been there, it's a wonderful place – magical! We particularly, well the excitement and the build-up to these holidays was enormous. We knew where we were going because we always went to the same cottage – my parents must have booked it from year to year – and part of the package was you got a beach hut, in the sand dunes. Well, I'll describe the geography of the village – it was like – *(She gestures with her hands)* – village, cottages, trees, church, that sort of thing. And then there's this amazing salt marsh – when the tide's in it floods it, but there's a raised road you can drive across. Then there's a golf course, with a golf club. And then there's sand dunes with all the beach huts, dotted in around it. And then the tide – it's a very sandy beach – the tide goes out for miles at low tide. But every day was the same. We used to go down to the beach. We'd stop at the village shop, and my mum would buy a loaf of sliced white bread and some sausages. And then we'd go down to the beach – and we'd either go swimming, or we'd play golf, or we'd play in the sand dunes. But then at lunch-time she'd get out this old-fashioned sort of Primus stove, it was called, a little cooking stove and she'd fry up the sausages. You used to get a slice of white bread, with the sausage on it,

and then whether you liked it or not she always put mustard dabbed along it, and then you rolled it up and ate it, piping hot. It was gorgeous, it was quite good because it was always freezing cold, the weather.

Audience laughter.

Well the year that I was fifteen was particularly exciting because I'd taken my 'O' levels a year early, and we were waiting for my 'O' level results. My family had decided I was a bit thick, so they weren't expecting much, but I had a sneaking suspicion that I might surprise them. So it was absolutely amazing when the results came in the post – not only had I passed them all, I'd done extremely well. There was general rejoicing, and amazement. *(Audience laughter)*. But my dad wasn't there – he'd got up early before the post came to go to the nearest town, Hunstanton, to do some shopping, go to the bank. And every three weeks he used to get his head, his hair cut, sort of shaved up the back so it was all stubbly when you stroked it. So we went up to the beach, the tide was in, quite rough, we all went swimming, it was really good fun – and then I went and stood on the sand dunes waiting for him. I waited and I waited because I was so longing to tell him the news.

Well eventually I saw him walking across the golf course and I *ran* over to him, and I told him, and I'll never forget he sort of went 'Oh!' *(She makes an expression of great surprise and takes a step backwards; audience laughs)* – like that, and then he came and gave me this huge hug, and it was just the best moment in my life. Well I said 'Are you coming to have lunch? Mum's just cooking the sausages' and he said 'No I think I'll just have a quick swim, while the tide's still in. I'll just go and put my bim-bags on,' which is what he always called his swimming trunks – and he went off across the sand dunes, they were sort of quite high, you couldn't see the beach from the beach huts. We all sat down around the beach hut eating our sausages, when suddenly we heard this strange noise. It got louder and louder – and then we saw, on top of the sand dunes, a woman, screaming 'Help! Help! Help! A man's been washed out to sea.' And in that moment my mother leapt off her stool and cried 'My husband! My husband!'

Well, my father never came back to eat his sausages. He was drowned.

She goes to retrieve the box of mustard.

(Quietly.) I think I'm going to need scissors for this. I'm

going to – it's quite difficult to get into this mustard. And – I'm going to put this in, as a tiny desert island, all on its own.

She pours the powdered mustard to form a mound, separated from the main pile of Corn Flakes and matches by a foot or so. Then she places the mustard box next in line on the large box at the back of the stage.

When I was twenty-one, my mother, poor woman, felt it was her duty and responsibility to give me a twenty-first birthday party. Well she wasn't very keen, because we lived in Bromley – I don't know if anybody knows that place – but I went to art school by that stage in the centre of London, and she didn't like my rowdy art school friends, but she knew she'd have to invite them to the party. *(She laughs.)* So she decided to have the party in two sections – there would be a drinks party for family and friends, and then other friends – or my art school friends – could arrive later. Well we went to a lot of trouble to get the house ready, we moved all the furniture back against the walls, and moved some of it out into the garden, and my mother went round very, very carefully, collecting all the china ornaments, including an amazing collection of pottery we'd just inherited from my great-aunt who was an archaeologist. And she put it all on the Welsh dresser in the dining room, on the shelves, for safety out of the way.

Well I had a special outfit. I got it from Etams – do you remember? I just thought it was amazing – it was this colour, nylon, so it was shiny. It had big floppy lapels which were fashionable then, with white piping around them. Then it had a kind of bare midriff, and then a white plastic belt, and a skirt that was about that long. *(She gestures – less than a foot; audience laughter.)* Which caused a bit of a stir – which was the point. And then to finish it off, I had these knee-high, silver platform boots. *(Audience laughter.)* Well I thought I looked fabulous.

I don't remember much from the first bit of the party, the speech was kind of a blur, it was really boring, drab – but then the fun began when my friends, my real friends, arrived later. And the drinking started. *(She laughs.)* Oh, there was loads and loads of bottles of Spanish white wine, lined up in the dining room, two litre bottles, and there was a lot of drinking – *(Laughs)* – mostly by me. *(An embarrassed laugh.)* Now since I haven't got a bottle, but I've got this boxed

wine, I don't know if anybody's discovered this stuff, it's fabulous. I've got a party trick – what you do is you put it on your head – *(She does so.)* – and you go…

She pours the wine into her mouth from on top of her head.

Audience laughter.

Shall I show you?

She turns, so the audience can see it in profile.

Oh, it's such good fun. It goes right down your front! It's hysterical. Ah! Whooh!

It was just a wild party. There was all this crashing around in the bushes in the garden, I can't remember a lot of it. So I remember very, very late in the evening – must have been, because there didn't seem to be many people around any more – I suppose they'd gone to get the last train home – and I was sort of standing next to the dresser just propped up against the wall, chatting to someone on my right, when I just sort of went like that – *(She drops to the side slightly)* – barely stumbled, and hardly touched the dresser – *(Audience laughter)* – but I looked round, and the whole thing swayed out of the wall. And all the china fell crashing onto the floor. And then it swayed back again. I looked with horror at this scene of devastation. But there were a few bits that weren't broken – and then I noticed a big china bowl, bouncing around and breaking every single thing *(Audience laughter)* that wasn't already broken.

Choir:

Bobby you silly girl.
Silly, silly girl.
What a calamity.
What a catastrophe.
A complete disaster.
A complete disaster.
Calamity!
Catastrophe!
Calamity!
Catastrophe!
A complete disaster!

While they sing, Bobby drinks more, looks embarrassed and then walks around in a circle, pouring the wine onto the floor, around the piles of Corn Flakes and Mustard Powder. She puts the box next in line at the back.

It's the sea! It's the oceans. The water has arrived at last.

I'd better just explain – it's terribly slippery up here

now, and I might just fall flat on my back. If I do, could you pretend you haven't noticed?

Audience laughter.

Great.

She takes the next box and puts it on the plinth at stage left.

When I left art school, I got a job teaching crafts in an adult education institute in Wandsworth. There were two problems about this – the first was I couldn't teach, and the second was I knew nothing about crafts. *(Audience laughter.)* I wasn't even interested in them. But it was a great opportunity for employment, so I applied myself to the – I'd got some books, I learnt basic candle-making, paper sculpture and leathercraft, but not very well. And the real problem arose when I tried to communicate these basic skills to my students. I – I just couldn't. *(Laughs.)* So what was so bizarre – people used to come back week after week. And they'd sit down and they'd say 'Make us a purse, Bobby', 'Make us a candle', whatever they wanted, and I'd get on and make them while we all chatted. Weird. But the bit I really liked was clearing up at the end of the class.

But this institute was amazing, because every summer it had workshops throughout the holidays for families, culminating in a big festival. And in my first year they put me in charge of the food – which was much more up my street, even then. *(Audience laughter.)* And I had so many plans, so many ideas, I was so excited. I stayed up night after night getting things ready, I mean I had helpers but – one of the things I did was make toffee apples, I've never done them before, made them in a domestic science room, and I used these sticks from a garden centre, the green ones. When I tried an apple I discovered the green dye had impregnated the apple. I had to throw them all away. But never mind. My *pièce de résistance* was the jelly worlds. I got three sand and water trays from the nursery, you know those ones on legs? I scrubbed them out meticulously. And then I made pots and pots and pots and buckets and everything of jelly and blancmange. It was all ready. And then on the day I sent them. There were three lots. All the food was down one side of the playground, with the worlds here. *(She gestures.)* There was a sea, a desert and a garden, and there was amazing attention to detail, although I say it myself. There were little sort of blancmange islands floating in the sea, with tiny

people and trees on them, and I was so thrilled.

Well everything was ready. Nobody, no one, no children in the playground because they'd all gone on a parade round the local streets to start up, in fancy dress. We had all the food ready, the helpers, the bowls and spoons for the jellies, and we waited. And we could hear them in the distance. And then they came in through the gates. Ah, the excitement!

I'd always imagined this orderly queue of children forming down the side of the playground, and I would lead them one by one past the worlds and they could select the bit they most wanted. I've never established what went wrong. *(Audience laughter.)* But it was just unbelievable. Suddenly this screaming horde of children came running towards me going 'Jelly! Jelly! Jelly!' And before we could stop them, they'd got in behind me, sort of pushed me away, and they started just digging their hands in. Like mad! I mean just wild, stuffing it in their mouths and laughing. And throwing it – it went all over the playground! I tried to get in there and stop them and I went wooeeeh, plonk, flat on my back. It was chaos. It was terrible, terrible mess. It was a complete and utter disaster.

The choir sing a wordless lament. Bobby removes the cubes of jelly and sets the box in its place at the back. She breaks the cubes apart and places or spits them into place on the two piles on the floor.

It's obvious, isn't it? It's the mountains. It's the glaciers. And over here – *(the small mustard island)* – this is the correct geographical term – we have an angry little volcano waiting to erupt. Actually you do get mountains under the sea apparently.

She picks up the Ariel washing powder box and places it on the stage-right plinth.

At about that time I lived in a squat in Anerley, which is a suburb of South London. I don't know how we ended up there, how we found this building, or *why* we selected it, because it was in the middle of a deserted high street, but we picked an empty butcher's shop! It was revolting. Really – the basement was flooded, it had kind of mushrooms growing up from the basement up the stairs. Oh! And the butcher's shop itself was all kind of blood-stained with great hooks hanging from the ceiling, it was sinister.

But we established one electric power source halfway up the stairs, and then we ran wires into the various rooms – incredibly dangerous – but we knew not to risk it by taking them right up to the top floor, where my bedroom and studio were. Bit of a drag, but there you go.

There's a terrible, terrible, terrible day, when I'd had a really – ugh – awful row with my boyfriend, I was very upset, so I decided to go to bed early to read, to take my mind off it. I took my little candlestick up with me, it was sort of one of those little flat plate things with a candle holder in the middle, a little thing. Carried it upstairs, put it on the bed, and then I lay across the bed to read – which is what happens when I do that, I almost go to sleep, I didn't sort of think. I don't know how long I was asleep for, but I suddenly woke up to this terrible – I can only really describe it as an experience – the whole bed was alight in front of me, just flames leaping up, and I suddenly realised that I was on fire, I was banging at my fringe, and my clothes, sort of rolling on the floor. And then I thought – oh, yeah, I got the bed-clothes and I folded them over the flames, ran round the bed, and it went out. But just to be sure I ran down to the kitchen, got a bucket of water, and threw it onto the bed. Oh! And I must have been in a state of shock, because it never occurred to me to tell anyone, or get help. I just wanted to go to sleep – and then I remembered I had a sleeping bag in my studio next door. So I went in to there, took off my burnt clothes, climbed into the sleeping bag and went to sleep on the floor.

When I woke up the next morning I couldn't work out what was going on. Why I was there on this dirty dusty floor, the sun streaming through the window. And then it all came back to me. I thought 'Oh god, I'm so lucky to be alive.' I was just sort of celebrating that fact, when I noticed a really strange sensation all over my body. I wondered if it was the burning, then I thought 'No, it's cat fleas' – it was a sort of itching, crawling. And I – I literally only just sort of scratched once, but I was on fire with itching. I was just rolling around on the floor, scratching, scratching, scratching, I've never experienced anything like it. Oh! Finally, I got out of the sleeping bag, and I looked down at my naked body. Oh, it was revolting! I was covered in these sort of huge, swollen, red weals where I'd scratched. Well, it took a visit to the doctor to establish that I had had a major allergic reaction – to the Ariel washing powder that I'd washed the sleeping bag in. And it was several days, and many, many cold baths, before the itching and the swelling died down.

She turns to the choir. They sing.

Choir:
Ariel Essential. Ariel Essential. Ariel Essential.
Automatic washing powder.
Ariel Essential.
Ariel Essential.
With biological action.
Enzymes.
Brightening agent.
Polycarboxylate.
Nonionic and cationic surfactants.
Oxygen-based bleaching agent.
Zeolites.
Bobby gets the box of Ariel washing powder.
Very, very late in the day, I think you'll agree, we have the ozone layer.
Audience laughter.
She pours the Ariel powder in a ring around the outside of the 'world'.
Getting sort of snug in there. I'm a bit anxious whether it's going to go around. Is there enough? Oh yup, we're okay. What a relief. *(Audience laughter.)* All snug in there.
She puts the box in its place.
Do you know I can't resist this?
She uses her foot to carve a line through the ring of washing powder.
Audience laughter.
A hole.
She does it again.
Two holes in.
Audience laughter.
I took an enormous amount of interest in my appearance in those days. I don't now I'm middle-aged. Only joking! *(Audience laughter.)* But I'd had the same hairstyle for years and years and years, it was really boring. From the kind of mid-sixties I had this sort of dead straight fringe, and long straight hair like that – *(She gestures.)* – I didn't know what to do about it. But then, one day, I saw in a magazine a photograph, and I just knew it was me. It was this woman who obviously had straight hair because the roots were straight, but then she had a halo of gentle curls round her face. And I thought 'Yes! I'll get a perm.'

So I went up to the high street. I'd never been to the hairdressers there. And there was this hairdresser, I swear, called Maison Gladys. I went in and I described what I wanted and she said – 'No problem.'

And so I booked an appointment for a couple of days later. I could barely wait for the excitement and, you know, my transformation. *(She laughs.)* When I went back she led me in – quite a young assistant, hairstylist – took me in, sat me down next to this trolley, with kind of pink sticks on it, and she took carefully one clump of hair at a time, wound it round the pink stick, put a bit of elastic on it – and she worked her way carefully round my head, in a sort of ring, like a kind of monk's tonsure of curlers. They were really stuck to my head, and I said 'Won't the curls be a bit tight?' and she said 'Oh no, we've got the blow-dryer for that,' and then I said 'But what about these bits?' because she'd left this whole section just hanging down over the top, sort of like the upside down petals of a tulip. I said 'What about them?' and she said 'I've got a plan for that later.' Well of course I entirely trusted her. She put a kind of noxious fluid on the curlers and a bag thing on my head. She told me I had to wait something like twenty minutes, half an hour, it was unbearable – so while I was waiting I just thought: go next door to the newsagent, with the bag on my head. Everybody stared, but I knew I'd swan in there in half an hour's time – whoooh – and impress them.

I got myself one of these box drinks that hadn't been out long – orange juice. And while I waited I sort of fantasised about my new appearance and sipped my drink. *(She drinks some of the Just Juice.)* Eventually, she came back, and she took out the curlers. I couldn't believe my eyes. The curls were sort of really stuck to my head, like sort of bum fluff. They were revolting. And I said 'But what about these bits?' She said 'I'm just dealing with that,' and she got a pair of scissors and just chopped, chopped it off. Honestly! And I just couldn't believe what it looked like. And ever so strange and I think peculiarly British – it never occurred to me to complain. *(Audience laughter.)* I even paid her! *(Audience laughter.)* By the time I got home I was square-mouthed with crying.

She walks over to the map.

Now, we're going to have the weather. Just a few drops of rain falling on the seeds, so they can grow. *(She pours a little orange juice out gently.)* But actually, I think what we'll have is extensive flooding – *(She squeezes the rest out of the carton quickly.)* – all in one place, and throughout, everywhere else. Ooh yeah, a little torrent. Oh,

disaster. Ooh, coming out, yeah that's right, that's the way of the world. *(Squeezing the last drops out of the carton.)*

I had, I have to admit, a kind of obsession with sugar, when I was in my twenties. I kind of started out quite small, I used to make little cakes, models of things. But then I made loads and loads of meringue women. I used to dress up like them. *(Audience laughter.)* Then I think I moved on to life-sized babies on meat platters. *(Audience laughter.)* Really caused a stir! *(Audience laughter.)* Then full-sized adults, lying on mattresses, but then I moved to a prefab in Stepney, and after I'd been there for a while I opened it to the public, and I called it 'An Edible Family in a Mobile Home'. I made a life-sized family of five out of cake, meringue, biscuits, that sort of thing. But – oh – I shouldn't say this, it was amazing – I covered all the ceilings, the walls, the floors, the furniture, the curtains, absolutely everything with newsprint, and then I piped sugar all over it, so it sort of presented this sugar bower of family life. It was just wonderful, because sugar kind of glimmers in the light, it was amazing. And then the public came and ate the family up, and it was terrible. *(She laughs; audience laughter.)* Then I – oh, I did all sorts of things – I know, I made a history of modern art out of sugar. I selected what I thought were the eighteen most significant works of art, and I copied them very, very meticulously onto these boards. I had quite a professional technique by these days. I used to mix up my stock of sugar in the morning, and then I'd mix it throughout the day with professional food colourings, I had all these little spatulas as my tools and I'd dab the sugar on carefully so that it was just right. But there were lots of techniques I'd learnt, by that stage. There's one amazing one which I did for hard-edge piping, you run out the sugar very liquid and when it dries it's just beautifully smooth and crispy. Oh!

Then they were eventually exhibited in the Louvre in Paris, and when they came back they were all licked. *(Audience laughter.)* How French! *(Audience laughter.)* I sort of adored the whole thing and I used to think I was entirely sugar because every time I touched the sugar I'd get a little bit on my hands or on the spatula, I used to suck my fingers – so that my teeth were permanently coated in a layer of sugar. I used to think, well because when you sieve sugar you get a kind of fine mist of it settles all over you. I used to think I was sugar on the outside, and sugar on the inside. I mean, so stupid! *(Audience laughter.)* Reality caught up with me. My teeth just got steadily worse, even though I brushed them – and finally the dentist said that unless I had extensive structural work done I would lose them, all. So in one six-month period, I went to the dentist seventeen times, each time for about three hours. It was very, very traumatic, very, very painful, and very, very expensive. Needless to say, I have not worked with sugar since then.

She picks the Tate & Lyle box up off the floor.

Until now! I just can't resist it.

Choir:

Sugar… (Repeated.)

Meanwhile, Bobby opens the icing sugar, tastes it on her finger, drops a pinch or two into her mouth and then throws a few handfuls over herself. Then she throws out the rest of it over the two islands, finally eating a bit more of it and setting the box in its place. She shakes the sugar out of her hair.

It's the ice age! It's the snow.

I did none of my own work when my children were small, I got another sort of job actually that was a bit more lucrative. But eventually the sort of pressure built up and I did a show about the first eight years, called 'Drawing on a Mother's Experience'. It proved to be a bit of a hit, and I started touring extensively, here and abroad. But I had lots of ideas brewing away, so I was very excited when I was invited by the Institute of Contemporary Arts to do a new piece for a showcase evening. They wanted something that lasted about ten minutes, and I'd had this idea for a while that I was really, you know thought was wonderful, that was called 'Chocolate Money'. Very, very serious, it was all about greed and lust. And the central image was to – well, I thought that if somebody was greedy they'd collect all this chocolate, you see, like chocolate coins and chocolate, put them all on a chair as a sort of bank, and then they'd sit on it to hide it from people, okay? And then when they stood up it would have all melted on their bottom. *(Audience laughter.)* In the right place. *(She gestures; audience laughter.)* But, it didn't work. I was obviously not hot enough. *(Audience laughter.)* But I wasn't put off, I went to a camping shop and I got those pocket warmers, and I stuffed them in my knickers, sat on the chocolate – imagine it was sort of chat, chat, chat, chat, chat – and yes, there was this huge blob of chocolate, just there. Well,

it went down a storm at the ICA – and word spread, very quickly. A couple of days later I was phoned up by a big festival in Glasgow called Mayfest, and they said could I turn this ten-minute show into an hour-long piece? *(Audience laughter.)* So of course I said yes. *(Audience laughter.)* I don't know why, I've never worked out why, but for some reason I decided to make it into a musical. *(Audience laughter.)* Which is particularly strange because I'm not known for my musical gifts. But I made up all the music myself, sang it myself and my – oh my favourite bit was me singing 'Chocolate' in eight different languages. It seemed to sound quite similar. Chocolate, choco-

The Choir interrupts.

Choir:

Chocolate.

Chocolat.

Chocolada.

Shokoletha.

Chocolatto.

Shocoloide.

Shokolada

and chocolate.

As they sing, Bobby waves at them enthusiastically, like a conductor. Then she gestures, in time with the video, for them to sit, rise and sit again.

Actually, you've probably gathered that mine was nothing like that. And I did have a very kind of sinking feeling that the show wasn't quite – quite right. I'd only managed to make it thirty-five minutes long, after a lot of work. But I had the booking and I had to go off as optimistically as I could to Glasgow.

My doubts were proved to be correct. I seem to remember that most of the audience walked out. *(Audience laughter.)* There's a terrible moment, when you're in the dressing room, especially when you're touring on your own, when you know that you've got to go out and face people, especially in the bar. But I went out, as bravely as I could, and, being Britain, nobody mentioned what had happened. *(Audience laughter.)* It was a great relief, we were all sort of drinking, chatting, about other things – when suddenly this young man came up and tapped me on the shoulder, and he said 'You're Bobby Baker aren't you?' and I went 'Yes', and he said 'I'm with a group of my friends over there. We're medical students. Would you come and join us? We're *really* interested in you.' So of course I was really pleased, and he bought me a drink, and I went over and sat down with them. They proceeded to ask me lots of questions about myself, my life and my work, and I was sort of chatting away, when there was this strange kind of – *(Coughs twice.)* – from the first man, and they all looked at each other with a little grin and he said 'Well, we just wanted to know more about you, before we told you that that was the worst show we have ever seen in all our lives.'

Audience laughter.

She picks up the Black Magic chocolates from the floor.

Now, absolutely wonderful, I've got a whole box of Black Magic. Whooh! I just adore it, when you open the chocolates, I don't know if anybody else has noticed this, you get a little – *(She sniffs them.)* – Ooh! Hmm.

She offers the box to some of the audience seated in the front row, then snatches it back again.

Audience laughter.

I was only teasing.

She does the same with the Choir. One of the choristers reaches out, but Bobby again withdraws the chocolates.

They are – all for me.

In here we have lots of chocolates – and for our map, lots and lots of people. And lots and lots of trouble. So, where shall we start? I think we'll have someone drowning. You see? *(She puts one chocolate down.)* Shall we have someone washed up on a desert island? *(Tosses another down.)* Ooh, yes. Now I think lost in space. *(Another chocolate, and so on.)* Um, I know, we'll have a mother and daughter who don't get on. Let's have a plane full of tourists falling from the sky into the Red Sea, um, oh I know, sort of sketching it in, we'll have a group of children being shot on the streets by soldiers, we'll have a couple of suicide bombers, a bit of murder, bit of rape – serial – a bit of incest, so we've got all the – Oh! Hang on, there's another tray… *(Audience laughter)* just put it in as war, plague, pestilence and famine.

She tips the remaining chocolates in and places the box in its place at the back.

Several years ago, my husband, who's a photographer, moved his studio into our house – you know, up the road in Holloway. And we didn't have quite enough room, so I had to sort things out and get rid of things. But I had to establish a new storage system, which I'm very addicted to. And I decided to get some new cupboards from IKEA, which is – well it *was* my favourite shop. I'm not so sure now. But it – you know the thing about going to IKEA – you can never get everything in one go. So you have to go back, again and again, to get all the bits.

Well one day I decided to go and see if some hinges were in stock, and I asked my son, who was about twelve at the time, whether he'd like to come with me. And he was excited because he loved IKEA too, so off we went. When we got there, no hinges, but we weren't worried. I bought a stock of these – I don't know if anybody's tried them – Anna's Ginger Thins. You used to be only able to get them from IKEA, now you can get them from other places. Just gorgeous! I bought Swedish meatballs, hot dogs, that sort of thing. And then my son had disappeared on his own, so I kind of wandered around just thinking 'Oh, I might have that, I might have that', you know, fantasising.

Eventually I decided we had to go home, so I looked everywhere for my son. Then I saw him, talking to some shop assistants. I called him, and he saw me, and he came rushing over and he went 'Mum! Mum! Look what they said I can have.' He led me over there, and he showed me this extraordinary object. It was about twelve foot high, bright yellow, made of cardboard. It was like a rocket, it had a kind of thing at the bottom to make it stand up – it was a giant cardboard display pencil. *(Audience laughter.)*

So I said 'Fine.' We took it to the car, the trouble was – no matter how hard we tried, every way we put it in the car it stuck massively out of the back. So I had to say 'Look I'm really sorry, it's dangerous, we're going to have to leave it behind.' He seemed okay about it, but all the way home he sat next to me and quietly sobbed. *(Audience laughter.)* I said 'Why did you want it?' and he said 'I have never wanted anything so much in all my life.' *(Audience laughter.)* I said 'Why?' And he said 'Because it would look so wicked in my bedroom.' *(Audience laughter.)* Well when we got home I felt really sorry for him, and so did my husband, and then I thought 'I know', my husband's car had a roof rack, so I'd just go back, I told my son, he was really excited – we rushed to get there before the shop shut, we didn't even put our coats on.

When we got to IKEA, we discovered that the giant cardboard display pencil had been put through the crusher. (Audience: Ahhh.) Well, that's life. So, we went home. *(Audience laughter.)* A sort of terrible atmosphere of gloom in the car. We got about half way round, we were pulled up behind another car at the lights – *(She mimes the car with the biscuit box.)* – on the North Circular, and I was thinking what can I do to cheer us up, and then I thought – music. And just at that moment the car in front of me pulled away, the lights changed, I was following him, and I literally only took my eyes off the road for a second, and in that second this car stopped and I went 'crash' into the back, really hard. I jumped out and I saw what had happened – this little elderly lady had tried to turn right and the car had stalled, and he'd stopped, and I'd pushed him so hard he crushed the side of her car, pinning her against the steering wheel, she was screaming, it was awful. His car was written off, he was furious. My husband's car was smashed in, my son was distraught – it was awful! Well I just gave up. I just sat quietly down by the side of the road and wept. And when anyone came up to me, including the police, I just said 'It's all my fault. Everything is all my fault.'

She opens the box of Ginger Thins and removes the biscuits, still wrapped in a plastic covering. She places the empty box in its place at the back.

Now – I'm just going to – *(She starts crushing the biscuits through the plastic.)* This is really enjoyable. *(Audience laughter.)* Smashing these up. Quite hard. Just imagine – how many millions and billions of particles and fragments are in here. Just trillions. Because we need them, for the map. That's it. Strong hands.

She gets her scissors out and cuts through the plastic.

Now I'm going to put this in, as all the human artefacts. So what shall we have? *(She throws down the crumbled Ginger Thins.)* Books, some mobile phones, some cars, some buses, some theatres, boxes, food, guns and bombs and tanks and toys and chairs and houses and *(throwing down the last of the crumbs)* absolutely everything. You name it, we've got it. *(Audience laughter.)*

She stands aside and looks at the map, horrified.
What a terrible, terrible mess.
She walks around to see it from a different angle.
What a – what a waste.
She walks further away, treading white footprints

behind her, and looks at it again, from a greater distance.

What a complete and utter disaster.
She leaves the stage. After a moment the choir stand and sing.

Choir:
Kelloggs Corn Flakes.
Wake up to the sunshine breakfast
Toasted flakes of corn.
Toasted flakes of corn.
Suitable for vegetarians.
Toasted flakes of corn.
Kellogg's Corn Flakes.
Wake up to a sunshine breakfast.
Toasted flakes of corn.
Toasted flakes of corn.
Toasted flakes of corn.
With extra folic acid.
Toasted flakes of corn.
Folic acid.
Because you are what you eat.
Because you are what you eat.
Ahh.
Some settling of contents may have occurred during transit.

As they sing, Bobby returns with a broom and sweeps the various elements of the map into a pile in the centre.

Choir:
Bryant and May
Cooks long matches.
Keep away from children.
Strike gently and away from the body.
Keep away from children.
As they continue to sing, Bobby uses a dustpan and brush to sweep up the mess on the floor, and throws it into the large box.
Bryant and May.
Cooks long matches.
Keep away from children.
Strike gently and away from the body.
Keep away from children.
This box of long matches
Has been designed to safely reach
Those awkward places
In the kitchen and the home
Such as the gas oven.
The gas oven.

Bryant and May.
Bryant and May.
Cooks long matches.
Cooks long matches.
Keep away from children.
Strike away from the body.
Keep away from children.

Bobby takes the smaller boxes from the top of the large box and places them inside it too. Finally, she sits and then crawls into the box herself. The choir continue to sing. Bobby closes the end flaps and seals herself in the large box.

Choir:
Colman's Double Mustard Superfine Compound.
Colman's Double Mustard Superfine Compound.
Colman's Double Mustard Superfine Compound.
Colman's Double Mustard Superfine Compound.
(Repeats, underneath.)
Established in Eighteen Fourteen.
Colman's Double Mustard Superfine Compound.
By appointment to Her Majesty the Queen.
Colman's of Norwich.
Colman's of Norwich.
Established in Eighteen Fourteen.
By appointment to Her Majesty the Queen.
Colman's of Norwich.
Colman's of Norwich.
To serve as a simple condiment with food.
As a simple condiment.
Only cold water should be used.
The water acts as catalyst
That helps yield the essential oil of mustard.
A pinch or two of dry mustard will perk up a vinaigrette dressing.
A vinaigrette dressing.
Colman's of Norwich.
Colman's of Norwich.
Colman's of Norwich.
Colman's of Norwich.

One of the choristers sings a wordless wail.

After some time a noise is heard and the box shakes. It is the sound of Bobby cutting through the box with a handsaw. The noise continues, intermittently, as the choir continue to sing.

Choir:
Vin de Pays de Cotes de Gasgogne.
Full flavoured dry white wine.
Keeps for six weeks after opening.

Rowntrees jelly.
Raspberry flavour.
Get set go!
Get set go!
Just Juice
One hundred percent
Pure orange juice.
No gunk, no junk.
No gunk, no junk.
Pierce here with straw.
Chill and shake well before use.

Bobby cuts a hole through the front of the box, then another, then a third. Her face is visible through the final hole. She manoeuvres her head and arms through the three holes and stands, with her arms spread out, exultant. The audience applauds. She dances round in one direction, then the other, performing a kind of ceremonial dance around the space, waving her arms as the choir continue to sing. Finally, she dances off into the darkness from which she came.

The choir finish their song.

Choir:
Ariel Essential.
Proctor and Gamble.
Ariel Essential.
Automatic washing powder.
With biological action.
Tate and Lyle icing sugar.
From pure cane sugar.
For all types of cake.
Icing, decoration, dusting.
Nestlé Black Magic.
An intriguing collection of rich dark chocolates.
Assorted chocolates.
Plain chocolates.
Assorted chocolates.
An intriguing collection of rich dark chocolates.
All sweets may contain nut traces.
Anna's Ginger Thins.
Ginger Thins.
Baked in Sweden.
Traditional ginger flavoured biscuits.

Opposite: *Box Story* (2004). BITE,
The Pit, Barbican, London.
Assorted foodstuffs, assorted boxes.

DAILY LIFE 5
Box Story MICHÈLE BARRETT

BOX STORY TAKES up some of the familiar themes of Baker's work in a conclusion that contains more openly tragic material than the earlier shows in the *Daily Life* series. All the performances are funny, of course, but this one has an emotional shock at its centre: her father's death in a drowning accident on a family holiday. Although this is dealt with 'lightly' in the show, the effects are clear to see. Drowning becomes one of the disasters invoked towards the end of the performance, along with plague, chaos, war and incest, and it is represented in Baker's 'drawing' during the performance as a solitary island. This shocking death, and its destructive long-term consequences, cannot be accommodated within the main framework of the depiction of a life.

Box Story links this experience to an awareness of the slow development and recognition of profound suffering. Baker's characteristic embarrassment with her audience, the trademark experience of the mess that she inflicts on herself, are seen in this show to follow from her father's death – she describes how she subsequently gets drunk and breaks things, gets into art and damages herself. There is an exploration of an abject lack of self-esteem in her years as a young adult, very different in tone from the cheeky child invoked at the beginning of this story. The culmination of the disasters is global in scale and – not surprisingly from an artist who thinks in terms of the meaning

of food – is represented by Black Magic chocolates.

Box Story, however, offers us an optimistic, indeed redemptive, look beyond death. As ever in Baker's work, the domestic activity of cleaning up has a restorative, therapeutic character – the ills and pestilences are physically swept up and swept away, opening the path to a statement of optimism and faith. This secular form of redemption figures in many of Baker's performances, often expressed through upbeat music.

Box Story was staged for its opening in 2001 in Baker's 'own' church of St Luke's, Holloway, in London. St Luke's previously hosted an event in the *Art in Sacred Spaces* festival in 2000, a service in which Baker delivered the 'sermon' (*The Woman Who Mistook Her Mouth for a Pocket*). Baker's performance on that occasion was reassuringly similar to her secular outings, complete with an on-stage wriggling of clothes and an ABBA dance routine. The first in the *Daily Life* series, *Kitchen Show*, will be remembered by the Baker faithful as including Action No. 8: saying the Lord's Prayer. The accompanying notes said, 'I always feel a bit embarrassed about it ... but it's such an important action that I *have* to include it.' Increasingly, Baker has been 'coming out' in the religious regard; the abandonment of her trademark white overall is significant in *Box Story*. Do not let the cycling shorts and the spangly high heels distract attention from the royal blue worn for this show: it is the exact blue traditionally used to represent the Madonna.

Box Story is not only about death, guilt and regeneration; it also deals with the more specifically Christian themes of sin and redemption. 'It's all my fault' is the ending to the catalogue of accidents that makes up the last story in the sequence. This plays with a gorily old-fashioned notion that sees sin as a stain that needs to be washed away in sacrificial blood; redemption here, as in the hymn by Cowper chosen for the 'Art in Sacred Spaces' service, is a 'blood-bought' reward from God for the unworthy. This notion of sin links with Baker's domestic agenda in quite complex ways: the biological washing powder of the obsessively clean woman may be sanctified here, but we are reminded that it also damages her skin.

The audience is free to take some distance from the specifically Christian aspect of the performance: it is merely an accentuated version of the more general way in which Baker sees mundane and daily life as the source of truth and vision. Linking the mundane to the mystical and sacramental, and in particular regarding the everyday as the route to special or privileged insight, has a significant history, even if the artists who have espoused this connection have often exposed themselves to criticism.

The 'Box' of the title is a cardboard fridge-freezer carton, on which Baker lines up the containers that she uses in her

Box Story (2004).
LIFT, Holloway, London.
Assorted food, assorted boxes.

performance as she finishes with them. While the box speaks for the mundanely domestic in any language, in a church it clearly works as an altar; the containers also have patent visual associations with altar furniture. The drawing that Baker created in the performance was associated visually with the island image at the bottom of the stained-glass window facing the audience. The setting is here particularly loaded with meaning, more so perhaps than some of the other shows in the *Daily Life* series, though *Kitchen Show* and *Grown-Up School* were also enriched by their settings.

Although the setting of *Box Story* favours a specifically Christian reading of the performance, there are far broader cultural resonances at work. The box is also a coffin: Egyptian funer-

Box Story (2004).
LIFT, Holloway, London.
Cardboard fridge-freezer carton.

ary culture is alluded to, and the formal placing of the shoes is very apt. Most of all, the box replays the myth of Pandora. In the popular version of the myth, Pandora brings a box to earth and, although she has been warned not to open it, her curiosity gets the better of her. When she opens it she releases, and is thus responsible for, the ills of humankind, such as war and plague. This version allies Pandora with the biblical Eve and represents women as the source of all trouble.

The myth of Pandora and her box, from classical Greek culture, has a complex history (Panofsky and Panofsky, 1991). It seems that it was not in fact a box, but a huge storage jar, and was not necessarily even Pandora's; she might have opened it, but possibly it was her husband Epimetheus. Pandora was herself created by the gods, animated by the fire that Prometheus stole from Zeus in order to help humans, then endowed with a variety of gifts (some good, some bad) from all the gods, and sent to earth. The ambiguities in the many versions of the Pandora myth are fully exploited by the way in which Baker uses the box in her story. What is often forgotten, though not by Baker, is the one spirit that remained in the container: Hope. Touchingly referred to as 'blind', Hope stays with Pandora 'in an unbreakable home under the rim of the great jar'. Hope, another word for optimism in the face of disaster and discouragement, is the most plausible secular alternative to a religious belief in 'redemption'. It is hope, blind hope, that inspires Baker's own break out from the box.

Box Story, as is fitting for the finale of the *Daily Life* series, reprises familiar elements of this sequence of shows, with a heightened drama, in part achieved through the commissioned music of Jocelyn Pook. The performance also acts as the artist's own mini-retrospective, including critical comment on her earlier work. Typically, Baker's history is self-mocking rather than grandiose: the legendary *Edible Family in a Mobile Home* was bad for her teeth, we are told, while the success of *Drawing on a Mother's Experience* went to her head. And we are treated to a priceless critique of one performance that other, vainer, artists might decide to forget.

Baker often puts her finger on recondite academic arguments – in this instance, about the currently fashionable vocabulary of 'cartography', the iconography of island and sea, the 'mapping' of culture. Earlier shows have in turn been obliquely informed by positively abstruse debates in psychoanalytic theory, semiotics, consumption and identity. She tends to position herself enigmatically in relation to the growing body of academic comment on the intellectual content of her work. Perhaps *Box Story*, in speaking of the dreadful coincidence between her teenage academic success and her father's sudden and tragic death, offers a biographical reason for such reluctance.

Opposite: *Box Story* (2004).
BITE, The Pit, Barbican, London.
Assorted food, boxes.

DAILY LIFE 5

Box Story **DEIRDRE HEDDON**

An edited extract from Deirdre
Heddon's 'Personal Performance: the
Resistant Confessions of Bobby Baker',
in *Modern Confessional Writing: New
Critical Essays*, ed. Jo Gill, London:
Routledge (2006).

Deirdre Heddon is a senior lecturer in
Theatre Studies at the University of
Glasgow. Her writing on the use
of autobiography in performance
has appeared in various edited
collections and journals and she has
recently completed a monograph,
Autobiography and Performance
(Palgrave Macmillan, 2007). She
is also the co-author, with Jane Milling,
of *Devising Performance:
A Critical History* (Palgrave
Macmillan, 2005).

Opposite: *Diary Drawing 385* (2001).

PERFORMANCE TEXTS, LIKE written texts, are capable of complex
engagements with the matter of experience, with the problematics
of memory and its potential representation, with the intricate
relationships between lived life and its telling. Weaving and
layerings and shifting perspectives are common devices of the
contemporary confessional performance, just as they are of the
written confessional text. One difference pertains, however: in
the performance text, there is an additional layer with which
to play, an extra ingredient to be thrown into the mix: the live,
and present, authoring body. The live presence of the confessing
subject prompts a questioning of the subject of confession.
Who is confessing? What is being confessed? Does the literal
performance of confession render its truth-status 'suspect', as the
act of confessing reveals the necessarily performative nature of
all confessional acts? Such a revelation might, arguably, be more
transparent in the live act that is witnessed by the spectator in
shared time and space.

An important property of most performance art that
distinguishes it from more conventional dramatic productions
is that in performance art the author and performer are typically
the same. As such, the 'author-performer' potentially has far

more control over the subject of representation. Translating this to the realm of autobiographical, confessional performance art, the subject has greater control over the representation of her or himself. This might also distinguish it from the gamut of currently available mass-mediated confessional opportunities. The word 'representation' is also important here. Within the frame of live performance, it is difficult to confuse the *re*presented with any realm of the 'real'.

The histories of performance art and autobiographical, confessional performances are, from the outset, linked. During the early 1970s, women, particularly in the USA, turned to performance art as a means of attaining some control over representations of themselves. Placed within the context of the second wave feminist movement, most particularly consciousness-raising activities, performance art (a relatively new practice, and therefore one without a dominant male genealogy) became a means by which women could both explore and represent hidden aspects of their everyday lives. Performance art enabled women to make visible that which had been forbidden, denied or erased within the dominant art movements. Such a turn to the everyday frequently involved the confession of personal details.

The attraction of personal material within performance art has remained constant, perhaps unsurprising given the contemporary cultural appetite to both confess and consume confession. I would argue, however, that autobiographical, confessional performances often attempt to position themselves as 'resistant' acts within this flow, with Baker's work just one example of such 'counter' activity.

The confession is considered a 'feminised space', and in a social world in which the 'feminine' continues to signify negatively, it is accordingly routinely devalued. The confessional performance, then, carries within it multiple risks for the female performer. It also, however, carries within it potential. If, as Foucault suggests, confession is a technique through which 'truth' is both produced and maintained, then the very operation of the confessional mode affords the opportunity for counter-discursive stories, the forging of other truths, other possible lives. As avenues for confession have multiplied, is it possible that so too have the stories that are being confessed? Equally, is it not also possible to play with the mode of confession, acknowledging its role in the construction of truth? 'Truth-telling' is the very condition upon which the confession rests. As Jessie Givner states, 'the very etymological traces of the word confession (confessus, meaning "incontrovertible, certain, beyond doubt") suggest that absolute truth is the basis of the ritual' (Givner, 1999: 126). But where is the 'truth' of confession inscribed other than in a convincing performance? And what if the confession were performed differently? Rather than assuming or subscribing to the 'truth' that confession reveals, one might deliberately use the confession to challenge that foundational assumption, making what Irene Gammel terms 'confessional interventions' (Gammel, 1999: 8). As I aim to show, Bobby Baker strategically deploys multiple interventions as she exploits the confessional apparatus.

In 1976, at the same time that Baker made *An Edible Family in a Mobile Home*, Foucault pronounced that Western man had 'become a confessing animal' (Foucault, 1976: 59). If we were already confessing animals in the 1970s, Foucault's statement begs us to consider what we are now. The number of confessional spaces available for occupancy in the mass media, and the sheer quantity of confessions elicited, is phenomenal. The embracing of opportunities enabled by digital technology, including weblogs, webpages and live webcams, reveals that our fascination with confession is far from abating.

Who is the Bobby Baker that is produced in these works, and what is her identity? Attempting to provide answers to these questions is surprisingly difficult, and that struggle is one sign of Baker's resistant mode of confession. Her unravelling identity is one means by which she resists becoming the confessing subject, even as she appears to be confessing. The various stories that Baker shares in *Drawing on a Mother's Experience* and *Box Story*, are all drawn from the life of Bobby Baker, and the person who performs these stories is Bobby Baker, so in classic autobiographical form the 'writing' subject is also the subject of the story – subject and object are one.

Between the Baker who performs, and the stories being performed, there are at least two other Bakers: the Baker who is performed and the non-performing Baker. (The last of these Bakers will remain outside of this discussion.)

In each performance there is what is best described as a *persona*, and it is this persona that Bobby Baker, the performer, performs. In the construction of her performed 'self', Baker self-consciously observes herself, and with the security of some distance is able, in a theatrically 'knowing' way, to make fun of what she sees. Her very process, then, admits to the gap between who she is outside of performance, and who she plays: 'I step on stage, I start performing, I become something else.' Of course, the moment anyone is on stage, they arguably become something else. However, Baker also admits to 'sort of develop[ing] that persona' (personal interview, November 2001), or developing a style of presentation.

Complicating matters, this persona is presented *as* Bobby Baker. Whose stories are these, then, that are being shared with us – Bobby Baker the performing subject's, or Bobby Baker the performed subject's? Who, if anyone, is confessing here? And if the Bobby Baker who offers up these stories is a persona, how referential or stable or truthful can these confessions be presumed to be? For Baker's confessing subject to trouble the act of confession, the presence of this persona must be evident and in fact the same persona appears in all of Baker's performances, although the 'eruptions' that she/Baker stages are different. This endurance of her persona, from show to show, is one of the means by which the persona becomes easily readable.

Baker's recent performance, *Box Story* (2001), invites a more explicit reckoning with confession, sited as it originally was in her own local church in London. This embracing of religious iconography is not a new departure. In *Kitchen Show*, Baker confessed to a daily recitation of the Lord's Prayer. In *How to Shop*, she takes John Bunyan's *The Pilgrim's Progress* as a sur-text,

Box Story (2004). BITE, The Pit, Barbican, London.

though her own 'quest' is tied to '"shopping for life" or "shopping for enlightenment"' (Harris, 1999: 113).

In her illuminating essay on Baker, Marina Warner claims that the 'principles and disciplines' of Baker's Christian faith remain 'intrinsic to her pieces'. One principle of this Protestant faith, writ in the resurrection of Christ, is the demand 'that sacrifice take place before rebirth and renewal can happen'. For Warner, Baker 'uses the idea of suffering and humiliation as a resource' (Warner, 1995: pp. 102–3 above). Baker's very public suffering and humiliation perhaps can be linked to the pre-oral confession of sins, by way of the act of *exomologesis*, 'recognition of fact', which is linked to penance. As Foucault writes, penance was 'not nominal but dramatic ... Symbolic, ritual, and theatrical' (Foucault 1988: 43–4). The exhibition of sin is the punishment, as well as an act of self-revelation: 'To prove suffering, to show shame, to make visible humility and exhibit modesty – these are the main features of punishment' (Foucault, 1988: 42).

Warner also reveals that Baker's father was a Methodist, and that the performer herself went to a Methodist school; also, on 'her mother's side there are "strings of vicars"' (Warner 1995: see p. 103 above). Though Baker is not herself a practising Methodist, there are nonetheless reverberations between *Box Story* and certain aspects of Methodism. For Methodists, as for Puritans, 'man' is born in original sin (and presumably one needs this sin in order to attain everlasting peace through forgiveness), but faith in Christ assures salvation. The experience of this new found faith results in the 'birth' of a new person. As one 'reborn' Methodist woman significantly reported, 'I found myself quite another' (Abelove, 1990: 89).

Methodist practice of self-scrutiny and public revelation – or confession – sits firmly within the Christian tradition. As Foucault notes:

> Christianity is not only a salvation religion, it's a confessional religion ... Christianity requires another form of truth obligation different from faith. Each person has the duty to know what is happening inside him, to acknowledge faults, to recognize temptations, to locate desires, and everyone is obliged to disclose these things either to God or to others in the community and hence to bear public or private witness against oneself. The truth obligations of faith and the self are linked together. This link permits a purification of the soul impossible without self-knowledge.
>
> (Foucault, 1988: 40)

Of course, this search for and disclosure of 'self', publicly or privately, carries with it an assumption of sin or guilt, accompanied accordingly by shame. Without guilt and shame, there is no contrition, and without contrition, there can be no forgiveness or absolution. Another shared feature of the confession, irrespective of its institutional location, is that it is generally considered to unburden, to cleanse, to release or lighten. As Peter Brooks writes, 'from Saint Augustine onwards, writers of personal confessions have claimed the need to expose their state of sin and error in order [to] regain the path of righteousness' (Brooks, 2000: 72–3). This purported 'effect' of confession can be found in the realm of the contemporary legal confession.

In this context, Brooks notes that 'Confession of misdeeds has become part of the everyday pedagogy of Western societies, normally with the understanding that recalcitrance in confession will aggravate punishment, while full confession will both cleanse the soul and provide possible mitigation of sanctions' (Brooks, 2000: 45). Brooks also suggests that, while it is generally thought that confession admits guilt, in actual fact it might be the very act of confessing that produces guilt in the confessant (to use the religious term), rather than any action or referent outside of the confession. The confession, then, performs guilt. Thinking about Baker's literal performance, I want to propose that the confession might also contain within it the possibility of performing innocence. Just as Baker uses the confessional apparatus to construct multiple identities, and to make uncertain the 'truth' status of both 'herself' and her stories, might Baker use the confession as a way to acknowledge that feelings of guilt are sometimes unfounded? Further, I will argue that it is the opportunity afforded by confession to create stories that has a liberating effect, rather than any admission of sin.

As in *Drawing on a Mother's Experience*, in *Box Story*, Baker, in spite of it all, has come through. But what needs to be remembered here is that the confessions that Baker shares are both carefully moulded, and then told and retold, first in rehearsal and then in performance. Though there is similarity here to the deliberate crafting of the written confession, and its desired effect, the fact that Baker's confessions are live (and ephemeral) renders them always available to be re-enacted, enabling a continual rewriting, or revising, of the confession. For example, Baker has been confessing in *Drawing on a Mother's Experience* for some 15 years, and over 200 times. The 'unburdening' that is supposedly enabled by confession might have less to do with admitting guilt (and being absolved) than with the opportunity that confession provides to craft a tale – to deliberately select, order, edit and perform. In confessional performance, the act of telling is most often an act of retelling, and it might be this that pulls Baker through at the end.

Of course, the belief that equates 'confession' with 'well-being' is found in non-religious contexts, such as psychoanalysis and other forms of counselling. In his seminar, 'Technologies of the Self', Foucault traces such 'technologies' in 'pagan and early Christian practice' (1988: 17). In both instances, Foucault contends that the focus was not on 'knowing oneself', but 'taking care of yourself'. Such 'taking care "of oneself"', within a pagan context, might include 'writing activity' (1988: 27), guidance by a master, silence, retreating into oneself, examination and review of conscience (based on 'stock taking' rather than on judgement and/or punishment). What is fundamental for Foucault is that the pagans' activities were pragmatic, focused on finding appropriate methods for self-care, whereas he perceives psychoanalysis as appropriating (ancient) methods in order to unearth some 'truth' about the self which will then lead to 'well-being'.

Baker's act of confession – or perhaps *craft* of confession is more appropriate, given the evident awareness and skill with which she practises it – may be, as she states, simply the act of '*making* stories up to *make* sense of the world' (personal interview, November 2001; my emphasis). Such stories are intended neither to provide a truth about the world, nor about the person who tells the story. They are merely one pragmatic response to the actual lived, messy, experiences of life: experiences that include, in this instance, such non-rationalisable tragedies as a parent being swept out to sea and drowning. Baker's confessions are, first and last, as her title acknowledges, stories. The private confessional box is knowingly reconfigured here as a story box. Returning to that other story that continuously ghosts Baker's, it is worth remembering that what is left in Pandora's box at the end is 'Hope'. And perhaps it is hope that Baker is, finally, offering us. I use the plural pronoun 'us' deliberately. One marked difference between the witnessed live performance and the read written text is that the former is experienced 'collectively', whereas the latter is more typically a private event. Though each spectator undoubtedly has their own individual experience, engaging with the performance in variable and unpredictable ways, the experience of spectatorship is shared. Baker has worried that her performances might be considered 'self-indulgent' (personal interview, 29 November 2001). However, capturing the paradoxical dialogic property adhering to this supposedly 'monologic' form, Baker reflects that the

> audience actually don't come away from the show very often talking about my life ... They actually relate to it as people, they've had that experience, or similar experiences ... I heard some ... fantastic stories about people leaving the show and then standing on the pavement for a long time telling each other stories.
>
> (personal interview, 29 November 2001)

The environment of performance, then, – its dependency on its audience, on its witnesses, in shared time and space – encourages the production of other confessions, the telling of other potential 'unburdenings'.

Comment

FRANKO B
MARIA LARIBOT
TIM ETCHELLS

FRANKO B

Dear Bobby,
Firstly, thank you.
Thank you for your warmth, your generosity, your openness, your humour, your directness and your militancy – yes your militancy, in the way you have presented and continue to do so, issues that usually are very personal and painful to talk about to the fore; you do this with dignity and without shame, using the simplest strategy available, which is to be human and to be you.

MARIA LARIBOT

I have always imagined Bobby being my mum, because she is big and generous, my aunt, because she can be mad, my daughter, because she is witty and naughty, and my next-door neighbour, because she is so sweetly British … but probably she has been always my best imagined sister. The one to follow with oranges as breasts running after the cat … leaving me blinded by fun, blinded by admiration.

TIM ETCHELLS
Artistic director, Forced Entertainment

Bobby Baker is an extraordinary inspiring artist, a hugely influential and significant presence in the UK performance scene. Taken together her work is both an investigation of domestic life, landscape and realities and at the same time a magical and political intervention, a sustained transformative act that makes the everyday seem very strange indeed.

Opposite page: *Cook Dems* (1990).
Publicity photograph. Baked antlers,
breast pizza.

$Spitting$ $\mathcal{M}ad$ SARAH GORMAN

Sarah Gorman raises the issue of what students can cope with, in a paper at the Performance Studies International Conference in 2006, held at Queen Mary.

Sarah Gorman is a Senior Lecturer in Drama Theatre and Performance Studies at Roehampton University, London. Her current research focuses upon contemporary British, North American and European experimental theatre, comprising of articles on The New York City Players, Forced Entertainment, Bobby Baker, Dood Paard and Janet Cardiff. Her work has been published in a number of journals; *Performance Research*, *Contemporary Theatre Review*, *The Drama Review*, *Theatre Journal* and *New Theatre Quarterly*, and she is currently preparing a book-length project about The New York City Players.

Dear Bobby,

I once showed a video of *Spitting Mad* to a group of first year students at De Montfort University. It was a mixed group of both dance and theatre students. They were new, I was new, we were incredibly wary of one another. I had yet to gauge where they were coming from, and had the mistaken view that they might be interested in experimental theatre and performance. I remember that I kept asking them if they thought various performances were 'political' and getting blank stares in response. It was a real education, for me, if not for them. When I turned on the classroom light after showing them the short film of you spitting out food to create a range of arts and crafts objects I was once again met by blank stares, I asked a few questions, and after an uneasy silence one of the more voluble members of the group offered that 'well, she's just mad isn't she? Just a mad woman.' I was completely stumped by this response as I had long dismissed this reading myself and come to celebrate all the subtle nuances and ironies in the work. This statement closed down the potential scope of further discussions and I seem to recall that we finished the class early. I resolved not to use material that I held dear again in class.

In subsequent weeks I was struck by how readily the students dismissed experimental work as 'abstract' or 'mad', and I would labour to point out how the transgressions within the work pointed to a way of resisting traditional societal customs and conventions. Again, I doubt that I was very persuasive. Whilst studying Artaud one student indignantly pointed out, 'If Artaud was mad and on drugs and everything then why are we studying him?' I began, hesitantly to talk about Descartes, about the mind/body dualism but these students were not ready for, or sympathetic to, anti-Enlightenment ideas. I resolved to only introduce 'mad' work into Year 2 or 3 of the syllabus.

I wonder about your fostering of these performances of eccentricity; I have to admit that the first time I saw you canter around your garden, with bin-liners pegged to your apron, I did consider this rather an improper act for a woman of your standing. However, I do have to say that I admire the way you retain such an impeccable demeanour of composure whilst making yourself look completely ridiculous. Your façade of composure is sometimes betrayed by an awkwardly crooked leg, or a subtle rising of your eyebrows, but even those signs, I now imagine to be deliberate. These students' insistence that the work should be dismissed as a manifestation of 'madness' alarmed me, as it made me realise how easily a great deal of people's work could, and has been dismissed once they have been constructed as 'unstable' or 'hysterical'. I am not just thinking of artists here, but colleagues and probably myself after I have been reduced to tears at work once too often. Reading back over my notes I see that a number of academics have picked up on your 'making a spectacle of yourself', of your Charcot-like representation of madness (with the exception that you are representing yourself rather than being represented). Had I only had those notes at my disposal in that De Montfort classroom.

Much love, Sarah

Page 240 and opposite: *Spitting Mad* (1996). Video grabs.

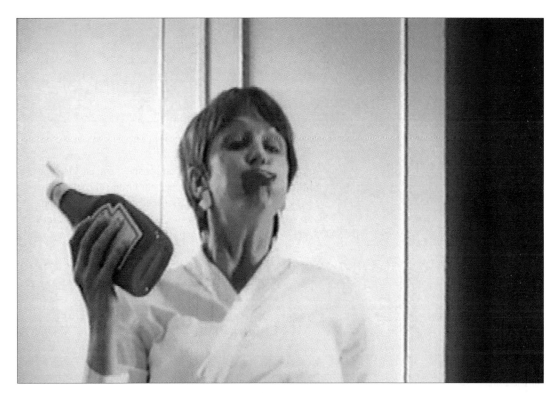

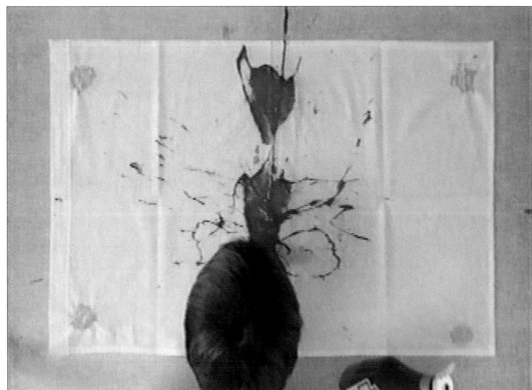

How to Live JON SNOW

I HAVE BOTH enjoyed and admired Bobby Baker's work for at least twenty years. Although it has always been a sumptuous fusion of the tactile, the sensuous, the humorous and the political, I have seen her work evolve, even metamorphose into something beyond both humour and art yet inclusive of both. Her latest work around mental health, courageously deploying her own personal experiences, provides an accessible yet light and sometimes downright funny insight into almost unexplored worlds. Bobby Baker starts us on journeys rooted in our own experience and then leads to destinations we never knew existed. Yet she does it so beguilingly, so irresistibly that her performances these days find every seat taken and more waiting outside.

$\mathcal{H}ow\ to\ \mathcal{L}ive$ JOHN DANIEL

Reprinted from *On Tour* 024 (2004).

Opposite: *How To Live* (2004). Publicity photograph.

A BAKER BY both name and nature, artist Bobby Baker rose to prominence in the 1970s for her edible art works. Food – shopping for it, cooking it, serving it, consuming it – is a consistent feature in Baker's work, which focuses on the seemingly mundane, everyday details of life. This time it's the humble pea. Small, round and, as foodstuffs go, distinctly lacking in glamour, Baker's chosen the pea as a symbol for the human psyche, in a show that's about mental health and the commercialisation of therapy. 'I think it's a fantastic image for our frailty and insignificance in the world', she explains, 'a symbol for the extraordinary minuteness of things'. Inspired by her own experience of being treated with Dialectical Behavioural Therapy (DBT) – a form of Cognitive Behavioural Therapy developed to treat people with mental health issues ranging from phobias to more critical personality disorders – Baker will take to the stage as a self-styled self-help guru to indoctrinate the masses with her own 11-step programme for a happy life, *How to Live*. 'My patients are peas', she explains with only the slightest hint of irony, 'and the basis of the show is that I'm giving an open session – with a patient who's agreed to be treated in front of the public – in which I'm teaching this set of skills that this patient needs in order to function as a normal person in society.'

It's typical of Baker's work that an issue of such profound social and personal significance should be approached so

irreverently. Yet the pea metaphor is designed to educate as well as entertain, and although Baker's stance is characteristically sceptical, her research for the show is backed up by hard science. With the help of a research grant from The Wellcome Trust, for the past two years Baker's been collaborating with psychologist and social anthropologist Dr Richard Hallam. *How to Live*, the fruit of that collaboration, is inspired by Baker and Hallam's shared fascination with the way in which psychology is packaged and dispensed to the public and by the fact that the language of therapy is now so bound up with the way society operates – in management strategy, reality TV, education and the media.

The process has taught both of them that, in the field of psychology at least, the worlds of science and the arts share much common ground, as Dr Hallam points out: 'Psychology does straddle art and science. I see it as a creative activity. There are some very hard nosed scientists that don't believe in dealing with questions that can't be answered or existential questions, but fortunately most aren't like that.' Baker continues 'We discovered we had a great deal in common in terms of our view; we are both, to a degree, sceptics, who like to explore things from the outside. There must be a lot of practitioners who, unlike Richard, find it uncomfortable to stand outside the practice and question it to this degree.'

Baker admits that her initial brush with DBT was not positive – 'I felt as though I was being indoctrinated, that I was being put in a mind control prison and that I was supposed to alter my way of thinking', she says – and her first response was to create a show that critiqued it. 'But as the years went by', she continues, 'I realised that it has an extraordinarily sophisticated way of operating and is founded on a scientific approach. I'm a rather belligerent, resistant patient, questioning everything exhaustively, and yet it's proven to have worked. It's also empowering, exciting and engaging. What I love is how it's heightened my ability to observe my own behaviour and thoughts and emotions. It's also intensified my gaze on society, which has really played into the way I make my work.'

For an artist whose work has always been confessional in nature, Baker's taking the bravest step of her career by going public with her own experience of the mental health system. 'It's been a concern to talk more openly about my own mental health problems', she admits 'but given that one in four people will experience mental health problems at some point in their lives, it feels very relevant to be open about it.' She's also eager to challenge the stereotypical notion that the individual who doesn't show his emotions is strong, whilst the person who responds with greater sensitivity to life's ups and downs, is weak. 'My experience is that the majority of people with mental health problems are phenomenally strong to cope with them', she asserts. 'There's an assumption that if you're severely mentally ill you just become a non-functioning member of society, and yet the evidence shows that there's an enormous number of people who actually function extremely effectively. People are encouraged to hide it away and be ashamed. And yet it's a part of life.'

If all this sounds a little earnest, don't worry: as in all Baker's shows, the serious theme of *How to Live* is likely to be subverted by the artist's left-field, often hilarious, sense of the absurd. Reviews of Baker's shows are littered with adjectives like 'dotty', 'batty', 'dippy' and 'quirky', and perhaps the secret of her success is to do with the fact that although, like many other performance artists, her work explores major existential themes, it's always served up with huge dollops of irony and wit.

It's this interplay between light and dark, mundanity and profundity, laughter and tears, that's made Baker a favourite of audiences in the UK and also increasingly in demand overseas, where she's seen as a quintessentially British middle-aged, middle-class housewife. As a mother of two grown-up children who celebrates her 25th wedding anniversary this year, it's a stereotype she simultaneously conforms to, reacts against, and self-consciously exploits: 'I am that but I'm also not that, because, I've got the very rebellious streak of an artist, which keeps me on the outside. I'm not the person I was brought up to be in a sense. I'm married with children and do the housework and those sorts of things, but I continuously question that. It's that questioning that I think people enjoy. I make fun of myself, which enables the audience to laugh. International audiences seem to genuinely want to laugh affectionately at the British and love the fact that we laugh at ourselves.'

Underpinning the project, as always with Baker's work, is her Zen Buddhist-like belief that little by little – like ripples caused by the drop of a tiny pebble into an ocean – the actions of one individual might change the world. 'When I perform,' Baker modestly asserts, 'I'm motivated in part by a somewhat simple desire to make people change their thinking, change their behaviour. I want people to leave the shows thinking differently or seeing things from a different perspective, even if only momentarily or only in fragments throughout their life. I'm hoping that they will leave the show in a state of hilarity and ecstasy with wonderful tools to change their lives.'

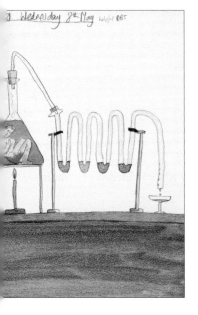

Diary Drawing 400 (2002). Wednesday 8 May. 'Helpful DBT.'

DAY 233   friday 21st August   HAVEN
                                      LAST
                                      NIGHT
                                      ALL
                                      NIGHT

Diary Drawings GRISELDA POLLOCK

Griselda Pollock is Professor of Social and Critical Histories of Art and Director of Centre for Cultural Analysis, Theory and History at the University of Leeds. Recent edited volumes include *Psychoanalysis and the Image* (Blackwell, 2006), *Museums after Modernism* (Blackwell, 2007), and *Encountering Eva Hesse* (Prestel, 2006). New publications include *Encounters in the Virtual Feminist Museum* (Routledge, 2007) and forthcoming, *Theatre of Memory: Trauma and Representation in the Work of Charlotte Salomon* (Yale, 2008) and articles on Agnes Martin, Louise Bourgeois, Christine Patten and Bracha Ettinger.

Opposite page: *Diary Drawing 233* (1997). 'Some of the "remarkable practitioners" that I have encountered in the NHS and mental health charities reaching out to me.' Watercolour paper, pencil, watercolour paint.

ONE OF THE MANY 'stories' told in Charlotte Salomon's *Leben? Oder Theater? (Life? Or Theatre?* 1941–2) is that of her own mother, who suffered deep depression which ultimately led to her taking her own life. Charlotte Salomon was only nine when this happened and was told that her mother had succumbed to the terrible influenza epidemic that killed so many during the 1920s. She only discovered the truth of her mother's death in 1940 when she struggled to bring her grandmother back from the brink of her depression. She too took her own life. The great cycle of paintings that Charlotte Salomon then undertook became a journey back to meet the women in her world whose psychological pain had made them choose death. Her questioning of *Leben,* which can mean 'to live' or 'life' was pursued over 1,325 gouache paintings and was created in a period of possibly less than a year. The work, only fully entering cultural knowledge in the 1990s, stands as one of the rare and profound studies, made by an artist, of the nature of feminine melancholia and psychic distress. In the introductory leaflet to the exhibition of Bobby Baker's *Diary Drawings,* Daniel Hinchcliffe links the two artists. I want to start my own reflections on Bobby Baker's work by pursuing this suggestion in order to move through it to identify for myself what is so specific and different in the work of Bobby Baker who now takes her place in that same field (see Pollock, 2006: 34–72 and, on representation or invisibility of feminine melancholia in a larger historical perspective, Buerkle, 2006: 73–87).

In Charlotte Salomon's painting we see her image of her mother in the grip of feelings of overwhelming despair by means of a painting that creates a three-headed figure. Facing front is Franciska Kann (Salomon recast her family members with Brechtian names); shown in profile and looking away, are her daughter and her husband. Those in whose gaze and thus social and emotional web she should feel herself safely ensconced and those by whom her emotional needs might be recognised and met look away. So close and yet so isolated, this simple composition creates a portrait of the cold solitude that is one of the deepest afflictions of depression: its incommunicability combined with the very fact in such a feeling of alienated loneliness, the world tends to turn away even more. Depression and worse in the field of psychic pain and illness does not bring us closer to those we need to meet us in a place that is incommunicable precisely because one of its conditions is the breakdown of what links us to life, the living, and the ordinariness of people getting on with their lives.

Charlotte Salomon's work is not in my opinion autobiographical, even though it is largely presented as such. Even if we imagine that she herself had to know something of such a state of traumatising psychological disintegration in order to imagine her mother's state of mind in so compelling and insightful a way, she is not documenting her own condition, but precisely, in retrospect reaching back to meet her in the place her own paintings restage for that missed encounter. Through painting, she is attempting to build a bridge back across the gulf in which her mother perished. For the work to be as affecting and effective as it is, as painting, Salomon had to be in charge of her processes, making *artistic* decisions, deploying her skills to realise an image, structuring into recognisability the emotional disintegration that she is painting by the very act of doing so.

Charlotte Salomon, *Why, oh why, am I alive?* (1942). Gouache on paper, 32.5 x 25 cm.

Bobby Baker paints a self-portrait on Day 12. Using the same striking format of a frontal portrait, a head-on confrontation with an image of a self, Bobby Baker works with intense economy to bring forth an image of her distinctive appearance: the short blonde hair, the long face, the fine features, that so many know from her brilliant series of performances in which this look, combined with a white medical/cookery overall, is a trade mark. I first saw Bobby Baker perform live when she was touring with her work *Drawing on a Mother's Experience* (Pollock, 1990). She arrived on stage dressed in her performance 'uniform' and took the audience through a carefully scripted and choreographed performance that set a mood of delighted laughter as the 'craziness' of childbirth and the early months was recounted by means of food and drink, used with artistic precision to create a gender-inversion of Jackson

Pollock's drip paintings. Working at so many levels to play off the gender-oppositions of artist and mother, the professional and the domestic, the heart of this performance was the unexpected and hence deeply shocking and moving moment in which Bobby Baker, telling us of her post-partum depression and a physical illness that also afflicted her at this time, laid herself down in the centre of the sheet, amidst the physical mess of her food art to create an image, which has remained with me ever since, of the kind of unspeakable agony that lies at the heart for so many women of their childbearing: post-partum depression. It is clear now from more

Right: *Diary Drawing 12* (1997). Watercolour paper, pencil, watercolour.

research, prompted by women's pressure, that for some women, the processes involved in pregnancy and giving birth actually precipitate prolonged depressive illnesses. Some recover, some relive its horrors with every child they bear, some are marked for life. It is certain that our culture does not fully want to know, understand, support or help a condition that so dramatically contradicts the ideologies of motherhood as blissful fulfilment. Independent

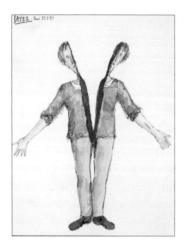

Top: *Diary Drawing 22* (1997).
'Day 22 Thurs. 27.2.97.'
Watercolour paper, pencil, watercolour.

Below: *Diary Drawing 25* (1997).
'Day 25 Wed. 5th March'.
Watercolour paper, pencil, watercolour.

of whatever delights in children or feelings, the often deranging emotional distress precipitated by this massive event must also have its own psychic as well as chemical structure.

How can we be brought to something beyond mere intellectual knowledge? How can we feel what all deep psychological conditions create: the gap that opens up between those who have never felt this way and the suffering subject quivering in the excruciating pain of every second, experiencing such pain that it seems unimaginable that one could endure even 60 seconds more, let alone 60 minutes of an hour and then 24 hours or a life?

This self-portrait drawing might firstly seem simply a register of the face. But it is a face full of the pathos of suffering. The energy is drained. The eyes are hooded and unfocused. The elegant and subtle lines with which this 'beautiful' drawing has been made all curve downwards, formally producing an effect of impenetrable sadness. But then all naturalism, finely realised, slips as we encounter two mouths. I do not know how to read their meaning. We have departed from the conventional techniques used by artists to produce effects: the slightest inclination of a line produces both likeness and affect. But here Bobby Baker has added a dimension that marks a deeper and less recognisable difference: something truly estranging. The following drawings pursue this search for a visual means to register what extremity feels like, to make images of it, by utilising the evocative capacities of the visual languages of figurative painting to such a degree.

Twentieth-century art such as Cubism and Expressionism pushed those inherited languages to their own kinds of formal extremity, demanding that their viewers accommodate to distortion and deformation as a necessary means to ensure authenticity. Surrealism added other kinds of extremity which included violence and mutilation as well as disturbing hybridisations and permutations. Bobby Baker's work does not belong in any of those categories precisely because she works with a different kind of contradiction: between the extraordinary clarity of colour, the sureness of drawing, the comforting familiarity of her figuration and the pathos they inscribe. Drawing perhaps more on a legacy of cartooning and children's illustration, she makes the domestic and comfortable ordinariness that in other circumstances might give rise to wry smiles and indulgent humour, split apart into a confrontation with agony. Literally, in this image from Day 22. The bloodied wound severs the head, dividing the self from the self, the right from the left, down to the groin and blood trickles on down the inside of each leg. In the gap created by the severing of the body and the mind is a terrible gap, a nothing.

The entry for Day 25 takes us further into this disintegrating sense of coherence, to place the sad-face portrait as now the benign and bearable mask that hides a more hideous and sinister presence, grimacing, staring, manic. The switchback of a certain condition is marked by a repeat of the bloodied severance, the face lifting off from the skull around which the ash-blonde hair now stands on end. The irremediable contrast between the dead, empty eyes and the fearsome identity now no longer invisible behind them, suggests a feeling of disorienting possession and alienness that in a terrible way, by the use of this device, becomes the hidden truth against which the sad-face seemingly has no resource: succumbing only further to a human emptiness in the battle with this manically alive but terrifying occupant of the place of the self. The only place of the artist-self as still a self is in the very courage of making such an image. Entry Day 43 shows us the façade of sad-face, the familiar image, tentative in space, now painted on to a flimsy construction of bricks, which is falling down. Part of the head lies on the ground. A section of arm has fallen off. Both physical identity and mental wholeness feel fractured. The brick divisions render what holds together the imaginary unity of person, body and soul/psyche suddenly visible as lines of potential breakage. We use the phrase, breakdown, for extreme mental suffering. Those who have never been broken or feared for their own capacity to 'hold it together' never notice those fracture lines, or how once one has been broken, the rebuild will look like this: scarred forever with the doubt that the unbroken never imagine in their feeling of cemented unity.

Other images in the diary return to the device of the doubled self. Diary entry day 496 reworks the contrasting faces of tragedy and comedy. In a bolder and more linear style of drawing the Janus-headed creature faces in oppposite directions, one manically happy, the other weeping. Diary drawing 543 gives a very different version of the duality but returning once again to the idea not of two competing facets, but a deeply divided being in which the appearance of the person who greets the world, and even performs in the Baker uniform, is a kind of strap-on carapace behind which a shrieking harpy tries to catch the world's attention.

This image brings to mind the famous poem by Stevie Smith, 'Not Waving but Drowning'. Some part of the self longs to be seen, to be heard, and all the gestures that attempt to solicit help and understanding at the level at which the pain is being experienced seem to be invisible to the others. They see only the opposing faces, happy or sad, not the appeal for help, not the recognition of what it feels like 'inside' beyond a seeing. The hugeness of the gaping mouth stands for a soundless shriek. It links across the work with two other aspects – the terrible anxiety resulting from what medication does to the body. In one image titled 'pre medication' and 'post medication', two bodies are shown. The first shivers, slight and fading. The second, ballooned into overweight sweats uncomfortably (Day 397).

Deprived of control over the housing of our own being by the chemicals proffered as the 'cure' or rather the means of manage-

Below: *Diary Drawing 43* (1997). 'Day 43 Mon 7.4'. Watercolour paper, pencil, watercolour.

Diary Drawing 543 (2005). 'Week 6th June To USA – Pea crisis'. (Forty foot container with entire set for *How To Live* and Pea rig impounded in USA Customs). Watercolour paper, pencil, watercolour.

Diary Drawing 397 (2002).
'Day 397 Monday 22nd April
Pre medication Post medication'
Watercolour paper, pencil, watercolour.

ment, who then is the subject? The artist seems to be showing us how a psychic disintegration and loss of wholeness and manageable consistency is further aggravated by what is done to the body so that the split is felt at a further level.

Bobby Baker's most brilliantly biting and cruelly truthful image-making is saved for her representations of those who would help her – psychotherapists and consultant psychiatrists. When I saw the exhibition these images of the professionals at first gave me most wicked pleasure, and then the deepest grief. Bobby Baker's keen eye, whatever her state, recorded those tell-tale details about the buttoned-up, closed, clean, carefully managed selves who in smart clothes and tight fashionable shoes sit opposite a desperate soul who is drowning in unimaginable daily emotional pain inside an unruly body and in self-distressing alienation from the calm and even plane of bearable psychic normality. The health professionals, it would seem from the drawings, are unable really to hear or to see the true state of their patients' feelings. Bobby Baker shows how *she* must manage her own self in their presence, to protect *them* from the true understanding of the wilderness and wildness of her illness. The drawings, so controlled in their mastery of the challenging art of painting in watercolour, so precise in their characterisations of self and others, so astute in reading the tiny and trivial signs that are the true indices of each person's state and condition, nonetheless, articulate a profound rage: rage that she who suffers the torments of psychic breakdown in a world so hopelessly unable to hold, contain or even recognise the pain lived in that internal landscape has to *take into her own consideration at all times* the feelings, sensibilities and capacities of those to whom she turns for help.

I do not pretend to understand what is the personal context of the drawing titled 'My Psychotherapist' (Day 165). It would be presumptuous to do so. But what I see in it is a dire reminder of the huge risks involved in that intimacy under the conditions of the psycho-therapeutic contract. Recently Christopher Bollas – speaking at CongressCATH, 7 July 2005, and in his novel *I've Heard the Mermaids Singing* – has joined with others in the field to express anxiety about the directions in which interrelational psychotherapy has taken us. The main problem is an interpretation of Freud's core concept of transference and counter-transference and the notion that the past is worked through in the present of the actual relation between analyst and analysand. This can frequently be reduced to a peculiar torturing of the analysand whose words, carrying often intensely experienced pain and produced at great emotional expense become empty signifiers turned back on the analysand as the analyst takes everything said to ultimately refer to themselves. The technique of seeing the analyst as a cipher of all the parent and other figures imaginatively addressed in the analyst's psychic theatre can so easily be perverted so that the analytical space becomes instead a replay of the very brutal battles and woundings by which the analysand is still scarred and bleeding. The image of the psychotherapist, with her figure-hugging peacock blue bodysuit and winkle-picker shoes, armed with a knife in her claw-like hands and a tongue as bloodied as the hugely elongated talons of the right hand is hardly reassuring. Instead it reminds us of the almost physically wounding power of words – especially those of the analyst who boldly tries to reflect back to the analysand or therapee so-called tough truths. I am of the opinion that few people in real distress should be exposed to analysts, since the work of analysis requires a psychic resilience

This page: *Diary Drawing 165* (1998). 'Day 165 Tuesday 13th January'. Watercolour paper, pencil, watercolour.

for the process, which is not tempered, in general, with love. Thus the images of therapists and psychiatrists in Baker's *Diary* need to be taken very seriously by those professions. They add their shocking visual representation to the growing unease about the psychological effects of current British practices.

Baker's visual self-analysis, a parallel register of living with psychic pain and worse, moves beyond the private space of a diaristic recording for herself. Entering, bravely, as she has allowed them to do so, into the public realm where art intersects with mental health care, the work offers itself as testimony in a public cultural court. Few people feeling the way Bobby Baker's images reveal to have been the inner world she has lived for so many years could retain enough outside of that experience to recast it in such vivid imagery – an imagery that works only because of such fine calculations of the technique, the materials and the repertoire of imagery. But if I construe one level of the *Diary Drawings* as a kind of evidence, a visual testimony, there is a danger of confining the work within an expressionist pathos of the artist as patient.

We need, therefore, before concluding, to draw back and draw a larger picture to ascertain yet another level of understanding of what Bracha Ettinger has called 'artworking' (Ettinger, 2000). One of Freud's key concepts of how psychoanalysis transforms the subject is the idea of working through. This work/*Arbeit* also appears in two other key concepts: the work of mourning, and dream work.

To these Bracha Ettinger has added 'artworking', suggesting not a purely therapeutic function for art, but rather the possibility that in making art and in responding to art thus made, certain transformations can occur, certain inner changes can be wrought in relation to the trauma we or others suffer. She calls art a possible 'transport station of trauma' and suggests that unpredictably, depending on the susceptibility of each participating subject, art may become an occasion for some kind of transmission, that causes changes in the partners it creates through the encounter-event. Thus art is not perceived as a simple vehicle for the expression of the solitary subject's contents that the viewer comes along and reads off, dispassionately or affectingly. Instead, art may open up a space between subjects, projected and imagined in the making, recalled and projected in the responding, that can, by mediation of the shared space of the work, cause transformations on both sides, even delayed in time.

What prompted and sustained Bobby Baker to keep a visual diary, what it did for her on a day-to-day basis, opens out to the space implied in the very act of making something to see. It builds upon a hope that someone might not only see it, but truly see it, see what so many of the drawings are about: the pain of what remains unseen/unrecognised by others but horribly felt by the artist herself. To fragilise her own boundaries to the point of daring to make the images, to share already with the paper and the other selves there depicted, is to invite others to fragilise their own frontiers to create shared thresholds. This means not merely looking at the work as either amazing drawing/painting or the voice of an anguished soul. In both cases the viewer would then maintain the boundaries, and keep a distance. Old Kantian aesthetic judgement is mastery at/by a distance. Identifying the other's subjectivity locked inside her expression is also to refuse to let the trauma leak out and seep into one's own subjectivity, where a different kind of responsiveness, what Ettinger calls response-ability, may, in receiving the transmissions from a place that is unknowable to anyone else, even if they have shared some similar kinds of psychic pain, becomes an active element in assisting the shifting of trauma. This is not at all about empathy.

I spoke earlier of the problem of love, or lack of love, in analytical and other kinds of therapies. Loving, in the ordinary sense, is obviously not enough. Indeed in the *Diary Drawings*, Baker shows the burden carried by family members, when one of their own is subject to a kind of perpetual weeping, a swamping of all of their joys with the stream of her tears. The darkening of the entire atmosphere by the black sun of one member's depression burdens the entire group who bravely mobilise love to help, a love that remains stubbornly helpless against the deadly negativity that has the loved one in its relentless grasp. So I do not mean that kind of love – which is exhausted by the struggle. To the pain one is enduring is often added the guilt of being relentlessly ill in the face of so much but ultimately limited 'love'.

Bracha Ettinger is trying to explain that beyond the current models of psychoanalysis and its theories of how subjectivity works and hence how it breaks down, there is another level of wounding to which depression and other psychic afflictions bear witness. Heretically, but with the wealth of her own analytical practice and art work as evidence in support, Bracha Ettinger identifies another dimension in subjectivity which she calls the matrixial that is distinct from what she has named the phallic (Ettinger, 2000: see also Pollock, 2004; Ettinger 2004).

The phallic is a legend about how we become a subject by separating out from the initial web of primary bonding and potential confusion with the Mother or the maternal fantasised as a holding and containing body. This may give rise to two fantasies: a terror of the collapse of our fragilely discovered boundaries with a subsequent return to a formless non-subjective mess. The other fantasy is born from the necessity energetically to police the frontiers of the constituted, territorialised self, to keep the self distinct from others. This generates a theoretical model of the subject as cut out from a cloth of formlessness, delineated via the imaginary within the boundaries of the body-imago as whole and unified. Supplementing this necessary level of formation of the subject that sustains the distance between subject and object, subject and other, Ettinger radically proposes that we are also formed through a much earlier, even more archaic, deposit of a different subjectivising potential for intersubjective co-emergence and co-affection.

Daringly, she suggests that this potential is laid down with the very late pre-birth sensations of a subjectivising encounter between several partners: the becoming-mother, not only produced as mother, but also imaginatively affected by the unknown not yet fully human entity she carries and the becoming infant impressed upon by the unknown subjectivising human other with whom the infant shares a borderspace that may be a threshold for affecting and transforming shared events. It is vital to stress that these 'partners' in *relating-without-relations* are unknown/unknowable to each other. Thus this encounter has nothing to do with mothers and babies, with psychological situations in which each are objects for each other's already emerging or already formed desire. The unknownness of this radical alterity that is, nonetheless, subjectivising, forming and affecting within a space of 'incestuous' intimacy, marks the matrixial dimension of subjectivity with its singular affective and ethical quality. It is, as Ettinger is now theorising it, a field of compassionate hospitality (Ettinger, 2006: 218–22).

The matrixial borderspace of the several proposes subjectivity at its very inception as an encounter. Its unknown partners are separated by a minimal difference caused by the co-presence of the several who are mutually (but in each partner differently) marked by common 'events' and 'encounters' that stretch across their shared borderspaces. The matrixial vision of the subject challenges the phallic model of an autistically isolated and cut-off subject, who only later begins to relate to its other-objects. In the matrixial dimension, we are always, at some level, susceptible to and moved by a co-emerging unknown subject-other that calls forth a primary potential for compassion. The condition of our human becoming in this prolonged and accumulating intimacy with a subjectivising other, produces a dimension in human subjectivity that later, after our phallic induction into culture under the sign of castration (separation and radical loss), may be activated. Although we are inevitably transformed by subsequent psychic events that will phallicise, but never utterly, the speaking subject, the matrixial makes visible a different kind of desire: not for unconditional reconnection with the severed Other. Matrixially, we yearn for a certain kind of co-affecting contact that already allows of a degree of difference. Thus the matrixial does not speak of the (phallic) longing to return to the womb, to be annihilated as a discrete subject, a longing for death which confuses our beginnings in a woman's body with death. Such a longing or dread is phallic since the opposition is between being and not being. Matrixial dimensions of subjectivity theorised by Ettinger propose states in which there is never absolute absence and not being and then presence and being. Instead the matrixial suggests that trans-subjective oscillations between partial subjectivities unknown to each other but co-emerging and co-affecting in which we can derive *either pleasure or trauma* from the fragility or potential response-ability to the events that vibrate along the strings that link us to a matrixial other which is feminine by definition – a m/ Other (a term that distinguishes this construct from the Mother of post-birth fantasies).

For Ettinger, the price we pay in life or art, as well as in her field as an analyst, for denying or refusing to recognise this potentiality and dimension is a repeated wounding of the often already matrixially wounded subject (wounded by the constant pressure of only a phallic account of subjectivity). The longing I am describing as matrixial is not a longing to be chorically contained, maternally held, put back inside a large, non-subjective space which is often miscalled the Mother. (Analysts who try this out, being Mother, only can perform a phallic concept of the Mother, and hence, like Freud, find it truly hard to perform this role.) Yet they try and, in doing so, like the health professionals represented in Bobby Baker's drawings, offering an invitation to the suffering soul to be open, to come to them for help, they risk worse because they can only perform their cure phallically, reincising a cut at the very point where the subject unconsciously desires something of being with, living beside, sensing human com-passion. The matrixial space is not a holding and containing (as the maternal is theorised in the British object relations schools); it is the possibility of a kind of moving with, being in a kind of contact that neither infantilises the subject in their neediness, nor refuses the luxurious comfort of that passing sharedness of the borderspace. It is not invasive, but creates the conditions for mutually transformative affects.

In recent years, I have found myself increasingly drawn to the study of matrixiality on three levels. As a feminist interested in psychoanalytically inflected theories of subjectivity and notably of femininity, it seems to speak to the blind spot in both. It enables us to imagine the feminine working creatively beyond its current definition as merely the negated other of the phallic. The matrixial feminine is redefined as a human resource for thinking and feeling with, for understanding a dimension of subjectivity that is intimated in so many situations (art, transference, friendship) but which remains unarticulated in theory or even common language. Secondly, one of the privileged sites of thinking about the matrixial is the aesthetic. By this term I do not mean art as the making of beautiful objects. Rather I am proposing that we understand art-making as a process of feeling, seeing, thinking with and through the aesthetic as an arena of trans-subjective transformations. In the manner of Freud's key concepts of 'working through', dream work and the work of mourning, Ettinger speaks of 'artworking' to suggest that the encounters and trans-subjective passages of both the initial 'event' that caused the making of art and the viewer's later encounter with the 'event' that brought the work into being – both radically other

and potentially unknowable – may bring about subjective transformations across an aesthetically invoked 'borderspace' where
the artist lends herself to her material in transforming it into art
and the viewer in turn lends herself to the artwork to animate its
potential to bring about affects or even new knowledge.

Finally, it has become clear that matrixiality is about a new
feminist ethics that challenges us in these varied fields to consider what harm is done to all, but especially women in their
moments of extreme psychic distress, *by the non-acknowledgement
of the kinds of relays and co-affections,* the kinds of longings that
Ettinger has identified in her dual work. Working across art and
psychoanalysis, her thinking is a gift to human subjectivity, masculine and feminine, of the recognition of matrixial severality
which is the effect on all subjects, *irrespective of later gendering or
sexual alignment,* of feminine sexual difference which can now
be theorised in relation to both the capacity for trans-subjective
encounter and hospitable com-passion (hence nothing to do with
organs or bodies).

If the matrixial dimension exists, capable of fostering our
capacity to respond, subjectively, with the unknownness of the
other, through the space of art, and equally capable of traumatising
us if and when the matrixial web is wounded, how would
acknowledging it shift not only theories of the subject and what we
suffer from in breakdowns and depression, but in the experience
of and working through and with such suffering? Might there
be a further gendered aspect to the way in which we experience
psychic collapse? Many factors will be at work, chemical as well
as psychological – but our cures so far are brutal or only partially
effective.

I can ultimately only speak for myself in knowing that the need
in profound emotional distress or psychological illness (whereas
Bobby Baker's work attests there is still a subject present to itself
and hence what I call the suffering soul) goes so far beyond what
is permitted in the usual transactions of family support or pro-
fessionally bounded help. It is not a longing for Mummy – so
often the psychological site of conflicted memories and ambivalent identifications and projections. Ettinger explains the difference between the desire forged phallically for the lost object which
makes desire aim at having its object, desire being the mark of
its lack, and matrixial desire, which is desire for a kind of being-
with-ness. This word involves both the partial relief offered by
a witness, as we know from work on testimony, and with-ness
which is not about empathy, sympathy or identification. Ironically
by tracking such a desire/longing back beyond the psychoanalytically policed demarcation of subjectivity as beginning only at birth
to the pre-birth severality, Ettinger avoids ideas of or encourage-
ments to regression to infantile states. Matrixial propositions of
the mutual significance of pre-natality and pre-maternity cannot

Dairy Drawing 323 (1998).
'Day 323 Monday 31st July'.
Watercolour paper, pencil,
watercolour.

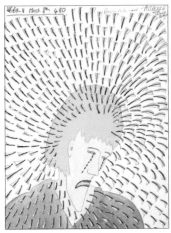

Diary Drawing 480 (2004).
'Week 11 March 8th
Drayton Park – mad – attacked with
sharp thoughts'.
Watercolour paper, pencil, watercolour.

reduce adults to children (Freudian regression, which is so hard for our narcissism to bear even when it is revealed, often with insensitive bluntness in analysis). Thinking about the matrix allows us to bring that archaically generated capacity forward from its genesis in the pre-birth encounter to facilitate acknowledgement of its potential for transformation in the transactions of our adult present.

This digression into the territory of psychoanalytical theory – towards the practice of which I have above expressed some ambivalence – is inspired by reflections arising from a limited encounter with Bobby Baker's *Diary Drawings*. I have seen an extended exhibition and had a small selection of images to study at leisure. What I sense by reading closely and then moving across their many intricate and elaborate spaces has shouted out to me that, in addition to the real and unspeakable suffering of her particular psychological affliction, there is an excruciating gap that seems unbridged by all those who, with good intentions, aim to help. What then seems so ungrateful, if the illness persists, and enough tears are wept to encircle the globe several times over (Day 323), can only be expressed by a rageous figure, a Bertha Mason in the psychic attic, shown in so many drawings stalking behind the clinically dressed Baker persona who tries so hard to present an apologetic or acceptable face to a world unable to see what is happening. I suggest that part of that gap is a matrixial wound, a sense of a deeper kind of being adrift and severed, heightened by the unavailability of a way to express what is missed, and missing, except by means of its visualisation through the invented and reworked tropes of a mutilated, bloated, weeping body used in Baker's highly personal yet culturally grounded drawings.

One drawing (Day 480) shows the weeping sad-face under attack from a swarm of metal shards – the note says, 'attacked by sharp thoughts'. Assaulted from inside and outside, the artist shows herself in another drawing as a tightrope walker on the rope called distress, balancing forces of therapeutic treatments and religion, that are identified with psychosis and self-invalidation respectively. Such images seemingly give a literal visualisation to a metaphorical state and use techniques with which we have become familiar from the study of 'other art' such as multiplication, annotation, diagram and miniaturisation.

In the nineteenth century, and at the turn of the modernist twentieth century, artists and art historians became extremely interested in art made from non-professional situations and extremity. The most famous and influential collection is that associated with Hans Prinzhorn which was exhibited by Cathérine de Zegher, with a catalogue with essays by Hal Foster and Bracha Ettinger, in 2000 (de Zegher, 2000; Foster, 2001; Ettinger, 2000b). Foster tracked the modernist enthusiasm for the art of the outsider, whose often untutored or inventive ways of registering disturbed inner worlds became, with the art of children and the aesthetics, often misrecognised naivety, of the art of non-European peoples, a renovating resource for modernism. Ettinger made a more surprising argument – that the art of the so-called

Dairy Drawing 244 (1999). 'Day 244 Wednesday 16th September. Group therapy'. Watercolour paper, pencil, watercolour.

'mad' was, in fact, very sane. It addressed itself to the other with the hope of communication and interpretation in the terms of the existing Symbolic. It was, therefore not art at all, but art as symptom, decipherable. Art for Ettinger, following Lacan's notion of a sinthome which is where the knotting of the three registers of Real, Imaginary and Symbolic slips but holds nonetheless and thus prevents disintegration into psychosis, involves a transformation of the Symbolic, the introduction into the Symbolic of what is not yet known in its terms.

The work of art as a sinthome, on the other hand, is a unique response that contains the enigma it co-responds to and that brings it about, an enigma that resonates a lacuna of a quite different status in the Symbolic; it does not correspond to lacks defined by the phallic mechanism of castration but to whatever is not yet there, to what is yet to come, to what resists

Dairy Drawing 303(1999). 'Day 303 Monday 31st January. Group therapy'. Watercolour paper, pencil, watercolour.

the Symbolic and to the mysterious and fascinating territory of that which is not yet even unconscious or to what is impossible yet to recognize.

(Ettinger, 2000b: 61)

I introduce Ettinger's distinction between art as symptom and art as sinthome by way of conclusion in order to suggest that we shall need to be very careful in responding to and placing the *Diary Drawings*. To render them simply confessional, expressions of a distressed subject, auto-therapeutic testimony to a particular threatening psychosis, would be to take their truth out from the aesthetic structures by which whatever that truth is, is articulated – that is, to make the art disappear.

Whatever the function or process of its making, the work we can now explore, because Bobby Baker has framed it through selection and representation, works for me as art as sinthome, not as merely art as symptom. That is because there is consistently more to the image than what we immediately see because of its visual clarity. There is the supplementary affective dimension arising from gestures, devices, themes that accumulate across the long-term undertaking. There is so much to be discovered beyond each day's summary of its most distinctive and hence recorded event or sensation. What is to be discovered is as much a revelation for the artist as for her attentive viewers, each bringing to the borderspace created by the presence of the drawings in the world whatever they have lived that will animate these drawings as subjective events. For some, the strangeness and extremity of psychological pain will remain other, reported on by a native informant of another planet. For others, the drawings offer landscape with shared landmarks, if slightly different features. For us all, there is the bare-faced courage of the turning of Baker's brilliant artistry to the service of showing how it is in that psychological territory which is most hidden away, medicalised and shunned, even if the suffering souls are 'in the community'.

I have used the phrase 'suffering soul' intentionally – bringing in a certain spiritual connotation while reminding myself that the word 'psyche' means 'soul' in Greek so that we remember that suffering, even when classified by neat medical labelling, is an affliction of the soul, of the essence of the person. The crisis of the subject, the suffering of the soul, can be treated with medication but that cannot be its essence. What is revealed in Bobby Baker's *Diary Drawings* is a speaking subject, finding a form to speak what seems otherwise invisible and incommunicable about a crisis of this subject and the suffering of her very soul. At the intersection of subjectivity and its reaching beyond its own limits to share and be shared, art-making can be, as it has often been in the past, a witness to the very dimension of the subject we used to call soul, which modern psychoanalysis calls the psyche and feminist cultural work reclaimed as subjectivity. Bobby Baker's work has so often amazed us in her ability to find formal means to give shape to the inner world – a paranoid and needy world full of Melanie Klein's good and bad objects, a world of intense rages and profound needs. Unleashed by whatever unbalances the mind beyond its own self-regulation, this inner world often finds words or, in failing to remain linked to language at all, becomes utterly psychotic, disconnected from any sense of self. Bobby Baker's *Diary Drawings* have found images.

In the discipline of the diary as a daily recording over time, a systematic recourse to the page as support for an imaging even of the self bloodily divided, possessed, haunted and rageous, the artist has produced artwork that is art-working beside the process/illness she has lived through. Its luminous colours, its clean lines, its accuracy and precision in drawing, characterisation and affectivity at first seem at odds with what it is we are lured in by such features to recognise. For me, the encounter becomes highly productive, precisely through her artistry's setting up the agency of art as work in excruciating tension with what that art is working through, and what range of human experience Bobby Baker has dared to confront and then invite us to confront with her, to know with her, to remember with her. Many artists work despite calamitous disabilities, mental and physical. Few have woven art and living together so perilously and precisely as Bobby Baker in her sustained practice of performance, with body, word and gesture as her medium. Now she has granted us insight into the texture of living against and with which she has maintained that practice at the edge of possibility. In doubling what we have learned from her performance with what she confided to this diary, she has put another kind of truth into the world about the nature of pain made worse by a gap, that perhaps her art in the world, and our response to it can however minutely reduce with the only gift we can give another: human recognition that she has spoken of herself but also called to a m/other.

BIBLIOGRAPHY & SOURCES

Abelove, Henry (1990) *The Evangelist of Desire: John Wesley and the Methodists*, Stanford: Stanford University Press.

Allan, Clare (2002) 'Bobby Baker: Pull Yourself Together', in Adrian Heathfield (ed.) *Small Acts: Performance, the Millennium and the Marking of Time*, London: Black Dog.

Aston, Elaine (2000) 'Transforming Women's Lives: Bobby Baker's Performances of "Daily Life"', *New Theatre Quarterly*, 61: 17–25.

Aston, Elaine (2002) 'Feminist Performance as Archive: Bobby Baker's "Daily Life" and *Box Story*', *Performance Research*, 7(4): 78–85.

Aston, Elaine (2004) 'Making a Spectacle Out of Herself: Bobby Baker's *Take a Peek!*', *European Journal of Women's Studies*, 11: 277–94.

Aston, Elaine and Harris, Geraldine (2007) *Performance, Practice and Process: Contemporary [Women] Practitioners*, Basingstoke: Palgrave Macmillan.

Atwood, Margaret (1969) *The Edible Woman* (1992), London: Virago.

Auslander, Philip (1999) *Liveness: Performance in a Mediatised Culture*, London and New York: Routledge.

Ayckbourn, Alan (1974) *Absent Friends* (1975), London: Samuel French.

Baker, Bobby (1990) 'Drawing on a Mother's Experience' (transcript of video performance, 1990), *n.paradoxa*, 5 (2000): 58–62. Reprinted above pp.149–53.

Baker, Bobby (1991) 'Kitchen Show: One Dozen Kitchen Actions Made Public', in *Kitchen Show*, London: Artsadmin; reprinted above, pp.164–170.

Baker, Bobby (1999) *The Berries Visit the Park*, London: Artsadmin.

Baker, Bobby (2001a) 'Box Story', in Clare Allan (ed.) *Box Story*, London: Artsadmin; reprinted in Adrian Heathfield (ed.) (2004) *Art and Performance Live*, London: Tate Publishing.

Baker, Bobby (2001b) 'Performance Artist Bobby Baker', in P. Allen *Art, Not Chance – Nine Artists' Diaries*, London: Calouste Gulbenkian Foundation.

Baker, Bobby (2005) 'Houseworkhouse' (website text reproduced in Spanish), in *Monografías: Casa/House*, 30: 285–99.

Baker, Bobby and Hallam, Richard (2003) 'How to Live', in B. Arends and D. Thackara *Experiment: Conversations in Art and Science*, London: The Wellcome Trust.

Baldwyn, Lucy (1996) 'Blending in: The Immaterial Art of Bobby Baker's Culinary Events', *The Drama Review*, 40(4): 37–55.

Barrett, Michèle (2001) 'Box Story' (essay) in Clare Allan (ed.) *Box Story*, London: Artsadmin; reprinted with minor revisions in Adrian Heathfield (ed.) (2004) Art *and Performance Live*, London: Tate Publishing; reprinted above, pp. 225–8.

Barthes, Roland (1954) *Critical Essays* (1985), Evanston, IL: Northwestern University Press.

Barthes, Roland (1957) *Mythologies* (1993), London: Vintage.

Beckett, Samuel (1961) *Happy Days* (1966), London: Faber and Faber.

Bennett, Susan (1990) *Theatre Audiences*, London: Routledge.

Blumberg, Marcia (1998) 'Domestic Place as Contestatory Space: The Kitchen as Catalyst and Crucible', *New Theatre Quarterly*, 55: 195–201.

Bollas, Christopher (2005) *I've Heard the Mermaids Singing*, London: Free Association Press.

Brooks, Peter (2000) *Troubling Confessions: Speaking Guilt in Law and Literature*, Chicago: University of Chicago Press.

Buerkle, Darcy (2006) 'Facing Charlotte Salomon', in Michael P. Steinberg and Monica Bohm-Duchen (eds) *Reading Charlotte Salomon*, Ithaca: Cornell University Press.

Bunyan, John (1678) *The Pilgrim's Progress*, ed. W. R. Owens (2003), Oxford: Oxford University Press.

Butler, Judith (1990) *Gender Trouble: Feminism and the Subversion of Identity*, London: Routledge.

Butler, Judith (1993) *Bodies That Matter*, London: Routledge.

Chicago, Judy (1996) *The Dinner Party: A Commemorative Volume*, London: Penguin.

Churchill, Caryl (1982) *Top Girls* (1991), London: Methuen.

Cixous, Hélène (1977) 'Aller à la mer', in Richard Drain (ed.) (1995) *Twentieth Century Theatre: A Sourcebook*, London: Routledge, pp.133–5.

Clément, Catherine (1986) 'Sorceress and Hysteric', in Hélène Cixous and Catherine Clément *The Newly Born Woman*, Minneapolis: Minnesota University Press.

Daniel, John (2004) 'The Performance Artist and the Pea', *On Tour* 024: 12–14.

de Certeau, Michel (1974) *Arts de faire*, trans. Steven Rendall (1984), *The Practice of Everyday Life*, Berkeley: University of California Press.

De Lauretis, Teresa (1987) *Technologies of Gender: Essays on Theory, Film, and Fiction*, Bloomington: Indiana University Press.

de Zegher, Cathérine (ed.) (2000) *The Prinzhorn Collection: Traces upon the Wunderblock*, New York: Drawing Center, Drawing Papers 7.

Derrida, Jacques (1995) *Archive Fever: A Freudian Impression*, trans. Eric Prenowitz, Chicago: University of Chicago Press.

Donkin, Ellen (1998) 'Occupational Hazards: Women Playwrights in London, 1660–1800', in Lizbeth Goodman with Jane Gay (eds) *The Routledge Reader in Gender and Performance*, London: Routledge.

Douglas, Mary (1975) 'Jokes', in *Implicit Meanings: Essays in Anthropology*, London: Routledge & Kegan Paul.

Ehresmann, Julia M. (1979) *The Pocket Dictionary of Art Terms*, revised by James Hall (1980), London: John Murray.

Elam, Keir (1980) *The Semiotics of Theatre and Drama*, London: Methuen.

Epstein, M. J. (1996) 'Consuming Performances: Eating Acts and Feminist Embodiment', *Drama Review*, 40(4): 20–36.

Ettinger, Bracha (2000a) 'Art as the transport station of trauma,' in Bracha Ettinger *Artworking 1985–1999*, Gent: Ludion.

Ettinger, Bracha (2000b) 'Some-Thing, Some-Event, Some-Encounter between Sinthome and Sympton', in Cathérine de Zegher (ed.) *The Prinzhorn Collection: Traces upon the Wunderblock*, New York: Drawing Center, Drawing Papers 7, pp. 61–75.

Ettinger, Bracha (2000c) *Artworking 1985–1999*, Gent: Ludion.

Ettinger, Bracha (2004) 'Weaving the Woman Artist With-in the Matrixial Encounter-Event', *Theory, Culture and Society*, 21(1): 69–94.

Ettinger, Bracha (2006) *The Matrixial Borderspace*, Minneapolis: University of Minnesota Press.

Ferris, Lesley (2002) 'Cooking Up the Self: Bobby Baker and Blondell Cummings "Do" the Kitchen', in Sidonie Smith and Julia Watson (eds) *Interfaces: Women/Autobiography/Image/Performance*, Ann Arbor: University of Michigan Press.

Foster, Hal (2001) 'No Man's Land: On the Modernist Reception of the Art of the Insane', also printed as 'Blinded Insights: On the Modernist Reception of the Mentally Ill', in *October*, 97: 3–30.

Foucault, Michel (1961) *Histoire de la Folie*, trans. Richard Howard (1967; 1989) *Madness and Civilisation: A History of Insanity in the Age of Reason*, London: Routledge.

Foucault, Michel (1976) *Histoire de la sexualité vol. I, La volonté de savoir*, trans. Robert Hurley (1978; 1980), *The History of Sexuality, vol. I, An Introduction*, New York: Vintage.

Foucault, Michel (1988) *Technologies of the Self: a seminar with Michel Foucault*, eds Luther H. Martin, Huck Gutman and Patrick H. Hutton, London: Tavistock Publications

Freud, Sigmund (1928) 'Humour, in James Strachey (ed.) (1953) *Complete Works, vol. XXI, 1927–31*, London: Hogarth.

Furse, Anna (1997) *Augustine (Big Hysteria)*, Amsterdam: Harwood Academic.

Gammel, Irene (ed.) (1999) *Confessional Politics: Women's Sexual Self-Representations in Life Writing and Popular Media*, Carbondale and Edwardsville: Southern Illinois University Press.

Garner, Stanton B., Jr (1994) *Bodied Spaces: Phenomenology and Performance in Contemporary Drama*, Ithaca, NY, and London: Cornell University Press.

Gill, Jo (2005) *Modern Confessional Writing: New Critical Theory*, London: Routledge.

Givner, J. (1999) 'TV Crisis and Confession: The Hill-Thomas Hearings', in Irene Gammel (ed.) *Confessional Politics: Women's Sexual Self-Representations in Life Writing and Popular Media*, Carbondale and Edwardsville: Southern Illinois University Press.

Goldberg, RoseLee (2001) *Performance Art*, London: Thames and Hudson.

Gorman, Sarah (2006) 'Rising to the (Table) Occasion, or How to cope with Bobby Baker', paper presented at Queen Mary, University of London as part of Performance Studies International's conference, London, June 2006.

Harris, Geraldine (1999) *Staging Femininities*, Manchester: Manchester University Press.

Heathfield, Adrian (1999) 'Risk in Intimacy: An Interview with Bobby Baker', *Performance Research: On Cooking*, 4(1) (Spring): 97–106; reprinted in full above, pp. 82–91.

Heathfield, Adrian with Templeton, Fiona and Quick, Andrew (1998) *Shattered Anatomies: Traces of the Body in Performance*, London: Arnolfini Live Publishing.

Heddon, Deirdre (1998) 'What's in a Name?', *Studies in Theatre Production*, 18: 49–59.

Heddon, Deirdre (2006) 'Personal Performance: The resistant confessions of Bobby Baker', in Elaine Aston and Geraldine Harris *Feminist Futures: Theatre, Performance, Theory*, Basingstoke: Palgrave Macmillan.

Iball, Helen (1999) 'Melting Moments: Bodies Upstaged by the Foodie Gaze', *Performance Research: On Cooking*, 4(1) (Spring): 70–81.

Iball, Helen (2005) 'Taking Ownership of "Her indoors": Performativity as a Theatrical Dis-location of the British "Housewife"', in Laura Lengel and John T. Warren (eds) *Casting Gender: Women and Performance in Intercultural Contexts*, New York: Peter Lang.

Joyce, James (1922) *Ulysses* (1937), London: John Lane|The Bodley Head.

Kane, Sarah (1995) *Blasted*, in *Complete Plays* (2001), London: Metheun.

Kintz, Linda (1992) *The Subject's Tragedy: Political Poetics, Feminist Theory, and Drama*, Michigan: University of Michigan Press.

Kirkland, John (1912) *The Modern Baker, Confectioner and Caterer*, London: Gresham.

Kristeva, Julia (1980) *Pouvoirs de l'horreur*; trans. Leon S. Roudiez (1982) as *Powers of Horror: An Essay on Abjection*, New York: Columbia University Press.

Langman, Lauren (1992) 'Neon Cages: Shopping for Subjectivity', in Rob Shields *Lifestyle Shopping: The Subject of Consumption*, London: Routledge.

LeWitt, Sol (1969) *Art-Language, No. 1*, reprinted in Gary Garrels (ed.) (2000) *Sol LeWitt: A Retrospective*, New Haven: Yale University Press.

Lupton, Deborah (1996) *Food, the Body and the Self*, London: Sage.

MacDonald, Claire (1995) 'Assumed Identities: Feminism, Autobiography and Performance Art', in Julia Swindells (ed.) *The Uses of Autobiography*, London: Taylor and Francis.

MacRitchie, Lynne (1980) 'Bobby Baker: My Cooking Competes', in Rozsika Parker and Griselda Pollock (eds) (1987; 1992) *Framing Feminism: Art and the Women's Movement 1970–1985*, London: Pandora Press.

Milne, A. A. (1928) *The House at Pooh Corner*, in (1986) *The Complete Winnie-the-Pooh*, London: Chancellor Press.

Morgan-Griffiths, Lauris (1999) 'Rummaging in life's underbelly: Domestic diva Bobby Baker takes her audience back into a real classroom', *Independent*, 21 June 1999.

Mulvey, Laura (1975) 'Visual pleasure and narrative cinema', *Screen*, 16(3): 6–18.

Nead, Lynda (1992) *The Female Nude: Art, Obscenity and Sexuality*, London: Routledge.

Oddey, Alison (ed.) (1999) *Performing Women: Stand-Ups, Strumpets and Itinerants*, London: Routledge.

Panofsky, Dora and Panofsky, Erwin (1991) *Pandora's Box: The Changing Aspects of a Mythical Symbol*, Princeton: Princeton University Press.

Parker, Rozsika and Pollock, Griselda (eds) (1987; 1992) *Framing Feminism: Art and the Women's Movement 1970–1985*, London: Pandora Press.

Pearson, Mike (1994) 'Theatre|Archeology, with Comments by Julian Thomas', *Drama Review*, 38(4): 133–61.

Phelan, Peggy (1993) *Unmarked: The Politics of Performance*, London and New York: Routledge.

Pollock, Griselda (1990) 'Drawing on a Mother's Experience', *Performance Magazine* (November).

Pollock, Griselda (1991) 'Kitchen Show: A Reading', in *Kitchen Show*, London: Artsadmin.

Pollock, Griselda (2004) 'Thinking the Feminine: Aesthetic Practice as Introduction to Bracha Ettinger's Concepts of Matrix and Metramorphosis,' *Theory, Culture and Society*, 21(1): 5–67.

Pollock, Griselda (2006) 'Theatre of Memory: Trauma and Cure in Charlotte

Salomon's Modernist Fairytale', in Michael P. Steinberg and Monica Bohm-Duchen (eds) *Reading Charlotte Salomon*, Ithaca: Cornell University Press.

Rose, Gillian (1996) *Mourning Becomes the Law: Philosophy and Representation*, Cambridge: Cambridge University Press.

Rothenstein, Elizabeth (1962) *Stanley Spencer*, London: Beaverbrook Newspapers.

Rowell, Margit (1997) *Objects of Desire: The Modern Still Life*, New York: MoMA.

Russell, Willy (1988) *Shirley Valentine*, London: Methuen.

Russo, Mary (1994) *The Female Grotesque: Risk, Excess and Modernity*, London: Routledge.

Schechner, Richard (1988) *Performance Theory*, London: Routledge.

Schneider, Rebecca (1997) *The Explicit Body in Performance*, London: Routledge.

Schneider, Rebecca (2001) 'Archives, Performance Remains', *Performance Research*, 6(2): 100-8.

Shahn, Ben (1957) *The Shape of Content*, Cambridge, MA: Harvard U ty Press.

Shakespeare, William (1594) *Titus Andronicus*, ed. Jonathan Bate (1995; 2002), London: Thompson.

Shakespeare, William (1604) *Hamlet*, ed. Harold Jenkins (1982; 1997), Walton-on-Thames: Thomas Nelson & Sons.

Shepard, Sam (1978) *Curse of the Starving Class*, in (1988) *Sam Shepard: Seven Plays*, London: Faber and Faber.

Shepard, Sam (1980) *True West*, in (1988) *Sam Shepard: Seven Plays*, London: Faber and Faber.

Shields, Rob (1992) *Lifestyle Shopping: The Subject of Consumption*, London: Routledge.

Showalter, Elaine (1985) *The Female Malady: Women, Madness and English Culture, 1830–1980*, London: Virago.

Slater, Nigel (1995) 'Nurse, the screens! It's time for choc-shock...' (review of *Take a Peek!*), *Observer*, 9 July 1995.

Smith, Paul (1988) *Discerning The Subject*, Minneapolis: University of Minnesota Press.

Storor, Mark and Year 5 pupils of Brecknock Primary School (1999) *Grown-Up School*, London: Artsadmin.

Toibin, Colm (1994) *The Sign of the Cross, Travels in Catholic Europe*, London: Jonathan Cape.

Tushingham, David (1994) 'Bobby Baker: "Food is my own language"' (interview), in *Live 1: Food for the soul*, London: Methuen Drama.

Warner, Marina (1995) 'Bobby Baker: The Rebel at the Heart of the Joker', *Art and Design: Photography in the Visual Arts*: 3–13; reprinted in an expanded form with minor revisions in Nicky Childs and Jeni Walwin (eds) (1998) *A Split Second of Paradise: New Performance and Live Art*, London: Rivers Oram Press; reprinted in full above.

Warner, Marina (1995a) *From the Beast to the Blonde: On Fairy Tales and Their Tellers*. London: Vintage.

Wesker, Arnold (1960) *The Kitchen*, in (1990) *Arnold Wesker*, vol. II, London: Penguin.

Wilde, Oscar (1895) *The Importance of Being Earnest*, in (1985) *Oscar Wilde: Plays*, Harmondsworth: Penguin.

Williams, Tennessee (1947) *A Streetcar Named Desire* (1984), London: Methuen Student Editions.

Woolf, Virginia (1927) *To the Lighthouse* (1965), London: Penguin.

Woolf, Virginia (1929) 'A Room of One's Own', in Michèle Barrett (ed.) (1993), *A Room of One's Own/Three Guineas*, London: Penguin.

OTHER MEDIA

Films

Gilbert, Lewis (dir.) (1989) *Shirley Valentine*.

Greenaway, Peter (dir.) (1989) *The Cook, The Thief, His Wife and Her Lover*.

Lamond, Carole (dir.) (1991) *Kitchen Show*.

Luna, Bigas (dir.) (1992) *Jamón, Jamón [Ham, Ham]*.

Luna, Bigas (dir.) (1993) *Huevos de Oro [Golden Balls]*.

Luna, Bigas (dir.) (1994) *La Teta y la Luna [The Tit and the Moon]*.

May, Deborah (dir.) (2005) *How to Live*.

Williams, Margaret (dir.) (1996) *Spitting Mad*.

Radio

Cash, Lucy (formerly Baldwyn) (dir.) (2001) *Shop Until Your Mind Goes Pop* (Radio 4).

Cash, Lucy (formerly Baldwyn) (dir.) (2003) *Behave Yourself* (Radio 4).

Imrie, Marilyn (dir.) (2002) *Box Story* (Radio 4).

Imrie, Marilyn (dir.) (2006) *How to Live* (Radio 4).

PERMISSIONS

We are grateful for permission to reproduce the following:

Images
Anthony Caro, 'Sculpture 2' (1962). © Barford Sculptures. Photograph: John Riddy/Tate, London, 2007.
Judy Chicago, 'The Dinner Party' (1979). © ARS, NY and DACS , London 2007.
Hugo Glendinning, 'Pull Yourself Together' (2000).
Deborah May, Housework image sequence (2000).
Claes Oldenburg, 'Floor Burger' (1962). © Oldenburg Van Bruggen Foundation, Art Gallery of Ontario, Toronto.
Charlotte Salomon, 'Why, Oh Why Am I Alive?' (1942). Catalogue ref. 04288-01. Collection Jewish Historical Museum, Amsterdam. © Charlotte Salomon Foundation.
Stanley Spencer, 'Scrubbing The Floor' (1927). The Sandham Memorial Chapel (The National Trust). Artwork © Estate of Stanley Spencer/DACS 2007. Photograph © NTPL/Roy Fox.

Reprinted text
Adrian Heathfield, 'Risk in Intimacy: an Interview with Bobby Baker', *Performance Research: On Cooking*, 4: 1, Spring 1999: 97–106. By permission of the author and Taylor & Francis.
Elaine Aston, 'Feminist Performance as Archive: Bobby Baker's "Daily Life" and Box Story', Performance Research, 7: 4 (2002): 78–85. By permission of the author and Taylor & Francis.
Helen Iball, 'Melting Moments: Bodies Upstaged by the Foodie Gaze', *Performance Research: On Cooking* (1999), pp. 70–81. By permission of the author and Taylor & Francis.
Lesley Ferris, 'Cooking Up the Self: Bobby Baker and Blondell Cummings "Do" the Kitchen'. From *Interfaces: Women, Autobiography, Image, Performance*, by Sidonie Smith and Julia Watson, eds (Ann Arbor: The University of Michigan Press.) By permission of the author and University of Michigan Press.
Lauris Morgan-Griffiths, 'Rummaging In

Life's Underbelly: Domestic Diva Bobby Baker Takes Her Audience Back Into A Real Classroom'. From the *Independent*, 21 June 1999. © *Independent*.
Geraldine Harris (1999) *Staging Femininities*, Manchester: Manchester University Press. By permission of the author.
Nigel Slater, 'Nurse, the screens! It's time for choc-shock'. From the *Observer*, 9 July 1995. ©Nigel Slater. By permission of the author and Lucas Alexander Whitley Ltd.
Deirdre Heddon, 'Personal Performance: The Resistant Confessions of Bobby Baker'. From *Modern Confessional Writing: New Critical Essays*, ed. Jo Gill, London: Routledge (2006).
Geraldine Harris and Elaine Aston, *Performance, Practice and Process: Contemporary [Women] Practitioners* (2007). By permission of the authors and Palgrave Macmillan.
Helen Iball, 'Taking Ownership of "Her indoors": Performativity as a Theatrical Dis-location of the British "Housewife'", in Lengel, Laura and Warren, John T., ed. (2005), *Casting Gender: Women and Performance in Intercultural Contexts*, New York: Peter Lang. By permission of the author and Peter Lang.
Lynn MacRitchie, 'Bobby Baker: *My Cooking Competes*', in Rozsika Parker, and Griselda Pollock, eds (1987; 1992) *Framing Feminism: Art and The Women's Movement 1970–1985*, London: Pandora Press. By permission of the author. Lynn MacRitchie's review was originally published in *Primary Sources* (Christmas, 1980).
Katy Deepwell, transcript of *Drawing on a Mother's Experience*. In *n.paradoxa* vol. 5 (2000). By permission of the author.
Elaine Aston, 'Making a Spectacle Out of Herself: Bobby Baker's *Take a Peek!*' European Journal of Women's Studies 2004 11: 277–294. By permission of the author and Sage Publications.
Sarah Gorman, 'Dear Bobby'. Unpublished conference paper, Performance Studies International 12, Queen Mary, University of London, 2006. By permission of the author.
David Tushingham, 'Food is my own

language', in *Live 1: Food for the soul*, London: Methuen Drama. By permission of the author.
Marina Warner, 'Bobby Baker: The Rebel at the Heart of the Joker', *Art and Design: Photography in the Visual Arts* 1995: III–XIII; reprinted in Nicky Childs and Jeni Walwin, eds (1998) *A Split Second of Paradise: New Performance and Live Art*, London: Rivers Oram Press. By permission of the author.
John Daniel, 'The Performance Artist and the Pea', On Tour 024 (2004). By permission of the author.

Material in the booklets accompanying *Kitchen Show* and *Box Story* is reprinted by permission of the authors and Artsadmin.

Every effort has been made to obtain permission to reproduce copyright material. If any proper acknowledgement has not been made, or permission not received, we would invite copyright holders to inform the publishers of the oversight.

Overleaf: *Diary Drawing 526* (2005) 'Week 6, 31st June. Better'.

INDEX

ABBA 67, 226
abjection 13–15, 84, 102, 107, 119, 142, 146, 191, 192
Acme Housing Association 35
acrostic conceits 112
actions 53–5, 70, 71, 85, 88, 109, 11–12, 120, 123, 132–3, 161, 164–71, 174, 180–1, 185, 204, 249
Adelaide festival, Australia 55, 56, 161
affect 110, 178, 203, 254
Alcott, Louisa May: *Little Women* 105
Alexander, Keith 62
Allan, Clare xi, 69, 70, 268
anger 43, 49, 62, 91, 105, 107, 152, 161, 175, 181
Anne, Princess 30, 34
archive 39, 81, 129–33
Archons 130
armature 15–16, 20, 33, 36, 37, 38
Art in Sacred Spaces 67, 226
Artaud, Antonin 16, 241–2
Arts Council England (ACE) 10, 35, 36, 55, 65, 81, 95, 96
Artsadmin 54, 67, 78
artworking 258, 261
Ashworth High Security Hospital 63
Aspinall, Mrs 143
Aston, Elaine 12, 81, 109–15, 129–33, 146, 188, 200–4
Atwood, Margaret: *The Edible Woman* 119, 121
audience, relationship with 14–15, 17, 38, 45, 46, 48, 53–4, 60, 66, 75, 84–8, 93, 97, 104, 109, 117–18, 123, 132, 156–7, 174, 176, 183, 185–6, 188, 195, 237, 249
Auslander, Philip 81, 129
Austen, Jane 4, 24, 27
autobiographical performance 83–4, 110, 131, 174, 176–7, 232, 233
Ayckbourn, Alan: *Absent Friends* 122

Baker, Bobby: childhood 23–4; DVD Set 49, 53, 55, 58, 61, 65, 66, 72, 77;early works 28–47, 135; education 4, 6–8, 24–7; gap in work (1980–88) 47–8; Guest Professorship (University of Giessen) 65; life 23–7, 47–8; overall costume 98, 106, 111, 174; performance persona 12, 39, 87, 109, 110–11, 131, 145, 183, 186, 189, 233–4, 263; *Time Out* Artist in Residence 70; work as a photographic stylist 48, 62;

artworks:
Alley Cat 28
Art Supermarket 44–5, 93, 145
Baby Cake 30–1, 128
Ballistic Buns 78
Baseball Boot Cake 4–5, 7, 28–9
Behave Yourself 75
Birthday Tea Party 29
Box Story (DL5) 12, 17, 70–1, 74, 75, 77, 111, 113, 130, 137, 140, 141, 145, 146, 211–22, 224–8, 230–7
Bread and Butter 77
Cake Christmas Dinner 29
Chocolate Money 49–50, 52, 219
Cook Dems 14, 50–3, 55, 56, 58, 59, 65, 70, 72, 105, 138, 207, 238
Dainty Feeding 74
Diary Drawings 10, 18, 20, 78, 147, 250–67
Dinner Party, The 39, 124
Displaying the Sunday Dinner 15, 119
Drawing on a Mother's Experience 10, 16, 45, 48–9, 50, 71, 89, 92, 100, 103–5, 112, 122, 130–1, 133, 138, 142, 145, 146, 148–57, 207, 219, 228, 233, 236, 252
Edible Family in a Mobile Home, An 8, 15, 16, 20, 35–9, 44, 52, 82, 84, 85, 101, 102, 105, 120, 121, 130, 138, 141, 145, 218, 228, 233
Elitist Jam 43–4
Game Fair 62–3
F.E.A.T. 78
Geography Dog 78
Grown-Up-School (DL4) 62, 65–6, 81, 96, 132, 146, 206–9, 227
Head cake 31
Hot Bauble Christmas Tree 35
Housewokhouse 70
How to Live 3, 12, 18, 19, 74, 75–7, 78, 110, 111, 112, 114, 137, 138, 140, 142, 145, 147, 244–9
How to Shop (DL2) 11, 13, 14, 56–8, 59, 61, 65, 85, 88, 98, 99, 101, 102, 103, 106, 109, 110–11, 113, 123, 137, 145, 146, 190–5, 207, 234
Jelly Game see *Grown up School*
Kitchen Show (DL1) 12, 53–5, 58, 59, 61, 62, 65, 67, 71, 84, 88, 90, 100, 101, 103–4, 111, 112, 113, 114, 121, 123, 132, 136–7, 138, 139, 142, 146, 61–3, 164–71, 172–7, 178–83, 185–9, 195,

207, 226, 227, 234
Life Piping 39, 43, 80
The Life Room 20, 26, 27, 31, 32–3
Mastering the Art of Piping 42–3, 44–5, 128, 144
Meringue Ladies 30–3, 34–5, 41, 42
Model Family, A 15, 78
My Cooking Competes 46–7, 49, 110, 139, 146, 158–9
Packed Lunch 46, 49, 52, 84, 139
Packed Supper 50
Perpetuity in Icing 22, 44, 45, 71
Princess Anne's Second Wedding Anniversary 34
Princess Anne's Wedding Day 30
Pull Yourself Together 11, 68–9, 112, 147
Shoeshopworkshop 78
Shop Until Your Mind Goes Pop 72
Smashing Lunch 72, 73
Spitting Mad 13, 15, 62, 95, 96, 109, 140–2, 147
Sweet and Sour 31
Table Occasions 64–5, 67, 88, 89, 113, 138
Take a Peek! (DL3) 10, 14, 16, 59–61, 81, 87, 88, 89, 96–101, 132, 137, 146, 197–204
To Bring a Sheep to Consciousness We Must Eat It. Therefore, to Bring the Staff of the New Art Gallery in Walsall to Consciousness We Must Eat Them 66–7
To Bring a Sheep to Consciousness We Must Eat It. Therefore to Bring Virginia Woolf to Consciousness We Must Eat Her 33–4
To demonstrate the effect of the popular press upon an artwork 44
A Useful Body of Herbs 58–9
The Woman Who Mistook Her Mouth for a Pocket 67, 226
Baloh Brown, Polona xi,12, 52–5, 58, 65, 71, 98, 113–14, 136, 186–7, 208
banal 96, 97, 100, 102, 124
Barthes, Roland 118
Bausch, Pina: *Kontakthof* 139
BBC 53, 62, 72, 74, 75, 77, 86, 96
beauty 43, 46, 123, 164, 168, 177, 181, 213
Beckett, Samuel: *Happy Days* 145
Berkely, Busby 61
Beuys, Joseph 38

Big Brother 137–8
Blake, William 112
blood 14, 97, 98, 102, 142, 192, 194, 202,
   216, 226, 254, 255, 257, 267
Bock, Frank x, 75–6
body in performance 125
Bollas, Christopher 256
breastfeeding 121, 156, 168, 175, 182
Brecht, Bertold 112, 252
Brecknock Primary School 62, 65
Breton, Andre 102
Breuer, Josef 131
bricolage 180
Briscombe, Bill xi, 72
British Council 189
British School of Sculpture 4
Bromley Evening Argus 25
Brooks, Peter 235–6
Bunyan, John: *Pilgrim's Progress* 56, 234
Burgess, Mrs (Art teacher) 24
Butler, Judith 12, 202
Byron, Dr Tanya 138

Camden Arts Centre 33
Cameron, Shirley 31
cannibalism 15, 102, 121, 194
Carluccio, Antonio 48
carnivalesque misrule 16, 106
Caro, Anthony, at Central St Martins 4–5,
   28; *Sculpture 2* 4
Carrier, Robert 48
cartography 71–2, 213, 228
Cash, Lucy x, 72, 75
Catherine Bailey Ltd 74, 77
Central St Martins 4, 8, 25, 28, 29, 30, 31,
   34, 99, 156
Cezanne, Paul: *Le Grandes Baigneuses* 25
Chadwick, Helen xi, 46
The Chapel of Love (song) 34
Charcot, Pierre 98, 131–2, 242
Charles, Prince of Wales 30
Chelsea Physic Garden 58, 207
Chicago, Judy: *The Dinner Party* 124
Chislehurst and Sidcup School for Girls 24
Christ 9, 101, 106, 192, 194, 234, 235
Christian ceremonies 101, 107
Christian references 101, 106, 191, 192–4,
   202, 226, 227, 234–7
Churchill, Caryl: *Top Girls* 124
Clement, Catherine 132
Cognitive Behaviour Therapy (CBT) 75, 136,
   147, 246
Come Dancing 86
compassion 18, 56, 57, 157, 190, 193–4, 260
conceptual art 1, 7–8, 114–15
confession 12, 147, 157, 230, 232–7, 248,
   265
consciousness-raising activities 232
cooking 24, 31, 32, 39, 44, 46, 47, 51, 52,
   53, 57, 79, 85, 86, 105, 110, 111, 119,

124, 159, 164, 166, 181, 198, 214, 246
Cowper, William 226
Coxhill, Lol 31
Crowley, Graham 4
cubism 144, 254
cultural translation 12, 19, 129–33,183,
   187–9, 200–4, 251, 266
Curious 75, 110, 113
Cutts, Mike 27

Daily Life Ltd 65
Daniel, John 246–9
De Certeau, Michel 12
De Lauretis, Teresa 203
De Zegher, Catherine 263
Deacon, Richard 4
Deepwell, Katy 146
DeMontfort University 241, 242
Derrida, Jacques 130
Descartes, Rene 242
Desert Island Discs 140
Dialectical Behaviour Therapy (DBT) *see*
   Cognitive Behaviour Therapy (CBT)
domestic work 83, 175, 226
Donkin, Ellen 176
Douglas, Mary 106–7
dream work 97, 258, 261
Duchamp, Marcel 5
Dusty Springfield Fan Club, Bromley
   Branch 24
Dyer, Fraser xi, 67

eating 5, 62, 67, 77, 84–5, 103, 117, 120,
   123–5, 145, 175, 182
eccentricity 16, 109, 121, 142, 186, 242
elitism 19, 43–4, 50, 140, 145
embarrassment 24, 52, 58, 75, 87, 91, 100,
   109, 140–2, 175, 187, 224
Emin, Tracey 67, 114
empowerment 140, 178, 189, 203–4, 248
English Chamber Choir x
English, Rose 35, 44
ephemerality 43, 129, 130, 146, 236
Epstein, Marcy 119–20
Escaping Gravity 63–4
Etchells, Tim 10, 68, 147, 239
Ettinger, Bracha Lichtenberg 18, 258–65
eucharist 107, 194
Euphoria Films 62
Everage, Dame Edna 198
exomologesis 234–5
experts 138, 140
Expressionism 96, 254, 258

FACT (Foundation for Art and Creative
   Technology) 63
Famous Five 105
Farrington's School for Girls, Chislehurst,
   Kent 24
Fegan, Tony 65

feminism 10, 13, 45, 81, 83–4, 85–6, 110,
   119–20, 129–33, 182, 197, 200–4, 232,
   261–2, 266
Fenton, Rose xi, 54
Ferris, Lesley 146, 172–7
fine art 6, 25, 26, 39, 113, 114
Finley, Karen 83, 119, 122
Floyd, Keith 48
Fool 16, 106–7; *see also* jester, joker
Forced Entertainment 68, 239
form 3, 4, 5, 6, 7, 18, 20, 29, 38, 58, 81, 86,
   88, 89, 97, 101, 106, 110,111–13, 114,
   137–8, 140, 141, 155, 178, 180, 185,
   189, 226, 233, 237, 266
Foster, Aisling 10, 81, 91, 146
Foster, Hal 263
Foster, Roy 4, 10, 81, 145
Foucault 12–13, 18, 141, 232, 233;
   Madness and Civilisation 16–17;
   Technologies of the Self 12, 235,
   236–7
Franko B 10, 75, 147, 239
Fraser Brown McKenna (architects) xi, 59,
   98
freak show 198, 204
Freud, Sigmund 131, 182, 258, 261, 263;
   museum 98; on humour 107;
   transference 256
fun-fair 198

Gammel, Irene 233
Garner, Stanton B. 117–18
gender performance 85, 106, 110, 120, 129,
   174, 183, 195, 202–3, 252–3, 262
George (cat) 167
gestus (Brecht) 112
Giessen University, Germany – guest
   professorship 65
Gilbert and George 99; *The Meal* 8
Givner, Jessie 232
Glendinning, Hugo xi, 68
Globe Theatre 28
Gnoli, Domenico: *Without a Still Life*
   (painting) 124
Goldberg, RoseLee 114
Goldsmiths College 6, 26, 32
Gorman, Sarah 147, 241–2
Goya, Francisco 16
Grand Union Design xi
grazing 123, 168, 175
Greenaway, Peter: *The Cook, The Thief,*
   His Wife and Her Lover 121
Greenbelt festival 89, 103, 112, 133, 151
Grenfell, Joyce 145
Griffin, Tamzin xi, 61, 98, 198
Grossman, Loyd 86
grotesque 132, 202, 204
Guardian (newspaper) 3, 19, 45, 124, 140
Gypsy Kings 65

Hallam, Richard x, 74, 77, 136, 140, 147, 248
Happy Families (game) 105
Harriott, Ainsley 86
Harris, Geraldine 10, 12, 14, 81, 109–15, 146, 191–5
Hayward, Tony 30
Hayward Gallery 28, 46, 84
Heathfield, Adrian xi, 6, 10, 11, 13, 15, 17, 19, 20, 68, 81, 83–91, 110, 112, 123, 135–43
Heddon, Deirdre 12, 147, 187, 230–7
Hill, Leslie 110
Hinchcliffe, Daniel xi, 18, 78, 251
Hinchcliffe, George xi
Hinchliffe, Ian 31
Hirst, Damien 67, 114
Hitchcock, Alfred 95
Hohki, Kazuko 114
home (arts organisation) 74
Homes Show 47
House of Tiny Tearaways 137
Houses of Parliament 62, 69, 96
Howell, Anthony 55
Hughes, Holly 83
humiliation 13, 14, 87, 102, 105, 132, 198, 203, 204, 234
hysteria 98, 131–2, 194, 242

Iball, Helen 12, 81, 117–26, 146, 185–9
ICA (Institute of Contemporary Arts) 23, 35, 9, 44–50, 56, 104, 110, 143, 59, 219
IKEA 220–1
Imrie, Marilyn xi, 74, 77
Incredible Hulk 34, 59
Independent (newspaper) 146
intersubjectivity 18, 259
Isaacs, Laura Godfrey 74

Jardine, Lisa 10, 14, 146, 197–8
jester 106–107; *see also* Fool, joker
John Lewis 48, 149
joker 16, 106–7; *see also* Fool, jester
Jones, Aled 50
Joyce, James: *Ulysses* 181
Junior Chef 86

Kane, Sarah: *Blasted* 121
Kant, Immanuel 259
Keidan, Lois xi, 49, 68
Keith and Marie (performance artists) 30, 31, 32, 42
Kenwood Chef 34, 51
Kenwood Chefette 48
Kirkland, John: *The Modern Baker* 42
Klein, Melanie 266
Knebworth House 28
Knight, Judith x, 54
Kristeva, Julia 13–15, 119, 146, 191–2, 194, 202

Lacan, Jacques 264
Lamond, Carole x, 54, 139
Lang, k.d. 61
Langman, Lauren 195
LaRibot, Maria 10, 147, 239
Last Supper 124
Leigh, Verity 68
Lennox, Annie 61, 197
LeWitt, Sol 7
Lichtenstein, Roy 27, 99
Little, Ted xi, 35
Live Art Development Agency xi
London International Festival of Theatre (LIFT) 13, 16, 53–7, 59, 60, 61, 64–6, 70–1, 87, 96, 98, 99, 101, 106, 111, 114, 164, 172, 178, 193, 195, 198, 203, 208, 224, 226, 227
London Nautical School for Boys 27
Lord Send Me (prayer) 192
Lord's Prayer 168–9, 226, 234
Louvre 43, 218
Luna, Bigas 121, 124; *Golden Balls* 124; *Jamon, Jamon* 124; *The Tit and The Moon* (films) 121, 124
Lupton, Deborah 119, 125

MacDonald, Claire 83–4
MacRitchie, Lynn 146, 159
Madonna (Christian) 72, 130, 226
Maison Gladys (hair salon) 217–18
marks and marking 43, 54, 67, 96, 112, 132–3, 150, 151, 152, 164, 170, 174–5, 181, 183
Martin, Ray 161–2
masochism 14, 109, 193
matrixial 18, 20, 259–63
maths 13, 142
May, Deborah 70, 73, 140
Mayfest, Glasgow 49, 59, 219
melancholia 251–2
Melville, Miranda x
memory 84, 91, 125, 126, 131, 132–3, 143, 174, 175, 181, 182, 188, 230
Mental Health Week 18, 78
mental healthcare 10, 18–20
mess 14, 51, 67, 86–7, 103, 122, 131, 149, 156, 166, 221, 224, 237, 253, 259
Methodism 101–2, 235
The Midday Show with Ray Martin (Australian TV) 161–2
Midler, Bette 145
Miller, Roland 31
Millican, Nikki 49, 52
Milne, A.A. 117
Miraculous Engineering x
mistakes 44, 161, 168, 175, 211
Modleski, Tania 200, 202
Monty Python 186
Morgan-Griffiths, Lauris 146, 207–9
mortification 14, 102, 193, 194

motherhood 49, 102, 103–7, 109, 122, 156, 178–82, 194, 207–8, 253–4, 260–1
mourning 258, 261
Mulvey, Laura 126
Muybridge, Edward: photographs 28

National Exhibition Centre (NEC), Birmingham 11, 46, 47
National Theatre 28
Noad, Lynda 118
Neal, Lucy xi, 54
New Testament 192
Nicholson, Lewis x, 54
Nietzsche, Friedrich 16
nudes (in painting) 118
numbers 13, 65, 89, 142
numerology 13, 65, 89, 142
Nuttall, Jeff 42

Oddey, Alison 189
Old Testament 191, 193
Oldenburg, Claes 8–9, 27, 38, 99; *Floor Burger* 8; *Store* 38
ontology 11, 129
Oppenheim, Meret 102
outside eye 12, 114
Oval House 30, 31, 33

Palmer, Jacqueline xi, 65
Pandora (myth) 72, 227–8, 237
parody 96, 100, 109, 111, 121, 137, 187
pastiche 86, 137, 138
Pavarotti, Luciano 169
pear-throwing 55, 146, 162, 163, 166, 175, 181, 189
Pearson, Mike 188
Peas for Peace movement 78
penance 235
People's Palace restaurant 197
Performance Art Collective 35
Performance Studies International 241–2
permeability of theatre space 118
Phelan, Peggy 11, 81, 129, 200, 202
Pine Street Day Centre 63, 78
Pollock, Griselda 18–20, 54, 90, 146, 147, 176, 178–83, 251–67
Pollock, Jackson 103, 130, 138, 145, 207
Pook, Jocelyn x, 70, 77, 228
Pop Art 43, 99
post-colonial concerns 186, 187
post-natal depression 16, 152, 207
Potter, Sally 35
prayer 67, 168–9, 180, 192–3, 226, 234
prime numbers *see* numerology
Primus stove 214
Prince Charles *see* Charles, Prince of Wales
Princess Anne *see* Anne, Princess
Prinzhorn, Hans 263
Private Eye (magazine) 28

psyche 93, 246, 255, 266
psychoanalysis 18–19, 140, 236–7, 258, 259, 262, 266
purity laws 191
Pygmalion (myth) 177

Queen Mary, University of London xi, 77, 78, 135–6

radio recordings 12, 53, 72, 74, 75, 77, 86–7, 137
Ramayana, The 95
recorded media 12, 49, 53, 54, 55, 58, 61, 63–4, 65, 66, 67, 72, 77, 132, 137, 139, 140
redemption 15, 67, 74, 146, 226, 228
Reindeer Werk 42
Reise, Barbara 6–7, 27
religious imagery 130, 191, 192, 194, 202
repetition 12, 49, 51, 138–9, 174, 192, 193, 195, 211
ResCen (Centre for Research into Creation in the Performing Arts) NightWalking weekend 73
risus paschalis 106
Robert Blair Primary School 62
Roden, Claudia 48
Rodenburg, Patsy 110–11
Rose Café 28
Rose, Gillian 97
Royal College of Art 7, 8
Royal Festival Hall 16, 60, 72, 73, 87, 98, 101, 197, 198, 203
Rudi (dog) 23, 66
rules 45, 58, 64, 65, 84, 88–9, 112, 191–3
Russell, Willy: Shirley Valentine (play) 123
Russo, Mary 202

Saatchi, Charles 115
sacrifice 101, 102, 157, 194, 226, 234
Salomon, Charlotte: Leben? Oder Theater? 251–2
Salpêtrière Hospital, Paris 98, 131
saturnalia (in ancient Rome) 106
satyr plays (in ancient Greece) 106
Schneider, Rebecca 119, 125, 129–30, 131
sculpture 4, 7, 9, 26, 27, 28, 30, 84, 99, 112, 121, 204, 216
semaphore 62, 96
sexuality 83, 87, 182–3, 195
Shahn, Ben 6
Shakespeare, William 28; Hamlet 16; King Lear 106; Titus Andronicus 121
Shaw, George Bernard: Androcles and the Lion 24
Shelley, Brooke x
Shepard, Sam: Curse of the Starving Class 124; True West 122, 123
Shirley Valentine (film) 193
shoes 57, 64, 70, 75, 101, 102, 111, 143,

152, 211, 213, 227, 256, 257
Sidcup Art School 24, 25
Simone, Nina: My Baby Just Cares for Me 48, 153
Sims, George R 31
sin 67, 100, 120, 193, 226, 234–6
sinthome 264–6
site-specificity 11, 65, 113
Slater, Nigel 10, 14, 146, 197–8
Small Acts at the Millennium 68–9
smell and taste 51, 85, 95, 113, 118, 125, 152, 168, 175, 194
Smith, Paul 177
Smith, Stevie: Not Waving But Drowning 255
Snow, Jon 10, 147, 244
South Bank Centre, London 58, 59, 64, 65, 84
Spencer, Stanley: Scrubbing the Floor 9
spillage 15, 65, 84, 122, 124, 131, 170
spitting 13, 15, 62, 95–6, 109, 240, 241, 243
Split Britches 113
Sprinkle, Annie 83
St Luke's Church, Holloway 67, 70, 113, 226
Stain Devils 67
stains 67, 101, 120, 149, 156, 177, 216, 226
Stevenson, Sîan x, 61, 63, 74, 79, 98, 198
still life painting 118, 124
Storor, Mark x, 65, 66
story boards 58, 102, 106, 190, 192, 194, 195
storytelling 131, 132, 188
street performances 11, 31, 42
sucre d'art exhibition 43
surrealism 102–3, 105, 124, 254
sympathy 52, 109, 157, 262

tableau 98, 200, 202
taboos 61, 88, 106, 110, 121, 156, 181, 182, 191, 192
talking cures 131
Texas Chainsaw Massacre 39
timelessness 139
Times (newspaper) 36
Tinguely, Jean 27
Tisdall, Caroline 45
Todd, Ann 95
Tomlinson, Dave xi, 67
Tomlinson, Pat xi
touring 3, 12, 50–78, 98, 187, 188, 189, 207, 219, 252; performance venues 52, 53, 72, 98, 110, 113, 189; politics of touring 146, 185–9
Toynbee Studios 74
Tushingham, David 121, 146, 155–7

Ukelele Orchestra of Great Britain xi
University of Bath, Institute of Interdisciplinary Arts 18, 78
unreason 1, 16, 20, 141

Victoria & Albert Museum (V&A) 74
Van Gogh, Vincent 16
video and DVD recordings 12, 49, 53, 54, 55, 58, 61, 63, 64, 65, 66, 67, 72, 74, 77, 95, 96, 113, 114, 139, 140, 188, 241, 272
violence 13, 15, 16, 20, 88, 90, 97, 100, 102, 109, 132, 166, 175, 181, 203, 204, 254
Virgin Mary 194
voyeurism 126, 157, 198

Wagner, Richard: Ride of the Valkyries 96
Wald, Steve x, 58, 68, 77
Walsall shopping centre 66, 67
Wanamaker, Sam 28
Wandsworth Adult Education Institute 27, 216
Warhol, Andy: Campbell's Soup images 124
Warner, Marina 3, 10, 13, 16, 18, 26, 81, 95–107, 124, 131, 132, 203, 234–5
Weaver, Lois 114
Weight Watchers 187
Welfare State (artists) 42
Wellcome Trust: Sciart xi, 74, 147, 248
Wesker, Arnold: The Kitchen 119
West Lodge Preparatory School, Sidcup 24
When The Boat Comes In (song) 193
Whitelaw, Mark 114
Whittuck, Andrew x, 1, 11, 18, 34, 36, 39, 44, 46, 47, 54, 65, 67, 70, 78, 98, 99, 112, 132, 152, 153
Whittuck, Charlie 78
Wilde, Oscar: The Importance of Being Earnest 120, 122
Williams, Margaret 62, 96
Williams, Tennessee: A Streetcar Named Desire 120, 123, 125
Winnie the Pooh 117
Woman's Hour (Radio 4) 53, 72, 75
Women's Institute (WI) 159, 207
Woodrow, Bill 4
Woolf, Virginia 26, 27, 33, 67; A Room of One's Own 4; To the Lighthouse 8–9

X6 Dance Collective 44

York, Simon x, 77